AF006372

The Story of
Twenty Questions

A Novelized Memoir

by Robert VanDeventer

THE STORY OF TWENTY QUESTIONS: A NOVELIZED MEMOIR
by Robert VanDeventer

© 2007 Robert VanDeventer

All rights reserved.
No part of this book may be reproduced in any form or by any means, electronic, mechanical, digital, photocopying or recording, except for the inclusion in a review, without permission in writing from the publisher.

www.Bearmanormedia.com
1-800-566-1251 (Order line only)

ISBN10: 1-59393-077-1
ISBN13: 978-1-59393-077-6

Printed in the United States

Book Cover Design by Paula Tarver-Leckey and Jill Ronsley
Book Design and Typesetting by Jill Ronsley, suneditwrite.com

Published in the USA by Bear Manor Media
PO Box 71426
Albany, GA 31708

Author's Note

I used the real names of all the famous people in the book who were guests on *Twenty Questions* and of cast members Bill Slater and Herb Polesie. The juvenile panel member, Bobby McGuire, the book's protagonist, is a rather stylized version of how I remember myself. I used that name in New York on the show and nowhere else. But in the book, I used it throughout the narrative, which created a small problem in the names of my mother and father. Dad, Fred VanDeventer, used his real name on the show. Mother, Florence VanDeventer, used her maiden name, Florence Rinard (pronounced Ri-nard'). But, since I am McGuire in the book, they would logically be McGuire in the book also, which might be confusing. So, I simply refer to them as Mother and Dad. All the other characters in the book are given fictitious names. But, with one or two exceptions, every character really existed and are characterized as I remember them. One exception is the leading lady, Mary Sue, who is a combination of three girls I knew. Honey is a combination of two others.

Most of the incidents and adventures really happened, pretty much as described. However, they did not all happen at the time described. For example, the scene backstage with the opera star, Regina Resnik, is placed in September 1947. She actually appeared August 23, 1947. The scene in the haunted house placed in the spring of 1948 actually occurred in 1949.

Much of the dialogue is quoted as I remember it word for word. More is paraphrased from memories of the conversations. Some is invented as any dialogue in a novel is invented.

Robert VanDeventer
Palmyra, Virginia
March 26, 2007

FOREWORD

Birth of a Quiz Show

(recollection by Bobby McGuire)

The radio quiz program *Twenty Questions* was first broadcast at 8 p.m., EST, Saturday, February 2, 1946, on the Mutual Broadcasting System. It originated from the Longacre Theatre on West 48th Street in New York.

I was there. I was a member of the show's panel of experts at the age of fourteen.

As a television program, *Twenty Questions* first appeared on WOR-TV, Channel 9, November 2, 1949. The program later appeared nationwide on the DuMont Television Network and finally on the ABC Television Network.

Twenty Questions was my father's show. It was his doing.

Dad had been a newsman in the Midwest all his life. He dreamed of becoming a foreign correspondent. But he wasn't the right age in either world war. So, in 1942 he became a newscaster on the radio, on WJR, the Goodwill Station, Detroit. This made him locally famous. His clock of fame had struck the hour. He gave speeches at high school commencements (I still have the scripts). He addressed company picnics. He did voice-over for Jam Handy films. He posed for publicity stills. And, since WJR had a vast Midwest market, he became known far beyond Detroit. By 1944, the year of D-Day, Leyte, and the St. Louis Browns, Dad had the highest rated radio news show in the area.

Meanwhile, Elmer Davis reached his peak on CBS. His five-minute news show at 8:55 p.m. made each minute count in a lean, homey delivery. To emulate the Midwestern twang of Elmer Davis, in October of 1944 WOR brought Dad to New York. He was assigned the 11:00 p.m.

news. Next, Frank Singeiser left the WOR 6:30 p.m. news and Dad took it over, beginning Christmas Day. This became the highest rated news show in New York. Among Dad's announcers for the two news shows were Charles Stark for Peter Paul candy and Bob Martin for *Look* Magazine.

Moving east in an epic journey of wartime America that I shall save for other pages, we came to live in Princeton, a long but fast commute via the Pennsylvania Railroad to New York. In no time, through the magic of radio, Dad became as well known in Princeton as he had been in Detroit. (Einstein was somewhat better known.) He did volunteer work for the OPA. He spoke for the Red Cross during Saturday matinees at the local movie theatre. He joined Rotary. Most importantly, he joined Springdale, the golf club. It was only natural for Dad to invite his announcers down for a round.

The morning of June 10, 1945, Mr. Stark came to play. I caddied. Mr. Stark would also stay for dinner. As dinner passed and words flowed, Mr. Stark asked me, "How do you like school in New Jersey compared with school in the Midwest?"

I had fourteen answers and opinions at hand but said only, "Okay."

Mother then asked Mr. Stark her own loaded question. "Have you been working in schools then, or education? I just wondered what you do when you're not announcing."

The question carried a hint of disapproval. Mother came from the frontier, where her family had cleared land and worked from sun to sun. Well, then, people who worked for a minute or two a day reading commercials must surely do other things.

Mr. Stark smiled with oil. "It is a little complicated, because announcers are usually producers as well. So, when I'm not announcing, you can usually find me kicking around ideas for new shows. We're working on a little idea right now that puts musical material in a quiz format. It's coming along."

Mr. Stark could not know that with those words he had pierced a dual underground pipe. I could see the white vapor of interest emanating upward from Mother's eyes. First, Mother was a musician, many people knew. Since girlhood, she had played piano and organ, church to conservatory. Second, we happened to be a family of quiz nuts.

Mother inquired for detail. "How do you put musical ideas in a quiz format?"

Stark's teeth appeared in grand grin. "It grows from an idea. Then you add a little here and a little there and change a little here and there and you come out with a show idea that can turn heads."

Mother pressed on. "How do you know when heads are turning?"

Mr. Stark eased back a little from his plate. "It's usually a case of a program director expressing interest."

Dad said, "Norm Livingston." He was program director of WOR/Mutual.

Stark nodded and went on. "Norm would be one example. Among many. It all comes down to a concept. From the concept you develop a cast, then hold a rough runthrough and, finally, an audition. Your principal ingredients are ideas, persistence, and patience."

Then, something popped from me. From my silly head. "What stage are you at with your musical quiz show?"

He paused, smiled, glanced slightly my way, and said, "We're ... still kicking it around."

Strangely, Mother persisted, smiling. "After the kicking is all over, what would happen then?"

He answered in double talk. Obviously, he could not say what would happen. It was all very complex and iffy.

Dad, seeing this, helped his rescue. "What Florence is thinking of is our own background playing quizzes. Not always but usually at the dinner table. And sometimes the car."

I had to add, "When we aren't playing the cow game, we play parlor games, such as, well, Categories, Ghost, and Animal, Vegetable, Mineral."

Stark said, "Animal, Vegetable, Mineral?"

Dad explained. "One of us thinks of a subject. Anything anywhere. And the others identify it by asking questions. Usually dividing the field in half."

Mr. Stark smiled, grinned. "This is a whole new concept for me. Especially this dividing the field in half."

Dad said, "That just means that if it's not upstairs, it's probably downstairs."

Mother said, "If it's not on this side of the room, it has to be on that side of the room."

"Sounds slightly familiar," Stark said.

Dad spoke with cool. "We'll play one."

We all had pushed back from the table by then.

Mother said, "Is it animal, vegetable, or mineral?"

Dad said, "Well, it's mainly mineral. With some animal and some vegetable."

Mother asked, "Is it right around the house here?"

"Yes."

Mother asked, "Downstairs?"

Dad assumed his judicial manner. "I would have to say no to that."

Mother asked, "Is it upstairs?"

"No."

Of course, I knew what it was. But sat tight. This was all so un-cool, although that word was hardly in use in 1945.

Mother asked, "Is it in the basement?"

"No. Bob, are you playing?"

I guess I made a face, as only idiot adolescents can. "All right. Is it outside the house?"

"Yes."

I made another face. "I know what it is. Mr. Stark's golf clubs."

Mr. Stark was impressed. He tilted his chair backward until its back rested against the doorway to the hall. "That was keen. Not an ordinary question-and-answer quiz. The fact is, plain quizzes are out of vogue at this time."

Mother said, "What's in vogue?"

"You need people involved. It's personalities that make your successful show."

Dad agreed. "That's why *Information Please* is the best quiz show on the air. Because of the people on it, the wits, especially Oscar Levant."

Mother said, "I haven't heard him play — the piano."

Dad said, "He's there for his dry wit."

Stark said, "That's very correct. It was the idea of a guy named Dan Golenpaul that made *Information Please* a hit and he went for personality from the very beginning. The same way that Louis Cowan generated the *Quiz Kids* naturally from it. In both, you need characters: Oscar Levant, Joel Kupperman."

Well, there I was. I had to say something. "I don't like Joel so much. I like Richard Williams. Harve Fischman. And, anyway, I don't think of Paul Wing's Spelling Bee as having characters." Contentious as always.

Mr. Stark said, "That was an adaptation of a known game, so characters were not needed as much."

I couldn't shut up. "So would the word game be an adaptation of a known game. So would Hangman. Categories. So would Animal, Vegetable, Mineral. If you were going to use something like Animal, Vegetable, Mineral on the radio, you wouldn't need characters, just like on the spelling bee. Is that what you're saying?"

I saw the oil start to flow. Mr. Stark would seek peace with his caddie. "That's a good point. What you really need is a balance. And a spark. Something to give it zip. On *Take It or Leave It*, you have the sailor on leave everybody is pulling for. *Dr. IQ* has the lady in the balcony."

I said, "Why couldn't contestants play Animal, Vegetable, Mineral?"

Stark smiled in tolerance. "One thing for sure. I have stepped into a house of quizzes." His grin shined showbiz. "However, not to disagree with Bob, Animal, Vegetable, Mineral would just never work with studio contestants. You see, you rarely get people like you. Audience members are usually awfully slow. Phil Baker has to prompt the sailor to keep the show moving."

Mother, hopeful and aggressive, said, "Couldn't we solve problems like that?"

Then Mr. Stark, still grinning, still leaning his chair against the doorway to the hall, turned the key. "No, look here," he said. "I can see it. What you've got is a *panel of experts. They* play the game. Our Clifton Fadiman has the subject like my golf clubs and the panel guesses it."

The rest of the afternoon has always remained a blur. I recall Mother asking time after time what would happen next. I remember Norm Livingston's name arising once again. But I remember most a great rising wind sweeping around me. I grinned, ecstatic. A radio show! We would have a radio show. Not just Dad on the news. A quiz show! That warm wind blew because it truly seemed possible.

Dad's way to work was inbound six afternoons a week on the 4:21 from Princeton Junction, right through the hole to Penn Station. A cab would move him to 40th and Broadway. Dad would arrive at 5:30, elevate to the news room on twenty-four, and start right in, reading through the script for the six-thirty News of the Hour..

On June 11, 1945, Dad went in early, on the 12:49. He wanted to talk to Norm Livingston. I had exams that day and scurried through them as if I might pass. I biked home by two: past the Catholic school, past Turney Motors, where we would soon buy a Packard, Evelyn Place, where Karin Artin, the 12-year-old exotic cellist, lived, and Joe the Greek's, where I bought my jaw breakers. Into the kitchen I burst. Had Dad called? Mother shook her head. She had been waiting, too. So intense had the quiz show hope become overnight that Mom permitted me to wait up till one in the morning.

Dad came in the front door to face us in some surprise.

"What are you doing up?"

In near unison we said, "What did he say? What did Norm Livingston say?"

"Oh. Well, look. These things take time. We didn't talk to Norm yet. Stark wants to kick it around a little first."

"Kick it around!"

He nodded. "I did speak to several of the announcers at WOR and they liked the idea."

"What did they say?"

"They'd heard of Animal, Vegetable, Mineral. But they called it Twenty Questions. The way these easterners play, you have to guess the subject by asking only twenty questions."

I said, "Why twenty?"

"I don't know. That's what they said."

I stood sleepily mystified. We had never played with any limit on the number of questions and had never referred to the game by any name other than animal, vegetable, mineral. "Twenty Questions." Although I turned up my lip in slight sneer, I thought it sounded okay.

With a slight shrug, Mother said, "Well, what's next?"

Dad said, "Stark wants to kick it around before anything else. He may want to approach his own contacts. Obviously, it's important who receives first approach."

Dad's other announcer, Bob Martin, came to play at Springdale the first of July. It developed at dinner, as he sat in Mr. Stark's chair, although not tilted back against the hall door frame as Mr. Stark had been, that he was doubly intrigued by the prospect of "this twenty questions idea."

First, as a producer himself, he could contribute toward getting the show on the air. "For one thing, I know as many people as Stark does. I'm a producer, too."

"We know that," Dad said.

Second, he suggested, with some allusions of shadiness, "There might be dozens of reasons why Stark wants to keep kicking it around."

At this, Dad's eyes rose, containing pristine in naivete from the clean playing fields of Tipton County, Indiana. "What kind of reasons?"

"It's a matter of who owns the rights. I know it's very early in the game for that kind of worry. But you might want to keep it in mind."

I asked, "What rights?"

"Rights to the idea of *Twenty Questions* as a radio property."

Dad's eyebrows were still up. "All right. That's noted."

Mr. Martin suggested one obvious move we ought to make. "Go see some quiz shows. I can get you tickets."

He did, and we all went to New York the Fourth of July and spent the evening watching *Can You Top This?*, *Detect and Collect*, and *Pot of Gold*. What we actually saw perplexed me. The shows were produced in plain old theatres, like the one where we had just seen *Life With Father*. All we saw were people on a stage talking into microphones. We could have accomplished as much staying home in front of the Philco. My view of the Lone Ranger riding toward Mustang Mag changed a bit, too. I felt that radio had been fooling me for years.

Twenty Questions was slow to materialize. On those occasions when the family had, for one reason or another, gone to New York, we had usually seen Mr. Stark up on 24 at WOR. Each time, I had glibly asked him if they were still kicking it around. Each time, he assured me they were, with a tolerant twinkle.

By now it was September (and I was a minuscule freshman at Princeton High School). The summer was over and Stark did nothing. By early October, we began nudging Dad to get this quiz show going. But still nothing happened, so, ever alert to Mother's every wish, Dad told Mr. Stark that, if he still did nothing by the end of the week, he would go to Norm Livingston alone. And he did. Stark still stalled. Dad took the ball.

As I stumbled on the rooty paths of high school, Dad was getting *Twenty Questions* to move in the womb. First, who would be in the cast — the panel and the emcee? From the beginning, I think all agreed that Dad would be on the panel. For the other panelists, they tried Dad's associates at the office, such as sportscaster Stan Lomax and a couple of the WOR announcers. They tried the blind pianist of show business, Alec Templeton. They tried women who had radio shows. Martha Dean. Mary Margaret McBride. For the emcee they tried men already emcees, like Paul Wing, of the National Spelling Bee. They tried the sports caster, Ted Husing. They sought Clifton Fadiman. He wasn't interested. They were doing things, but weren't getting anywhere.

Then, one Sunday late in the fall, Dad asked me if I remembered that day in June when the *Twenty Questions* idea began. I assured him I recalled every detail. All right, who had actually suggested that animal, vegetable, mineral be made into a radio show? I said nobody had. It just developed. He said to remember well, because it looked like the show was going to be a hit.

By December *Twenty Questions* began to take hold of my thoughts. Bob Martin was involved now. Norm Livingston had already taken a personal hand. They seemed to be holding more meetings than before. They held more auditions. Major progress occurred when they chose Mary Margaret McBride for the panel. Then, a week later Mary Margaret's head cold happened to change the orbits of the family. Sniffles kept her from the next scheduled audition. The audition must go on, with others already scheduled, so Mother agreed to substitute for Mary Margaret, just to help out. She wowed the whole crew. She could play, she had a pleasantness about her that sounded sincere on mike, and she was willing. Very willing. I recall that they all came home exhilarated.

So, the show was forming. Dad and two women would be on the panel of four. For the fourth panel member, they wanted someone with a dry voice and a dry wit, another Oscar Levant. They tried Ned Sparks. They tried other old vaudevillians I had never heard of. No step forward, then one step backward. Mary Margaret McBride pulled out altogether. Her crowded schedule could not fit in a quiz show.

All right, said Norm Livingston, instead of a newscaster, two women, and a wit, let us try something different. Let us try a *juvenile*. The Quiz Kids still rated high. But where do you get juveniles? Norm Livingston knew that the Quiz Kids talent came from schools somewhere in the Chicago area. New York had so-called "genius" schools, too. But the juvenile idea itself needed a try out first, before developing sources for weekly juvenile geniuses. That meant another audition.

They asked me to help out. I at least knew how to play.

This grand audition, took place a Saturday morning in January 1946 in one of Mutual's new ground-floor studios at 1440 Broadway. Because of scheduling, this would be a three-pronged audition — testing the juvenile idea, another possible Oscar Levant, and an emcee.

I felt pretty secure about it because I was just really a stand-in. I was not trying out for a part. I was just helping out, and not really thinking much about it. I would do this thing and get back to my regular teenage worries. I had never met any of these people but didn't much care since I would probably never see any of them again. Uncounted droves of people, too, all grownups, were milling around. I felt even smaller than I did roaming the halls of PHS.

Herb Polesie, on hand for the wit audition, milled less and settled more, seated back against a metal table, one leg up on a wooden chair. He held a curved pipe, less in the literary way of coziness than in the showbiz way of laughs. His face worked bright humor, somewhere between wag and droll.

Bill Slater, on hand for the emcee audition, was a big man, poised like the captain of a ship. He moved with deliberate power. His hair was combed straight back in that bright gray of cosmopolitan experience. This man was in charge. When they were ready to begin, I heard Dad ask him if he needed *Twenty Questions* subjects to use for the audition. He dismissed the offer, saying, "I have subjects." There would be no discussion.

Dad was more accommodating than he usually was, but, of course, he had many people to please. He offered exuberance to some, serious discussion to others, especially Bob Simon, who was Norm Livingston's assistant. I gathered that, although Mr. Simon must be pleased, they viewed him as a Devil's advocate and nit picker. Dad would hold him at arm's length while awaiting Mr. Livingston, who was on his way.

Mother was smiling, nodding, standing back. She always mixed easily, soon a friend to all, if more or less without opinion.

I was standing back even further, sensing that anybody looking my way would wonder what this kid was doing there. Worse yet, those who knew about the juvenile test would be looking at me with the thought, so this is what a juvenile looks like. I knew, of course, that at fourteen I was not really what they wanted. A real kid is no older than nine or ten and preferably six or seven. After that a kid begins to lose the special accommodation he receives because he is a kid.

Pretty soon we were ready to start. While the other people in the room retreated to the fringes, we sat at two tables facing each other, Mr. Slater at the short one, the panel at the other. Without knowing exactly when or how he did it, Mr. Slater assumed command. He announced that he would play the subjects in the order in which he had them, calling on any panel member who raised his hand. Any questions?

All right, we started to play. I suppose we went through somewhere between fifteen and thirty subjects. Nobody lagged or paused. We had played this game for years. If anybody expected stumbling contestants, he did not find them that day. One hand at least was always raised, and usually hands fought for attention. Dad would shout Ho. I would jump with a flailing arm. Mr. Polesie exclaimed that he felt like he was in a hurricane. We sailed through the subjects. After the first few, I could see that Mr. Slater had chosen lots of golden oldies. The Tower of London. Adam and Eve. The apple on William Tell's son's head. George Washington's false teeth.

Well, to put it perhaps too bluntly, I got almost all of them. They just flowed. I felt like a gunner who couldn't miss from the key. About halfway through, Mr. Livingston came in. He waved us on, sitting back near the rear wall. I got two or three more. Mr. Slater, by now, would pause in posed amazement when I named the subject. He would hold the card in frozen posture. Dad or Mother would get one here and there and, when they did, some felt a certain relief.

Suddenly it was over. Dad was talking to Mr. Livingston. Mr. Livingston was talking to Mr. Slater. Mr. Slater said he wanted to shake my hand. I was amazing. Mr. Polesie told me that I had a very good presence. Mother's attitude was mixed.

I had no idea if what we had shown that day was what Norm Livingston would accept. Herb Polesie had made some cracks that went in pretty well. He won a spot. I certainly got the impression that we had found our emcee. Producer would be Bob Martin. Apparently, Mr. Livingston liked his idea of a juvenile on the panel because he wanted Dad to make sure I would be available in two weeks to do the formal audition in a theatre — and maybe the first show, if all went well. That was the first time I had heard anybody say that *Twenty Questions* really was going to go on the air.

On January 19 in the Longacre Theatre, someone, probably Norm Livingston, asked the audience, on hand for the witty feminism of *Leave It To The Girls,* to remain for the audition of a new quiz show. It would be a new quiz show called *Twenty Questions.*

Of the event itself I still carry two memories. As the theatre audition began, I happened to look forward and beheld out there endless rows of real people, looking at me and at times laughing or applauding because of something I said. The other memory was of words I heard on the stage after it ended. Norm Livingston said to Dad, "Now, you'll have Bobby for the first show, won't you?"

Two Saturdays later, we drove in early. Dad did the Six-Thirty News. Stark, who knew *Twenty Questions* was about to calve, said, "I sue on Monday." And we rode to the Longacre in a cab.

Bob Martin, who as producer was responsible for finding a guest panelist, had delivered Guy Lombardo. Norm Livingston loomed. The show would be "sustaining." No sponsor. But advertising agencies had sent scouts. *Pageant Magazine* had agreed to pay the guest. In return, the prize for using a subject was a year's subscription. If we failed to name the subject in twenty questions — in radio phrase, if we were stumped — the sender would receive a twenty-five dollar prize and a *Pageant* subscription for life.

The Longacre was about half full. Shills had handed out tickets to people around Times Square who looked like tourists. At seven thirty-five Mr. Slater walked onto the stage. He looked left, then slowly right. "This is the best looking audience we've ever had here."

I recall getting four of the nine subjects on that first show. One was Robert E. Lee. The rest the fade of time has obscured.

James Stewart was a guest during Twenty Questions' later years,. Here, backstage with Dad and Mother.

After the green *On the Air* sign went off, the stage became a bedlam. Little knots of blue suits surrounded Mr. Slater. Bob Martin spoke in earnest with ad agency types. Dad and Mom were talking to everybody at once. Before long Dad and Norm Livingston drifted together. I sort of tagged along. Dad asked what we would do about the future of the juvenile panel member. "Should we start the weekly search?"

Mr. Livingston shook his head. "Bobby, could you do it every week?"

I shrugged. "I guess so. Except for camp."

Dad said, "He goes to Boy Scout camp."

Mr. Livingston nodded, eager to confirm this minor matter and get on toward finding a sponsor. "Let's leave things as they are."

Twenty Question's last radio broadcast, still on MBS, occurred over eight years later, March 27, 1954, from the Roof Theatre of the Chanin Building on East 42nd Street. I had taken four years off for college, but at the end I was still on the panel.

Chapter 1

Rails to Disaster

Nineteen Scouts were heading home from Philmont Scout Ranch aboard the *California Limited*. They had made the old rail car into a rolling club room, turning some of the seats lengthwise facing windows and all the others facing each other. Two of them were playing Twenty Questions. It was Spade's turn for a subject, Bobby's turn to guess it.

Spade:	Vegetable.
Bob:	Does it exist?
Spade:	No. I guess not.
Bob:	Did it ever exist?
Spade:	Sure.
Bob:	Was it wood or a wood product?
Spade:	No.
Bob:	Was it cloth?
Spade:	No.
Bob:	Was it edible?
Spade:	Probably not.
Bob:	What does that mean?
Spade:	It means yes. Yeah, it was edible.
Bob:	Would you usually eat it with a meal?
Spade:	You could.
Bob:	If you did, would it be the main course.
Spade:	No.
Bob:	Was it dessert?
Spade:	Yes.
Bob:	Would this be used on the show as a subject?

Spade: I don't think so.
Bob, after a pause: Oh. The pudding.

"Too easy, Young Bobby will always be famous for the pudding."

"Very funny." Young Bobby had thrown the kettle in the brook to cool it, but not exactly as expected. Now he looked out. A cloud of soot and smoke from the engine billowed by. Beyond it, the plains stretched far away, tan to the horizon, so deep that the train never seemed to pass the far edge. He said, with obvious hesitation, "Hey, Spade, I got a serious question. About girls. I mean, when you're dancing there, holding onto her and all, you ever get worried you might, you know, touch her the wrong way or anything?"

"Look," Spade said, munching a pear serenely as they swayed and bumped, "We all know you're the most famous person in the school. Hell, you're the most famous person who's ever been in the school." He grinned in motion with the old rail car. "But Bobby McGuire dancing with a girl? Shit, Man. You'd be staring at her chin." Spade, accredited philosopher of teen, went on. "*Twenty Questions* for you's got to be logical. I mean, you're always answering the teacher in class. You're in plays all the time. You do skits at campfires. But, with girls, *Twenty Questions* cuts no ice at all."

"I'll go out for football."

"What as? The ball?"

They were interrupted by a hard curve. Both young men skidded over canvas-covered seats. "There's dancing in New York I gotta go to."

"And you dance?"

"Sometimes."

"Who with? Your mother?"

"Sponsors and advertising agencies have parties."

He stared out the window. Personal probing by a classmate like Spade made him feel embarrassed. Bobby would not learn until years later that most child performers — radio, movies, sports — eventually went into analysis.

Spade went on. "When are you going to have Elizabeth Taylor on *Twenty Questions*? Did you see *National Velvet*?"

Bobby looked aside, then bit into a pear. "We could, you know. Peggy Ann Garner and Barbara Ann Scott were both guests. Both less stuck up than I am."

"If you have Elizabeth Taylor, let me know and I'll be there."

Bobby flipped the pear core out the window with majestic disdain. "I'll get you tickets. If we ever see another sunrise. But, let's face it. This bucket will never make Kansas City." Bobby said grimly, "The whole trip's been scary."

Spade wadded up his sandwich paper. "Not for big guys." Spade tossed the wad of sandwich paper out the window. "How can you come out here anyway for three weeks? Don't they care?"

"If they cared, they would have sent me to Paris."

Young Bobby had gone to Philmont Scout Ranch only because they wouldn't let him miss more than two shows. He would have missed four if he had gone to Paris for the 1947 International Boy Scout Jamboree. But there were ratings worries with this and he went out west instead, with stunning result. To this day around the embering campfires of Troop 43 in Princeton, New Jersey, and around similar smokers throughout the world, his two weeks on the trail in New Mexico became marked as an historic mid-century crisis similar in stature to the Berlin Airlift, Senator McCarthy, and Margaret Truman. From Cimarron Bench to the Tooth of Time, he found himself dodging daily calamity. He hiked with his head down. His burro's load always managed to slide off. Then there was the great pudding episode.

"That Paris trip was five hundred dollars," Spade said.

"Instead of thirty-nine ninety-five."

Bobby was absorbing the train ride home from Philmont as a Janis of ladhood. It looked backward to campfire ballads, merit badges, and square knots and looked forward with terror to the Princeton Playhouse movie palace, dance programs, and dark rec rooms beyond. Both Scouts and *Twenty Questions* had always been welcome fortresses against the need to take on that coming disaster, Females. His freshman year, a luscious girl in his class, Betsy Baldwin, complained in student council of her parents' limiting how many dates per week she could accept. Up to now Bobby had felt safe from clutches such as hers. But very early on, especially from Spade's campfire braggadocio about girls, Bobby could perceive the devil moon of *women* rising all over Ponil Base Camp, and all over him.

"I could have gone to Paris. Climbed the Eiffel Tower on the outside. Had some wine for the first time. Seen bare tits maybe. But no. They ship me to a state full of red rocks by way of an antiquated roller coaster."

Spade said, "Can you pull down that shade without ripping it like you did last time?"

"Tells you something, doesn't it? Sixteen years old and my big success of the expedition is pulling down a window shade."

Minutes and miles jumped by. Then, "Thurman told me they're going to form an Explorer troop or post or whatever you call it."

Spade's eyes shifted slightly. "You really want to join? Don't kid me."

"What can I lose? It would ease the agony, and, if there's one thing upon which Young Bobby thrives, it's agony. Why else would I stick myself with four miles of Indian cactus and eat four yards of pork roll?"

"But they have dances and things."

"I could I learn how to dance." He wrinkled his brows. "I can see my mother going up to Al Nathan, our Ronson contact man, and telling him Bobby can dance as well as he plays *Twenty Questions*."

Spade, concentrating on the sandwich, spoke to it. "Their functions are always Saturday. What's going to happen when *Twenty Questions* starts to get in the way?"

"I'll just tell them I quit. Then they'll have to go find another teenager for their quiz panel, and what they'll find is that we're in short supply. I happen to know they've gone looking without finding any. The witty kids can't play the game and the ones who can play the game lack my ethereal charm."

"Even if you could go on Saturdays, you don't just press a button and start going out."

"I'm working up a fully defined sense of lust."

A Milky Way wrapper was shifting on the seat beside him. Bobby wadded it into a ball and tossed the ball down the aisle.

"You think you just pick up the phone and you got a date?"

"More or less."

"You're really nuts. You know that, McGuire? For being so smart, you don't know a damn thing."

Chapter 2

Twenty Questions

It was nine p.m that Saturday before Labor day. The family was seated tensely at Toffinetti's, corner of 43rd and Broadway, for an after-show supper. To emphasize the weight of the moment, Dad's nose exhaled twin jets of blue smoke. Neither cigarettes nor radio quiz shows were evil in 1947.

"Kid, you can't play both ends against the middle."

This was one of Dad's favorite phrases. He had many and he depended on them, which seemed odd to Bobby—cliches from a man so big so soon. Just twenty years before, Dad had been a kid reporter in Chicago, in those glorious Hildy Johnson times. Only six years before, he had been a country newscaster in Detroit. Now he had the highest rated news program in New York and owned a quiz show heard coast to coast.

Young Bobby grunted. "I didn't." He was half furious and half powerless, the typical kid condition. He was absently using a fork to push around the grated cheese container as if it were a hockey puck.

"I had to go to bat for you in this late business, Dingfod."

"Where? With who?"

"Fineshriber."

Bobby looked at him sideways. "Is he a big gun or something?"

"I think you know." He drew on his cigarette.

"All I do is play a game. When it comes to details, I'm a dunce."

"Well, you should know."

Dad was wearing a blue surge suit and he was leaning forward with his elbows on the table and his cigarette poised. He might have been provincial once, but he showed no hint of it now.

Bobby said, raising his voice slightly, "Dingfod could have stayed till the end of the movie and taken a cab. So, he leaves early and takes a subway, which is supposed to be faster, and winds up with a free ticket to the dog house."

"It's not just tonight, Bob. It's your whole attitude during the last year. You just go off in your own direction."

"You make me feel like I just got another D minus from Miss Gilman."

"He *is* our boss, Jinky Bob," Mother said.

Mother was hanging back from the table like a revered relative hanging above the mantle. Her gloves were folded beside her plate. Mother was a seasoned mediator and frequent referee.

"He's my boss?" He looked to Dad. "He's my *boss*?"

This was the 1940s. In that long-ago, simmering summer of 1947, Young Bobby was still ensnared by a problem that had first emerged in early 1946. "Step right up, radio listeners. He's smart and he's only a teenager. He's our amazing fourteen-year-old schoolboy." Oh, yes. He was billed as wise beyond his years. One guest panelist that month was Harry McNaughton, star of a deliberately dopey radio show called *It Pays To Be Ignorant*. Harry was especially ruinous. "It pays us to be ignorant. It pays Bobby to be intelligent." Just what the doctor ordered for a teenage panelist's id and ego. Show business lent to him fame and it also lent the illusion of importance. On account of that illusion, he believed himself so wonderful that he could afford to disparage the whole affair. Their radio show was a light lark and he couldn't care less. His apathy was discussed from Keene's English Chop House to Danny's Hideaway. Had Truman decided to hand the A-bomb to the Russians, the impact would have been similar.

Harry: Where's that Clark Clifford when I need him?

Young Bobby's making light of the program made the sponsor, Ronson Lighters, and its agency wince. They thought that appearing on *Twenty Questions* was surely an ace Bobby had been dealt in the game of *teen*. Girls would swoon. Not hardly. Girls were still as worthless to him as shaving cream.

Of course, Bobby was not the only one on the *Twenty Questions* panel who was paid to be smart, whether they were or not.

Mother: Bobby certainly wasn't the only one on the panel.

She was known on the panel as Florence Rinard (Ri-*nard*) and she got her share of subjects.

Mother: I got as many subjects as Bobby got, and people liked me more.

Herb Polesie was the panel's wag. He said funny things in a funny voice.

Herb: My mother-in-law is a fine lady. She fines me every time I see her.

Bobby's father was the panel's anchor. He scored less often but held the panel together. Dad had been a newscaster on WOR for years.

Dad: Here's a brief recapitulation of the news at this hour.

Bill Slater, Herb Polesie, Bobby, Mother, Dad are presented with an award, one of many the show received.

The family usually drove from their new home in Princeton to New York Saturday afternoon in their new '47 Cad. The show didn't go on until 8:00, so, while Dad did his WOR 6:30 news show, Bobby would go to a second-run movie on 42nd Street. This Saturday it was *Gunfighters* with Randolph Scott. At 7:15, just as Randy was about to gun down Forrest Tucker, Bobby, conscientious for once, skipped the climax and beat it to the Eighth Avenue Subway. But there, alas, he encountered municipal disaster. The train froze in its hole just short of 50th Street. When it finally made the station, he sprinted from the north exit a quarter block down 52nd Street to the stage entrance of the Mutual Guild Theatre. Sweltering fans, hoping against all reason to encounter Young Bobby, were waiting in line along the sidewalk, when he broke through to enter the stage door. He bounded up the steel steps to the wings of the theatre, where Dad was standing.

Bobby entered saying, "Well, here I am at last. You can call in Mr. Kean."

Dad, the WOR newscaster, anchored the panel

Dad was rather round with a dark handsome face. His hair was black, what little was left. In days before radio, when weekly paychecks were the meaning of life, he had concocted some crazy laughs for his son, but, since he went on the air, much of his funny abandon had abandoned him.

Bobby asked, "Where's mother?"

Although stage hands, other cast members, and hangers-on from the network, the agency, and the sponsor, were milling about, none was paying any attention.

"In make-up." Mother always obtained extra make-up, even though it was a radio show. It was applied in one of the rude dressing rooms down a hall near the stairway, one of the old theatre's passages and dim niches that seemed to flow away to nowhere. Everything was dark and high, spooky and very grand. Some famous people had trod those boards, and here was Young Bobby.

"Lucky make-up."

Dad shook his head. "No buy, Ashtray." He was pointing his finger. "You're late and, when you're late, somebody has to tell you. It's in the contract."

"Contract?"

Contract. Bobby felt the weight of the word in his hip pocket. So did all showbiz people. They do to this day. That he had never seen a contract tells you how far from the center of the business Young Bobby really was.

"Yes." Dad's mincing yes. "It's in the contract." He nodded his head with emphasis.

Bobby was ill-at-ease talking business with Dad, the same Dad who had thrown him softballs and baited his hook.

"Oh, yes, the contract. Those white papers grown-ups wave around. Those billet-doux we pay George thousands to write. They'll engulf us like we're in a Broadway parade. No wonder my grades are so low."

Dad said, "It's part of the union contract and you belong to the union."

The guy who played Superman was president of AFRA, somewhat less powerful than a locomotive. Bobby had attended a few smoky union meetings, palming his card with exquisite finesse as the union steward checked him in.

"I know I belong to the union. I carry a union card, along with my Eagle Scout card, my Social Security Card, and my membership card in Captain Midnight's Secret Squadron." Short shrift for unions. "Who's the guest?"

"An opera singer. Regina Resnik."

The guest on the show was like the hood ornament on a car. As it was, Miss Resnik was near the high end, not Hollywood but several billings above Yankee ball players and Ted Malone. Lucille Ball, who had been a guest the first summer the show was on the air, two years before, had been their biggest name. At the time, she was not yet a comedienne but still a glamorous redhead, and she managed to rub some of that glamour off on Bobby. He sat next to the guest on the panel, and, when he got a subject that night, she reached over and rubbed his cheek. He turned bright red. Fourteen years old.

"Never heard of her. A coloratura?"

"Mother has. A Wagnerian. You might ask George about the contract." Dad turned away to greet Al Nathan and two other men from Ronson. These were not hangers-on.

Bobby looked toward the nearby circle of chairs. "We going to warm her up or let her suffer in ignorance?"

Before each show, they would sit in a circle backstage and try to train the guest to play. The game they played, and the show itself, was a panel version of the old animal, vegetable, mineral game. The listening audience sent in subjects for the panel to guess. They received thousands of suggestions each week, and most of them were Churchill's cigar. As the fifth panel member, the guest would play the game with them, to little effect, which didn't matter much, because they were there to plug a book or movie or to keep their name before the public. Few seemed to mind looking foolish. A few looked good.

"We did. She's played the game. Ask George about it, Crab Cake."

Bobby nodded as he turned, saying rather loudly, "Speaking of lines, did you see the crowd outside? People in their right minds are standing on 52nd Street in the heat to see a quiz show."

Dad pulled in his chin. "Maybe you don't quite realize what this show means to you." He swung away and cordially greeted the Ronson people.

Bobby wandered through the wings and crossed the stage behind the show's shell, passing harps in cases, racks of steel chairs, and a pin rail to fly scenery for other Mutual radio shows. He found George on the other side, talking to Gary Stevens, who had succeeded Bob Martin as the show's producer, and Flo Cahn, publicity agent.

Flo was slick, pungent, and trimmed out for show business like a table at Sardi's. Gary, a broad, dark pro who had produced movies before the war, was half way through his life as a knower. He knew everybody in show business. He looked up, smiled and nodded. "We were looking for you."

"I got stuck in the subway."

Gary was full of Manhattan wisdom. "Never take a subway when you got a show to do. A cab is cheaper in the long run."

"One stop on a four track line, paying full nickel to revel in the reliable transport the city provides and what happens? The *Titanic* was faster."

Bobby turned to George Adler. He was agent, lawyer, and dirty-work factotum to the show and the family. Every show needed a George, a shot of serotonin among the many ganglia that dangled from the network, the producers, the agency, the sponsor, and Walter Winchell. Young Bobby had developed admiration for this guy because he knew how to take heat and bumps without bruises — bruises that showed anyway. He could even kowtow. Some job for a brilliant lawyer.

"Dad asked me to ask you."

"Ask me what?" He even grinned, although he probably felt more like frowning. He was a tall, good looking guy with a professional puss something like Gary's. Bobby envied him for several reasons, one of which was that he drove an MG-TC.

"He says I got a contract I never heard of between me and the show."

"You're kidding. Right?" The grin broadened. Gary and Flo slid away, each sensing that a mess was about to gush.

"Me? Kid? I'm just a little game player. I guess animals, vegetables, and minerals. When you talk about parties of the first part, I come in second. No. It's just that, if I have a contract, I want to know about it is all." He wanted to make a point with George, but George wasn't interested. In the 1940s big guys weren't interested in little guys.

"I still think you're kidding."

"I thought Dad was. But he had that Hoosier Schoolmaster frown on his face, thinking hickory stick, and he said you would tell me about it."

"Well, let's talk about it after the show. If you still aren't kidding."

So, Young Bobby, dismissed by his forever elders, returned to the other wing, pouting in discontent. He would deal with these Philistines later.

In the guests's circle on folding chairs, he found Miss Resnik and her agent talking to the emcee, Bill Slater. To Bobby he was always Mr. Slater. He was a big, strong man Dad's age, very erect, with a handsome face and straight-back silver hair. He was a graduate of West Point and the rod was still rammed.

Slater said, "Bobby, have you met Regina Resnik?"

They had booked opera singers before as a shine on their cultural image. Most of them were females — attractive, intelligent, and rather spunky. But this one was spectacular and close enough to his age — if still a long way off, who was he kidding — that Bobby was instantly self conscious. She was shorter than others and svelte with dark stunning features including great shimmering eyes.

He nodded and almost smiled, which was rare for him. "Well, hello. I'm merely the kid on the show."

"Hello." She smiled back, somewhat unsure what to make of this kid amongst adults.

Everybody else was unsure, too. Bobby didn't know what to make of it himself. How could he? It had never been done before. You had the Quiz Kids in Chicago but they were kids amongst kids. The juvenile on the *Twenty Questions* panel always made people around Mutual very uneasy, mainly because they could never figure out why it worked.

Bobby said, "They tell me you've played the game."

"I sure have. But I'm no expert."

Gary leaned in. "Stand by. Five minutes, Bill." Gary went away.

Bobby said, ignoring the others, "I have to ask you, Mr. Slater. Are you going to mention my birthday?"

"Hasn't come up, Bobby. It might be you're getting old for it. Sixteen isn't quite as amazing as fourteen."

"I just wanted to know so I can, you know, act surprised."

"Let me find out." He rose and excused himself.

Left alone with Miss Resnik and her female agent, Bobby felt almost frightened. He caught himself looking from side to side, like a tailback who doesn't want to fumble but knows he's going to.

Miss Resnik said, "That's a coincidence. My birthday is a week from today."

Bobby blurted, "Is that so? How old are you gonna be?" His silent cry reverberated among his synapses. Aaaagggghhhh!. It was out before he could drag it back. What a dunce. What a dodo.

She smiled with toleration. "Now, that would be telling."

The silence was dismal, like midnight in the mortuary. His tongue groped for sound. He finally said, "Three thousand human feet in the theatre and I have to stuff one into my own mouth. I apologize for both the question and for the smelly theatre."

Bobby wanted to fly to the outer planets. He wanted a cannon to shoot him through the grid over the stage.

"The Met is smellier. Really."

"We had Mimi Benzell last year and she said the same thing."

Miss Resnik very likely understood his embarrassment. She smiled. "It must be exciting for you, smelly or not."

Bobby nodded reluctantly. "I guess so. It's supposed to be. But actually, you know, all I do is play a parlor game."

"Even so." She leaned forward. This would be a secret revealed. "I'm always excited when the curtain goes up. Any curtain."

"You are?" He looked right at her. "You're not kidding, are you?"

"Will I remember my lines? My blocking? My phrasing?"

"That's amazing. But then I'm still amazed by the Radio City Music Hall and the Gilbert Hall of Science."

Mother came up and Bobby rose. She said, "I'm Florence Rinard." Miss Resnik rose and they shook hands. As they started discussing *Die Walkure*, Bobby slipped away.

He found Mr. Slater standing at the right stage entrance. In a minute or two, he would walk on and do the warm up.

Bobby and emcee Bill Slater backstage

Bobby inquired, "Big house?"

He nodded down at him. "Your father says skip the birthday."

"One of his more rational judgments." He looked out and could see the long draped table where the panel sat and the shorter table where Mr. Slater sat beside Gary.

Slater said, "Sixteen is dating and growing taller."

"People say both are compulsory."

"You'll want to skip shows because they're Saturday night." Mr Slater had been principal of a prep school for many years and knew kids like Bobby for the fools they were.

Before Bobby could continue, Slater walked out on stage. Applause greeted him. He would pore over the audience, then nod and say, "This is the best looking audience we've ever had here."

Bobby looked aside. Ruby Shepherd had appeared. She was almost as short as Bobby, very cute and dark with an engaging smile. Her job was to turn down the big white cards from which the audience learned what the subject was. Mr. Slater always introduced her first.

"Hi, Ruby."

"Hi, Bobby. Feeling smart tonight?" She had an airy, husky voice. He had once felt like grabbing Ruby. But, when he learned she had a child, he didn't know what to make of her.

After she went out, Herb Polesie appeared beside him. Like Gary, he had produced movies before the war, one starring Bing Crosby, before the *Roads* were built. He was a round man like Dad with an egg-shaped head and twinkling eyes. His voice was dry and had a comic sound like a bassoon.

He looked down at Bobby, grinning. "I like your tie." At one time Bobby had insisted on competing in wearing the loudest tie, not realizing that in doing so he was stepping on Herb's lines.

Herb went out with a shout and Bobby was next.

From "Is it a whole animal?" to "Is it east of the Mississippi?" Young Bobby tore up the kilocycles that night. He got a warm-up and three subjects.

This is Ronson's Mystery Voice offstage in a soundproof booth. I'm here to tell you that the subject is, well, cheese — the green cheese the moon's made of.

Bill Slater:	All right this one's animal. Who'll start?
Dad:	Is it a whole animal?
Bill Slater:	No
Mother:	Is it part of a human being?
Bill Slater:	No
Herb:	Is it part of a four-footed animal?
Bill Slater:	Uh, well, yes.

Mother:	Is it cloth?
Bill Slater:	Not cloth
Bobby:	Is it edible?
Bill Slater:	Uh, I don't believe so. Not in the form in which I'm thinking of it.
Dad:	Is it part of a domestic animal?
Bill Slater:	You mean like a dog? No. Not in that sense of the word.
Bob:	Did it come from a domestic animal?
Bill Slater:	Yes
Mother:	Is it part of a cow?
Bill Slater:	Yes. Or a product therefrom.
Mother:	Is it leather?
Bill Slater:	No
Dad:	Is it a product of milk?
Bill Slater:	Yes
Herb:	Is it cheese?
Bill Slater:	Yes
Mother:	Is it in a saying or expression?
Bill Slater:	Yes
Bob:	Is it any particular color?
Bill Slater:	Yes, now that …
Bob:	The green cheese the moon's made of.
Bill Slater:	Bobby McGuire! (Applause) You got it in fifteen questions.

Miss Resnik was charming, as she was at the Met for years to come. You would think everybody concerned would have left the theatre that night brimming with gaiety and good cheer.

"Where shall we eat?" Mother inquired as the family entered a cab.

Dad rejoined, "Ask Bobby. He knows everything,"

In this atmosphere of internecine suspicion, the cab bounced through Times Square to Toffinetti's, a bright Italian eatery only three blocks from WOR. Dad still had his 11:00 PM news show to do.

This was a tourist spot larded up with dazzle and razzle. He ate up that stuff, an early exposure to what later became known as Marketing.

Dad ordered an Old Forester and soda. He had become caught up in the cosmopolitan panache of ordering by brand in these, his salad days of drinking. Years later, when Dad began to succumb to alcohol, he used euphemisms to order booze. Dry martinis among friends became "Juniper Junction." Mother had not yet begun to drink or smoke.

Bobby said, "Wasn't Miss Resnik great?" He wanted to lighten things.

"Yes, she was," Mother admitted. "I thought she was all right. She's only in her twenties. And she sings Wagner."

Mother very likely felt very comfortable, like a revered image. She had been a town belle in early-century Indiana and assumed she was still a belle in mid-century New York, so that she would smile with poise and restraint as she assumed New York belles did.

Mother, who appeared on the panel as Florence Rinard, had been a town belle in Indiana.

Bobby said, "At least she isn't built like Helen Traubel." Bobby grinned at his earthy suggestion.

Dad nodded. "She did all right. We all did all right. It was a good show. But."

His drink came. He lit a cigarette.

Bobby said to him, "My whole life is full of *buts*, like an ashtray after your bridge club."

Which brought on jets of blue smoke and the name Fineshriber.

Now Dad had said, "Nobody's your boss. Is that it, Ashtray?"

Bobby leaned back, probably rolling his eyes. Didn't they understand anything? "Nobody's my boss is the phrase of the week. I apply it to *Twenty Questions*, when you recall that I can quit any time. You said George had drawn up the contract that way."

"I don't buy, Sugar Spoon. I said the contract provided for replacement when you went to camp and when you went to college. That's all."

Bobby turned up his palms in adolescent disbelief. "You mean I couldn't quit, even if I want to?"

"Why would you want to quit?" Mother said with her pacifist smile.

To Bobby, off in his own direction perhaps, that was the whole issue. To almost anyone else, being drafted to appear every week on a radio quiz show at age fourteen would amount to some incredible dream come true. And in the first year or so, Bobby felt that way. He floated on clouds. He dreamed of paradise only to awake to find things even better. But by the second anniversary, the dream had begun to have subplots. Bobby was on the radio, after all, because he was a freak. He had told himself, "On the radio I'm a low magnitude star; everywhere else I'm still a drip."

He said, "I'm like Columbus halfway across. I sail on and who knows what lies ahead? Maybe I'll be drafted to run for Congress, with my boyish charm. Maybe I'm going out on a date some Saturday night with a wholly worthy young lady." Okay. He got it in. Not too subtle. But there it lay, an ember of warning. The show would have to deal with it.

"We could make allowances for that," Dad said. But he said it as if he were confronting a problem of the coming millennium, with fifty-three years to solve it.

The waiter hovered. He wore a silky black suit, not quite a tux, and had a long, dark face. He seemed exotic. It was a strange factoid that Young Bobby identified later in life that almost every waiter in New York looked exotic. Bobby ordered the spaghetti and meat balls, the house specialty. Dad did, too. Mother ordered a hamburger. That was her constant order. At the Roosevelt Grill, with Guy Lombardo at their table, she would order a hamburger.

"Remember," Mother said, "we've got a big stake in *Twenty Questions*."

"Did you say steak? With *Twenty Questions* gravy? Dad's news remains our bread and butter?"

Dad was withdrawing. He did not like to argue with his son. "Well, Bob, maybe there are a few things you just don't know much of anything about."

Bobby shook his head doggedly. "But that's what I heard Mother say. I heard her."

His problem was obvious to those who have either studied adolescent behavior or who have gone to camp. The kid was still naive enough to depend upon absolute truth for success. How naive can you be? At sixteen! The real world of cynical reality was lurking just outside Bobby's door, but he would lose many encounters before he opened it and stepped out.

She was all smiles and reason. "But, Bobby, you wouldn't want us to give up *Twenty Questions*. Now would you?"

The problem here was that his adolescent condition was normal. Bobby did not know what he wanted. Finally, through the stiff silence, he crinkled his eyebrows. "What ever happened to the plan to get a different teenager every week anyway? I could have gone to Paris and become an international traveler instead of to Philmont to become a bungling burro packer."

Dad said shortly, "You know the answer to that. Fineshriber said to stick with you."

Bobby grimaced. "Yes, and he hardly knows me."

Before anyone could continue, the food arrived. Bobby loaded his spaghetti with grated cheese. A free bowlful was there for the taking and, somehow, the stuff being free made a difference.

Dad spoke as he seasoned his meal. He used pepper on everything. "He isn't very happy with the camp and college clause either. When you went to Philmont and we had replacements, the ratings fell."

"So did my arches."

"Not much but some, and Fineshriber let us know about it."

Bobby waved it away. "Alas, poor ratings. Mutual should send him to manage their three hundredth station in Oil City, Pennsylvania."

"I can't agree with your attitude, Bob. He's built up the ratings for the whole network, you know. He's quite a manager."

"So was Mussolini." Bobby forked spaghetti. "But I have a piece of good news for Mr. Fineshriber." He looked aside for spies. He awaited a fanfare. "I doubt if I go to camp again. After what I did to Philmont, where could I go?"

Dad paused to let the sounds pass, then said, "He also hopes you'll go to Princeton, so you can stay on the show."

Bobby dismissed this plan. "Princeton's an eastern school."

"Yes, it is. And I can't blame you for wanting to avoid the eastern establishment. But you want to remember, there really are other people to be considered. Not just Robert."

"Not Robert at all. If I was being considered, I'd be home right now, where I'm a very small high school student. The first day of school I went into the principal's office and asked him to show me personally to my home room. And he did it."

"We know you're a good student, Bob," Mother said, almost ready to grip her hamburger, "I think what Daddy means is that, if you left the show, it might affect the ratings, and we'd all suffer in the long run."

Bobby faked a tad of exasperation. Why did they always have to argue? "Mother, I'm only a junior in high school, starting week after next. College hasn't even crossed my mind."

"Very little crosses your mind, does it, Gumball?" Dad said.

Chapter 3

PHS

That first Wednesday in September, first day of school, Young Bobby, now a junior, swept into 124 as if he were crossing a stage. Even though nobody was looking at him any more than at anybody else, he felt dozens of eyes on his backbone. Like most people in show business, he awaited the applause and ignored the silence.

It was a typical classroom, a bank of windows on one wall opposite a blackboard on the other. Yes, black. The green chalkboards — they changed the color, it was said, so that the word black need not be used — came later. One-arm chair/desks made ambiguous rows. The teacher's desk was up front. Flag in one corner. Bible on a lectern in another. Since home room assignments reflected the alphabet, Bobby had seen the same kids in home room every year. Freshman year they had elected him to student council. Sophomore year Bobby had fostered Mort Manion's election, describing Mort as "an agreeable seed from north of town." After waves and hellos, it was Mort who this day Bobby drew aside.

Behind his hand he whispered, "Hello, Mort. I see you're smiling in reaction to the educational possibilities of the first day of school, one of which is election to student council, for which I think we can get Dick Mickleson." He let his eyes sneak aside, like a spy making sure the desk wasn't bugged.

Mort said, "Fine with me. Not Kimberly Manners?"

"Not this year." Kimberly was a jolly girl he had known since eighth grade. Bobby was saving her. For what he never said. "Kimberly's of great reputation, but a Fascist, while Dick will rule with a wet hand. I'll nominate. You second."

"Yeah." Mort grinned. "Still on the radio?" His glasses reflected the windows behind.

"Only in my sober moments. A career in movies is next. I'll rival Roddy MacDowell."

Mort said, "Seen the new girl?"

New girl! This was, of course, was an interjectional phrase, somewhat akin to "open fire" in other venues of struggle, forcing Bobby's hands up in mock consternation. "Girl? As in gym shorts?"

New girl. Bobby suspected this could be the first step by which all journeys are begun, a step that up to now Princeton High School society had postponed demanding of him. They all knew, or so he figured, that Saturday nights he was going steady with *Twenty Questions.*

Bobby: They knew that I was going steady with a freak show named Twenty Questions.

But Bobby had seen the handwriting on the wall.

Bobby: I had seen the handwriting on the boy's room wall.

So he was all set to ask somebody out.

Bobby: Like whom?

Either get a girl or you're through in this school. Maybe this new girl is her. Maybe not. But find out or do fifty words.

That very morning, his mother at breakfast had brought it up.

Bobby was saying between spoonfuls, "How I love Grape Nuts Flakes. Boy! Another spoonful and I turn into a Post Toastie. Why can't I have something exotic, like Ralston?"

The hint of sarcasm came at the expense of Checkerboard Square in St. Louis, where it was propounded in those years that eating the cereal advertised by Tom Mix would inevitably transform each eater closer to the physical ideal Mr. Mix represented. Ovaltine would accomplish the same toward Captain Midnight, Wheaties toward Jack Armstrong, and Quaker Puffed Wheat Sparkies toward Terry (if not the pirates). Bram-ah, hee-too, he-ta-poo, how!

"Your father likes Grape Nuts Flakes."

He spooned. "He's not going out for cross country. Taking American history with Miss Hight." He spooned. "Or, going out with girls."

Dad was still in slumber, with reason. He took the 11:25 train home from New York each weeknight after his eleven o'clock news, arriving around 1:00, and, so, rarely saw Bobby between weekends. By that age it didn't seem to matter much.

"You will need energy, Jinky Bob" his mother said. Then, after a pause, "Girls?"

Theirs was a sunny kitchen. Almost balmy, in some ways. The east end window over the sink looked out over the patio and down the slope to the mossy pond beyond. The window at the other end, where they ate most meals, overlooked the flagstone front porch. It was essence of suburbia.

"Girls. Known from Northwest Angle to Key West as the unfair sex. Ready to rend the family and shatter my eternal calm."

She sat back a space from the table. She was not showing surprise, whether she felt any or not. She was looking out the window at clumps of white birches. Then, turning back, she said, "You're not continuing in the Boy Scouts?"

"I'll be a Scout when I'm thirty." He spooned. "I list my triumphs as follows. First to use gasoline to start a cook fire. First to take my fourteen-mile hike on roller skates." He spooned. "Explorers are next and Explorers invite girls. I'm not sure how."

Some mild surprise here. But not much. "That's what you want?"

They used place mats on the black enamel table. His was more stained than the others. The radio on the shelf behind him stayed off in the morning. He couldn't stand noise at breakfast. But they would listen to Dad's 6:30 news show at supper and leave it on for Stan Lomax.

"I can't stay young forever." He spooned. "Or can I? Goodness knows I've been trying long enough. Explorers could force me into it. Since everybody but me's already gone out."

"Everybody but you?" Her tone was mellow, almost suave. There was certainly no spite or disappointment quite showing.

He picked up his milk and stared at it. "I wonder. Do I continue to tie sheep shanks, or do I tie knots of romantic exploration?"

"So, here you are, going to escort young women?"

"Scouts will survive. Pete can take over the Post leadership, even though he lacks my sense of the ridiculous. Of course there is one general problem. Girls don't like me much."

"Oh, Bobby." Thus she sat, blank — Bambi's mother.

He lifted the glass. "I'll probably start drinking coffee someday, too." He flipped a thumb toward her cup. "Or does it stunt your growth?"

She drew it back slightly.

He rambled on. "Can going to the movies with girls be that different from going to the movies with the boys? That is today's question. If the females keep saying no, I'm back to overnight hikes at Camp Buck and all I've lost is my sense of innocence."

"What girl?"

"I'll run a raffle."

With that exit line, this essence of the naive biked the two country/suburban miles to Princeton High. If you narrow your vision enough, you can probably place his passage within most any Hardy Boys adventure. And, like Frank and Joe, he was not sure which way to turn, which course to choose. Was he still, "Yes, Mother?" Or, was he ready for, "Hey, Babe"?

He approached PHS from the tail end of Moore Street. The bike rack stood behind the gym (nobody locked bikes). He jammed his front tire into a slot. It had been the first post-war bike for sale at Kopps Cycle Shop, well equipped with saddle bags, a Stuart-Warner speedometer, a generator, a horn. When Bobby got it the previous Christmas, he was full of pride. But that was nine months ago and now, about here, cars loomed in his wish list. Parking a car in the PHS lot would be a giant social step above sticking his bike in the rack, so giant, in fact, that it loomed in something of a mist.

The school was red brick, two-story, in the shape of a square U upside down, with the gym an added el to your left. In the middle was a paved circle around the flag pole. All the entrances were gothic arches, including a main one beneath a gothic bell tower. This rose an extra floor to contain the faculty lounge with a belfry above that.

Into this theatre of adolescence, young Bobby, dumb, struggling, and shy in corduroys, red sweater, and loafers, stepped, like a mid-century gargoyle not quite set in stone. He went in the back door into the hall past the gym. Near the tower door, he turned left into the main hall, feeling almost exhilarated by the bustle and by the sense that he belonged here.

In front of 106 he ran into Fred Darkly. Fred wore a tan, buttoned shirt, pants like Bobby's, and oxfords. Fred was a tall, literate red head — everybody's idea of a model high school student.

Fred: I was everybody's model of an ideal high school student.

Fred was as active in the school as Bobby was and just as smart.

Fred: I was more active than McGuire and smarter, too.

In fact, there was some evidence Fred resented him.

Fred: I secretly hated his guts.

They were going opposite ways down the crowded main hall. On Bobby's right, leaded casement windows looked out upon the flag pole in the circle. Although the halls had not been used since June, an aroma of red cleaning granules pervaded the air. Yes, public schools were known as much for their aromas as for their heartbreaks.

Bobby swung back and shouted, "Hey, Fred. We've managed to run into each other on the first day of our junior year."

Fred's armload of school stuff looked precarious, as herds of indigenous animals thundered by. Nobody had back packs in those days, and the few who carried briefcases were considered weird or super intellectual.

Fred said, "Seen the new girl?" If Fred was Bobby's equal in many activities, he was clearly more advanced in the lead story of the day.

"New girl? You mean on the block and what am I bid?" He waved empty hands. He wasn't sure he had time for this. Everything was moving.

"Going out for cross country?" Kids were sliding by him and bumping into him.

"What new girl?" Bobby flexed with the current.

"You said cross country and I already told Mr. Miles." Fred's open hand waved outward, brushing a passing sweater.

Bobby nodded. "Our cross country coach is a rabid Democrat."

Fred's eyes rolled upward. He swung back and was gone. Bobby wondered why his cronies' eyes were always rolling upward. A little inside-the-Beltway gamesmanship long before it was built.

Further down the hall, at the other main intersection, where Bobby would turn left toward his home room, he encountered John McFarland talking with John Ham. They were seniors, a class ahead of him. Both wore white shirts and dirty white bucks. He knew Ham a little, but McFarland was his closest friend in the senior class.

Bobby said, "Hello John and John." He unfolded both palms toward them.

They nodded. Ham was tall, McFarland about Bobby's height. Both were scholars, the closest thing in PHS to preppies.

McFarland said, "Mineral and vegetable."

Bobby:	Show subject?
John:	No
Bobby:	Is it in Princeton?
John:	Yes
Bobby:	In Princeton High School?
John:	Yes
Bobby:	Is it mine?

John:	No
Bobby:	Yours?
John:	No
Bobby:	Does it belong to anybody?
John:	Yes.
Bobby:	A student?
John:	No
Bobby:	To a teacher?
John:	Yes
Bobby:	Female teacher?
John:	Yes
Bobby:	Is her home room on the first floor?
John:	No
Bobby:	Is it situated on the north-south hall?
John:	Yes.
Bobby:	Does she keep it on her desk?
John:	No
Bobby:	Does she wear it?
John:	Yes.
Bobby:	So, it's clothing of … no. Miss Hight's eye shade.
John:	Yes. Thirteen questions.

Bobby said, nodding, "I guess so. Celluloid? Rubber?

McFarland nodded. "I saw your new Cadillac."

Bobby nodded. "You mean the blue one?" He spoke lightly, tossing off the symbol of status and at the same time admitting note of it.

McFarland said to Ham, flicking his a thumb, "Those bright red wheels were his idea."

It was important to Bobby that he could talk to these guys and they would listen. Besides being a caste up, they knew they were smarter than he was and tolerated his *professional* smartness on the radio without envy. Guys in his own gang weren't quite so tolerant. Radio or no, to them Bobby was snooty. To other guys in the school, the athletes and rowdies, Bobby was just a jerk. He would walk past the Penero brothers and they would mimic how Bobby walked and define with their hands how small he was. Because of this, he started hunching his shoulders, and did so for forty years.

He arrived at his home room, 124.

The pre-class home room period consisted of roll taking, announcements, chatter, and Bible. Somebody read a passage each morning. There were not yet enough atheist, Jewish, or Islamic students in the school to generate dissent, complaint, or law suit, so Scripture, which was babble to most anyway, got read and lost on a need-to-know basis.

When the bell rang, they jammed out to class. First period Young Bobby was vouchsafed American History with Miss Hight, who was teaching the class for her eighty-fifth straight year. Second period was Caesar with Miss Philmore, who was proclaiming *Omnes Galles* in her eighty-fifth consecutive declension. Third period was physics with Mr. Seward, who would proclaim that, standing at the north pole, the north magnetic pole was south and a little east. Of course, that kind of gaffe was obvious enough on a globe, but there wasn't one in the room and no GPS either.

The annual election he had discussed with Mort would occur fourth period. This was known as *home room,* quiet chaos before heading for lunch. Miss Eiseley asked for nominations. It was time for sordid politics to raise its head. The class Machiavelli would take over.

Bobby rose. "I am proud to nominate Dick Mickleson."

Mort rose. "I'm proud to second." He smiled. This boy knew how the power structure was tilted and was happy to form one of its buttresses.

Then dead silence, as Bobby expected.

"Any more nominations?" asked Miss Eiseley.

Nobody said anything. She looked about, slightly surprised, gently waving her board pointer all the way around to the blackboard, where white chalk lay whole and unbroken. "Well, then, I guess that's it. Dick, you're our student council representative." She encouraged a smatter of applause. Dick arose and bowed in a mocking way. They also elected an alternate, who turned out to be Kimberly, obviously being groomed for bigger things.

Sixth period, after lunch, was algebra with Mr. Leppard. The class crammed the back chairs and milled around.

Among the millers, Bobby saw a new face, with dark brown hair and a silhouette that his mother would describe as pleasingly plump. A sweet smile, too. What? Sweet? Really? Was he sure? Was James Marshall holding the first nugget in his pan? This was not just welcome. It was climactic. Vintage readers will recall the atmosphere, laden with Victorian residue. Most girls of that era were ready to repel all advances — first with grimaces, and, if they didn't work, with Salem-like accusations of conceit.

Ah, conceit. That was their surest charge, their swiftest arrow, envenomed with shame or curare.

After class, in the harried hall, between algebra and English, Bobby asked Fred, "Is that who you meant? That fat vagabond? That Gypsy porker wallowing in the sty?"

"Yeah. Harnessall said he's going to ask her out." He neither smiled nor frowned, holding a subtle position on the matter.

What? That ace, that stud, was going to ask her out? This was hard news to hear and harder to accept. Jack Harnessall was in the class and in the gang, and in a month or two he would be seventeen, old enough to own a drivers license. Bobby was forced to ease off a campaign not yet started. He resorted to grapes of tart vintage. "He can have her with my blessing, along with the mold and all the lead you can pour into it."

They walked along, lockers at their elbows.

Fred continued, "They come in on the same bus." He looked down at Bobby with a smirk. "Something new for PHS, isn't she?"

Bobby said, "New for PHS I'm sure she is, in the same sense that mumps were new to the Iroquois? What's her name, besides Vampire?" He did not want to ask, but he had to ask.

"Hurley. Mary Sue Hurley. Listen, what'll I tell Mr. Miles?"

They swung around a traffic patrol member. Between classes the student patrol anchored the hall intersections like pylons. "Cross country, I guess. Harder work but gentler. From Princeton?" Caution to the gale. He had to know.

"What do you care?" Fred's knowing smile was far ahead of Bobby's reluctant interest.

"I'm interested in Gypsies. Just saw Dietrich in *Golden Earrings*."

Kids brushed by. Some cutting in at speed. Some lolling along.

"From out of town," Fred said. "I think Monmouth Junction."

"Looks very young."

"So do you."

Word since the cave, of course, holds that the stuff of female attraction is in place by first grade. That's the earliest placement. Some would insist on seventh grade, depending on the latest book suppressed by the school board. But the board could not deny that girls at the senior prom filled the same spaces as those at the Tiffany ball.

Seventh period was English with Dr. Seascott, who held the school's only Ph.D. Bobby's Gypsy porker somehow wasn't there. What? Shock and disappointment. The situation did not follow school hierarchy. Unless there was a conflict, all the academics were in One Sections and she wasn't. She must be in a Two Section. The kiss of academic death! How could this be? He had to know, but he couldn't go asking. You just couldn't show interest, fearful of some adolescent version of the school-yard chant, *Bobby's got a girl friend.*

After the class began, the classroom phone rang. Dr. Seascott answered, mumbled a few words, then turned. "Bob, could you see Miss Hazard after class." Dr. Seascott let his brow wrinkle as he hung up. "Have fun. Now, back to Thornton Wilder. *Our Town* will likely become his most enduring work, of course."

After class, in Room 105, paper and students were always crowded in. Bobby ducked in the door and tried to look pleasant. He couldn't imagine what she wanted. He'd never had a class with her. "Miss Hazard?"

She was a younger teacher, still dressing for men. "Oh, yes. Bob. Uh, this is Clark Janicki. Wants to ask you something." She smiled. Very cordial. "And then I do." She was faculty advisor to the *PHS Chronicle*, the student newspaper.

Bobby didn't know the kid. He was probably a freshman, almost as short as Bobby. It was common knowledge that the new kids got smaller every year. He shrugged. "I hear that you're Clark Janicki and you want to ask me something?"

The kid took a breath and plunged. "Well, you've given interviews to *Seventeen*, and *Time*, and *National Scholastic*, and all these other magazines. How about giving the *PHS Chronicle* a chance?"

Bobby felt worry, not sure whether Clark was an accomplished reporter or just a little kid who had agreed with somebody to take a chance. Others in the room, mostly girls, looked around from their focuses. They stood there holding papers, books, or pencils poised, as if the future of the newspaper would teeter on his response.

Bobby swallowed. He felt several extra breaths in his chest. "I would. I'd give the *Chronicle* a chance except for the rule that states in appropriate language that we never mention *Twenty Questions* here at school." He made a feeble shrug.

"Yeah, but all the other magazines…"

"That's another world somewhere out with the furthest planets and gets lost in the rule that we never mention *Twenty Questions* here at school. You can interview me about school or home or Scouts, boy or girl.

Just that we wouldn't want to mention the show." He had long assumed that the faculty had gathered soon after the show began and decided that nobody would ever mention it, since nobody ever had.

Miss Hazard, holding a clipboard, eased it under her arm.

Clark was saying, "That's just what we'd want to mention. And then about what you read, what you listen to on the radio, where you go on vacation. That sort of thing."

"I think it's in the contract actually. You've heard of contracts. Those little papers that say don't, don't, don't? You can talk all you want about my reading Big Little Books, Hardy Boys and Tom Sawyer and how I listen to *I Love a Mystery, FBI in Peace and War*, and *Fibber McGee*, and how I go to Scout camp or to my uncle's farm in Indiana. Used to. Just no mention of the show. Sorry." He flipped his hands. The issue was out of them.

"You say you have it in the contract?" Miss Hazard inquired.

"Even though contracts confuse me. It's the rule." He looked at her for confirmation. "The show's been on for a year and a half and I never heard a teacher mention it."

She nodded. "Not right out anyway."

"Put me down as a plain student with bad eyes. Or a bad student with plain eyes, the choice being yours." He blinked a few times and squinted them almost shut.

As Clark slunk away, Bobby felt a little sorry for him. His memorized spiel had failed. The others returned to their foci.

As he turned to go, Miss Hazard was looking over his shoulder. He turned and saw a girl entering with an envelope.

"I'm sorry," the newcomer said. "I forgot to bring it fourth period. I guess I'll be taking regular English with Mr. Chesterton instead of journalism after all."

"Thank you, Mary Sue. We'll be sorry to lose you."

The girl wore a white blouse buttoned way up and a plaid skirt of a thousand pleats. No golden earrings in sight. She took a breath, flashed Bobby a breathy smile, and rushed out. The doors were of stained oak with multi-pane windows in the upper half. Through them Bobby watched her turn outside and disappear down the hall. Something froze his chest. He needed to breath but couldn't get a breath out.

Bobby said, swallowing hard, "Was that the new girl?" He felt as if he had not moved fast enough. Something was flowing right by him.

"I believe she is new. Mary Sue Hurley."

Young Clark leaned in. "Yeah. Her father was in the FBI."
Bobby felt his chin tuck in. "A chilling fact to learn. Her father's in the FBI, starring Alan Ladd, with guns and buttoned trench coats."
The ceiling's fluorescent lighting grew brighter.
"At one of the A-bomb plants," Clark continued.
Bobby offered a Bob Hope-ism. "Shake hands with a chain reaction."
Bobby floated out, ready to learn Romany. He floated down the hall and who knows where else. She could not, he thought, flash everyone a smile as dazzling as the one he had just seen. Porker or not, the fat was in the fire. "Hey Babe."
He took several deep breaths. He felt the presence of a new world and in it he would feel like a fish out of water in a serious way, as he had felt nineteen months ago on the stage of the Longacre Theatre. As he walked the halls, among the elbowing crowds, he could dimly see ahead dark rec rooms and hear phonographs tracing the grooves of something called *Stardust*
You can guess what Bobby did next day, Thursday, Sept 18. He went to the main office before home room period and had his schedule changed. He explained it was nothing big. He would have English with Mr. Chesterton instead of Dr. Seascott. He told them he'd read *Our Town*. The office secretary, the benign and longevous Miss Ulp, looked at Bobby as if he were goofy.
So, seventh period next day, when Bobby walked into 206, Mr. Chesterton looked up and frowned.
Bobby said, smiling, "Hello, sir."
"Bob. You in this class?"
"Yes, sir." He held books high.
"Where were you yesterday?"
"I had a schedule mixup."
"Know anything about English?"
"Only what I read in the papers."
"All right, sit anywhere to start and maybe next week we'll make some changes."
He could see that Mary Sue Hurley was halfway back in the row nearest the door. There was no way to take a nearby seat without razzing. He didn't even dare to look. Guys loaded from the back. He knew some, most of them his enemies and detractors, and they had taken all the back seats. Bobby crossed to the window row and took the first available seat, about

halfway back. He set his books down on the slanting desk top. Dan Rechio was behind him. The seat in front of him was vacant and stayed vacant until Friday, when a girl named Honey Winderlick took it, and Bobby forgot all about Mary Sue Hurley. The paradigm of *Babe* had arrived upon the scene.

Chapter 4

Wrote on Your Slate

So, what do you do when your chosen one is a banana split across the room, and right in front of you is a five-ounce martini? Young Bobby, never having tasted either, wasn't sure. He had gone through all this paper work just to get into the same class with Mary Sue and there she sat, six rows away on a 'so what' basis.

Mary Sue: There I sat six rows away. So what!

She was no doubt awaiting his approach.

Mary Sue: I didn't know Bob from Adam.

Undoubtedly sweating from primal fear that Bobby might sit near her and invite her to New York.

Mary Sue: Nice girls don't sweat.

And, there was Honey an elbow away. She was well designed in many ways, most of Princeton High agreed, and Bobby had to admit that, whatever Mother might say, she looked very fetching.

Honey: Mother should have seen the angora sweater I was wearing.

She was obviously the sweetest thing this side of heaven.

Honey: Size thirty-six.

And she seemed to keep finding excuses for turning around.

Honey: Can I borrow your eraser?

So, whatever her own plans, Bobby thought the least he could be was polite and attentive. After all, maybe she would let him copy her papers.

Honey: Good luck.

That Friday afternoon Honey wasn't thinking much about help and assistance anyway. "I heard you. You know that?" She had swung sideways.

Bobby grunted, then started taking deep breaths, and shied back an inch. "Heard me what?" He moved his lips as little as possible.

Mr. Chesterton had asked them to read a scene and somebody front right — Bobby thought it was jolly Kimberly – had asked a question about it, so, the teacher was bending over her desk to answer. This did not mean, of course, that he would be unable to detect Bobby and Honey in proto-passionate conversation. It has been determined over the decades that teachers of the 1940s had already developed hyper-tympanic perception, often attributed to leaks earlier that year from Roswell, New Mexico.

"You got four subjects." Late summer warmth flooded in the open windows of 206. Light breezes ruffled the long blonde ringlets across her ear. "Now, tell me you remember."

He was using his bright chuckle mode. "Oh. You mean on the show."

This girl, this close, was a pleasant surprise. Bobby had seen her before, of course, for the two previous years. But residents of Agra seldom notice the Taj Mahal, and Bobby was noticing for the first time a spectacular, intimidating figure along with her dark blue eyes. He was intimidated, all right. When she reached up and brushed a strand of hair, he watched the movement in awe similar to that shown when Eve suggested apple sauce with the pork.

"You ought to be proud of it." She opened a book across her lap. A finger tabbed a page of *Macbeth*, as if she had read it.

Bobby swallowed, following her finger in ecstasy, saying, "Pride goeth before some inconvenience."

She shot a glance right onto him. "You must be absolutely brilliant."

Honey was still half turned toward him. His eyes circled her face, but never stopped right on it. In classrooms Bobby did not dare to smile when he talked to girls because it would show that he liked what he was doing. The sophisticated young man frowned and screwed up his lips to show disdain. "That would be showbiz, making me brilliant in the same sense that it makes a magician a genius. I just know a few stupid facts."

She half folded the book closed and looked right at him. Her left angora shoulder was toward the front of the room. "They're not stupid. You even..."

Mr. Chesterton interrupted. His voice carried. "Honey, are you and Bob talking about Macbeth?"

Bobby smiled. His eyes glanced upward. "We're leading up to it."

"You sure it isn't Romeo and Juliet?"

The class broke into laughter along lines of their exposure to blank verse. Some guys in the back seats didn't get it. He knew Honey did. She swung back and lowered her face into her hands.

When class was over, Honey gathered her books and her other paraphernalia and rose. Bobby thought she was going to march right out and leave this embarrassment behind. People were always holding something glorious in front of him and snatching it away. But she didn't leave. She turned in the aisle and Bobby was very pleased. Maybe he wasn't such a nonentity. Such a little jerk.

"You'll have to help me. I don't understand this Shakespeare and you understand everything."

Bobby slid up to his feet and faced her, their eyes close to level. His smile was apologetic if not apoplectic. "Helping you would be a privilege highly sought, but I never really read any Shakespeare."

Bobby was jostled from behind. Dan Rechio wanted out. "Move it, Big Shot. Right now."

"Sorry." He sat back down. He was used to backing away and had developed various schemes to avoid confrontations he could not win.

Rechio pushed on by, forcing Honey along ahead of him and, Bobby thought, out of his life. It wasn't fair. He would report it to the authorities.

The weekend was forgettable, with his entire head crammed full of Bunnies and Mary Sues as the Cadillac moved through Rahway crammed with friends of the family who were riding in to see the show. They saw that week as guest on *Twenty Questions* Danton Walker, a columnist Bobby had never heard of, which only showed how little Bobby read the papers.

Seventh period Monday, Mr. Chesterton decided to assign seating. Bobby had some vague idea of why he was doing it. The guys in the back were going to be brought forward toward enlightenment.

"Bob? You there?"

Bobby looked up. He knew what Mr. Chesterton was going to do. He was going to rend Romeo from Juliet. "You think you can sit over there in front of Mary Sue without talking her head off?"

Amid some muted cheers and jeers, Bobby rose and walked past Honey, across the front, past jolly Kimberly, and up the aisle by the door. This was the walk in which you know your fly is open and you're so panicked about it that you tend to walk sideways, which, of course, tells the guys in the back what you're worried about, and maybe some of the girls, too.

She was fifth seat, first row. He would be fourth seat. Bobby saw that her eyes were low. She was smiling at a book cover, like a bridge player who has taken a trick and is preparing to lead from her hand.

Not looking up, she said, "Don't say anything." She opened the book.

Bobby had not seen her this close before and he went immediately to his appraisal mode. Her smile was impish, coy, as if she understood the follies of the world and often tolerated them.

"Pardon?" He sat down and glanced back. She wore a maroon V-neck sweater over a white blouse and a bright scarf over the sweater. Her hair was dark and medium length in a sort of permanent Bobby knew nothing about. In fact Bobby knew almost nothing of how girls dressed or why.

"Don't say anything or he'll see you and give you fifty words because you were already talking." She shuffled through pages. "To her." Her brow wrinkled in explanation. "Keep quiet and he'll go on to something else."

Bobby couldn't believe she was talking to him in such a commanding way. The rest of the classroom was beginning to revolve around her like the view from a merry-go-round.

"I was asking who . . ."

"Just remember, if you get fifty words, it isn't my fault." When her eyes looked right at him, they turned a deeper shade of blue. Not burning blue. Electric blue. Atomic blue. "Turn away now."

"What?" He was unsure which way to go.

She was at pains to explain. "He doesn't like girls. If he sees me talking to you, he'll give me fifty words."

Bobby swung to the front again. A cat foot fog was expanding all through him.

After a small pause, she said to his back, "Do you agree?"

Bobby wasn't sure. "No. He. . . "

"I'm not doing fifty words today. Or tomorrow."

Bobby glanced halfway back and spoke from the side of his mouth. "Girls never get fifty words anyway." Injustice reigned all over. "Some girls just talk their way out of trouble with teachers."

"I don't like getting punished. So stop whispering with me before he notices and . . ."

"I think I'll keep whispering." He paused for effect. "Not minding very much getting caught. Speaking as an individual who used to stay after school on several likely occasions." He slowly dragged out a textbook, the one that contained *Macbeth*.

She took a short breath. "Then I'll be quiet and when he starts noticing all the noise from over here I'll raise my hand and say it was all my fault. I put you up to making it all, which is just like Lady Macbeth anyway."

Bobby shuffled papers. Sought a pencil. Closed the text.

She said, "Why don't you say something?"

Bobby felt a new weird discomfort that he was to feel for years thereafter. Wildy curious. But also put upon. He said, "It would be risking the wrath of the leader before us. He's going to give us our assignment and I can't find my pencil."

"Here."

"Thanks. Hey, the point's broken."

Mr. Chesterton finally spotted them. "What are you two talking about?"

Bobby looked up and grinned. All innocence. "Us? Talking?"

Mary Sue said, "We were talking about Macbeth."

"So was I." He leveled a glance on their row. "We're going to start reading it tomorrow aloud. Maybe I better put you two in the lead roles."

After that, class procedures took over and Bobby felt itchy, not sure what was going on behind him. For all Bobby knew, she was making faces or sticking out her tongue. When the first bell rang, Bobby gathered his stuff, rose, and turned back toward her, not sure he would be welcome. Not sure if he would be branded aggressive or backward and unfriendly. Not sure of anything.

She was still seated, arranging papers. He looked down. "I have to ask. Is it true your father's in the FBI? Or is that just one of the rumors started by Henry Wallace?"

She looked up and smiled, rendering him helpless. He did not know what smiles meant. He seldom saw one. "It was true. Just during the war. Why?"

"Why nothing. I was asking to expand my grasp of the general scene. Wondering in my grasping way if that explains why you weren't here last year, is all I'm asking."

"Last year this time I was in Knoxville. Now I'm in Monmouth Junction, where I grew up. I guess you grew up in Princeton?"

"Far from it. You're looking at Mr. Corn Belt with Michigan his latest home and Indiana before that. We've just lived here a couple of years."

She had gathered her books onto her looseleaf notebook and slid out and up. "Maybe I should read the fan magazines." She was his height.

Maybe an inch shorter. Her face was angelic but her small mouth, even smiling, held a trace of cynicism.

"The fan ... Oh, sure. Skip to the kiddie page."

Kimberly stepped up the aisle from her seat in front. She said in a wry voice, "Don't listen to him. He's a liar from birth."

Kimberly was obviously waiting for Mary Sue, so Bobby ambled away and out the door. Unsure how to ride, Bobby fled the corral. He felt all sorts of other metaphors, too, but overriding all of it, Bobby felt angry. He knew he had botched something and, much worse, that he would be afraid to try harder for fear he'd botch it again.

After the day's final bell, Bobby hurried uptown where drills and amalgams awaited him that fine fall day. Dr. Majarian's office was near the far end of town at Number Twenty on Nassau Street, the town's main thoroughfare, a binary alignment with the shops and stores on one side and the university on the other. As Bobby passed the Garden Theatre, he saw Fred Darkly on ahead, coming out of Farr Hardware.

Bobby said, "You hear about the Explorer meeting tomorrow?"

"No. What time?"

"I'm calling the big leader to find out. Thurman gave me the number."

They were walking calmly on the forty-foot-wide sidewalk. Suddenly, Fred said, "So you found out who I meant."

"Who?"

"Mary Sue Hurley." He was looking right ahead. "I saw Kimberly. She said you're moving right in."

It didn't matter if Fred were serious or just kidding. Young Bobby was slightly shocked. "Me?" He was incredulous and apologetic at the same time. He was learning what it meant to be a factor. "I didn't ask to sit there."

"You sure took advantage of it."

"In my little, unassuming, unprepossessing way."

"You know — you are the luckiest person who ever lived."

"Me? Small me?"

"In every goddam way, too."

Bobby wanted to reassure Fred that they weren't in competition for anything. But he didn't know how.

Fred ducked into Zinders and Bobby continued alone, past Nill's, Western Union, Palmer Square, to his dental fate.

In the chair, between "Open" and "Rinse", Bobby inhaled the nitrous oxide into a stupor of vivid scenes. He saw the orderly orientation of Nassau Street dissolve into Highland Park, in the heart of Detroit, and the concrete trash bunkers into which they dumped the ashes from the apartment incinerator. He was five then and used to play in them. He saw the rear bumper of the car that hit him on Second Boulevard. It left a dent in the back of his head many have blamed for some of his problems. He saw the flat streets of Redford a year later. They tantalized him because he deduced that there were always more streets beyond, generating his first awful longings in the romance of faraway places. Then, the final move around the Detroit rim, where Bobby at last grew into the Scouts, with that first hike to Nankin Mills. He was coming to, when the last vision took focus, the incredibly romantic trip east, during the war, through the snow, across Pennsylvania on US 6. He had never seen hills before.

Without admitting it, stored as a deep secret in his silly brain, Bobby found himself creeping around the school next afternoon to watch her climb on the Monmouth Junction bus.

Chapter 5

On His Honor

Doc Foss took a deep breath. "Well then it looks like we may have to allow more planning time. See here, I have lots of ideas to schedule. Football playing cookout, roller skating party at the Capitol Arena, a dinner dance, and a long weekend at Camp Pahaquarra." He looked up from the list to sense reaction. There was none. "But I wanted to get things going with a simple little overnight hike. Now it looks like it ain't so simple. Pardon my grammar."

Pete said, "We can schedule it. But to make it simpler and smaller, maybe we ought to start with just one night."

"But really now that's troop stuff. I wanted two nights. It gives you more chance to practice Scout skills."

Spade Harmon said, "Two nights is always going to conflict with something at school on a Friday. Until some vacation time comes up."

Bobby grunted. He dropped the doily he'd been fiddling with back into place. "Friday wouldn't matter to me. I don't go to wild dances and uncivilized parties."

Nobody really knew how frightened he was of females. His friends and even his parents simply assumed he was totally normal and that he looked upon females as normal, too.

Doc Foss said evenly, "You'll go to our dinner dance, won't you? You'll go to our roller skating party, won't you?"

Bobby stared, then blurted, "With women?" His eyes almost closed. Spade said, grinning, "You ain't gonna dance with me, Young Bobby." They had been close enough out west that Bobby was fair game back east.

Bobby grinned grimly. "Indeed I ain't." His eyes roamed wildly. "What about the roller skating?"

Spade was still grinning. "You ain't gonna skate with me neither." That brought general laughter.

Bobby swallowed, which felt like a walnut in his throat. He wanted to crawl in bed. "I thought this was a scout outfit, in the shadow of James E. West and Elbert K. Fretwell."

Doc Foss said, "Let's save our philosophical discussions for later, shall we?"

"But it's already later." Bobby had to talk through the pain. "Why don't we switch around? Go roller skating stag and take girls on the overnight hike?"

Itchy said, center davenport, "You got a sleeping bag big enough for two, McGuire?"

Fred said, half humor half challenge, "You got one big enough for you and Mary Sue Hurley?"

Bobby smiled in thanks. He was unused to being talked about as if he mattered.

Doc Foss raised a low hand. "Uh, gentlemen, let's save our scout camp memories for another day. Let me suggest Friday, October 31. We can have a post-Halloween over nighter to Camp Buck."

Spade said, shaking his head slowly, "That's what I mean. The school Halloween dance is that Friday and I'll be going to it."

Itchy said, "I too."

Pete said, "Me too."

Bobby looked at him. "Pete? You? Ah, Mussolini, whose hand held the dagger." Bobby looked around at the silences. He said, half cloudy, "I'm never sure what may spoil my Ralston Straight Shooter image. Will my fans know I've stayed away from fast stuff?"

Fred said, "Fast?" His smirk of derision suggested pity. Bobby was used to it. Guys were always mocking how stupid he really was.

Doc Foss interposed, "Far be it from me to enter your social life, but it's hard to see how a Halloween dance is fast."

"Fast is in the eye of the siren. I've vaguely heard about growing up, and other frightening propositions, but I've also got the show to think of. I'm supposed to be this amazing kid. When I get older, it won't be so amazing."

Doc Foss said in resignation, "Well, I don't see how there's much you can do about it."

Pete, his friend, said, "He's just scared of girls."

"Why you young Greek fraud. You never forgot that Latin Tea, when we learned that Lesbia est puella."

It wasn't the Scouts' noble proclamations that had attracted Young Bobby since the age of twelve. He would do his best to do his duty, but Bobby didn't even know what *morally straight* meant and neither did they. No, it was probably the campfires. The uniform, too, but mainly the campfires. Those fountains of smoke had wafted the kids many heights above cowboys and Indians. Scouts turned things once bad to things now good. Now you could set things on fire and get rewards for doing it. So, when Bobby heard that a gentleman named Doc Foss was going to be leader of the new Explorer Post, first meeting Tuesday night, Bobby listened. Of course, with Bobby's Philmont experience taken into consideration, it was obvious that word had reached him accidently.

Bobby: Of course, with my Philmont experience taken into consideration, it was obvious that I should have gone to Paris.

The problem was, his new challenge with girls made Bobby feel confused about the continued role of scouts and his former life.

Bobby: I felt confused between the continued role of scouts and my former so-called life.

He had trudged home from school Tuesday afternoon, wondering if he really wanted to ride his bike to some Scout meeting somewhere in Jugtown, especially since he was feeling early tingles of a sore throat. Maybe he'd rather moon about Mary Sue or Honey Winderlick all evening in the sun room. Let's face it. His mind now was providing limited room for the old campfire ikon. While he still looked back fondly on those Scout hikes to Cradle Rock, what Bobby saw now was some other kid rocking the rock and that other kid should have been riding to Doc Foss's.

At least Pete Likasatus still supported his view on scouts.

Pete: I supported his view on very little.

Unfortunately, Pete was just too bloody perfect. He was a well built athlete, friendly enough, and got the best grades in the class.

Pete: Two girls got better grades than I did.

However, Bobby could still beat him in ping pong.

Pete: He could beat me in ping pong on his table.

So, as they sat around the Foss's cozy living room — Pete, Fred, Spade and Spade's friends Itchy, Joel, Moose, and Rinehart — Bobby adopted a coolly detached, totally confused, attitude, his throat feeling larger by the minute, while Doc Foss, a blustery, deep-voiced blusterer, was saying,

"Yes. Yes. Instead of meetings every week, we schedule them as needed. This is the first year for Post 60, but there's been a lot of planning. A lot of planning."

While the others had spread themselves on the davenport and on straight chairs brought in from the dining room, Bobby had taken the easy chair, obviously Doc Foss's, who had taken one of the straight chairs. The puzzled host didn't mention it, or even stare a little. He had leaned over an open notebook spread across his knees. "What shall we start with? Social? Overnight hike? Field trip?"

Pete had said, "Overnight hike to Camp Buck."

Fred said, "If the fireplace hasn't caved in."

Pete said, "It's a good place to cook, with the indoors fireplace, and you can roam up and down the Raritan River, too." Pete could be so blunt, so forthright. He would ponder then take his time and state the facts of the situation, as a smile covered his face and his eyes squinted into near laughter.

Bobby had held off because his throat hurt more when he spoke. But now he grumbled, "Last overnight hike this individual nearly froze. My feet were as blue as my blood. The kabobs were shivering on their stick."

Pete said from his end of the davenport, "They'll pick you up?"

"I was so frozen . . . By goodly that's another item of interest you've broached." He stopped. He had, of course, forgotten his Saturday commitment. "Sorry. I was caught up in the excitement of roaming in the Arctic. Maybe I can get the night off."

Doc Foss said, a weary smile on his face, "Don't forget me. I'm new here. Who's picking you up and for what?"

Pete said, "He has to go to New York every Saturday night."

Doc Foss's brow wrinkled. "Well, uh, I think we can go into personal conflicts later." He looked about the room's eager young faces, most of them dull, flat, and smudged. "So, we're in the hiking and camping business, aren't we? So, let's start with an overnight hike. Did somebody say Camp Buck? Uh, what's Camp Buck?"

Pete said, "It's sort of a dump on the upper Raritan."

Doc Foss was holding back exasperation. "Yes. Yes. Leave it to an Explorer Post to turn a dump into a nightmare. Raritan? What's Raritan?"

Bobby's fingers were scratching like a cat at the lace doily on the chair's arm. "Camp Buck, on the Raritan River, sort of a Waldorf with flies. Two cabins with board bunks. One with fireplace. The cabin not the bunk. The fireplace is smokey and the bunks hard as cement. Or it was my can that was smokey and the cabin's hard as cement. Either way at Camp Buck your mind turns to Jell-o."

Doc Foss was mystified but game. "Our kind of place. Go Friday and come back Sunday?"

Pete said, his own brow slightly wrinkled. "How about we go Saturday morning."

Doc Foss said calmly, as a challenge, "That was when you were in Troop 43. Now you're senior scouts. How about going on Friday with Post 60? Make it a two-night outing."

Fred said, "Could we get drivers?"

"Let me handle transport." He cleared his throat. "The question is when. This coming weekend too soon? The twenty-seventh of, uhm, September?"

Bobby said, "So, if we're hell bent for goose bumps, why put it off? Even if it comes at a bad time. The guest being Governor Driscoll, who fixes Dad's speeding tickets. The old saying, walkers are talkers, but the back seat of a Nash turns into a bed."

Doc Foss stared a full five seconds. Then he said, as if overleaping some mound in the way, "Well, that's very perceptive, I'm sure. Is this night you might get off from something in New York, may I inquire?"

Fred said, "*Twenty Questions.*" He swallowed, hating to say the words.

Bobby said, "Being a little radio program I'm on. Saturday nights at eight." He explained with an increasing sense of heat and glowing pain below his chin. "And don't forget to buy Ronson Lighters. Press it's lit. Release it's out. Safely out the instant you lift your finger."

Doc Foss spoke calmly to explain his position. "Yes. Uhm, I don't have much time for entertainment, I'm sorry to say." Then he looked right at Bobby. "So, the governor of New Jersey is going to appear as a guest? My, my."

"I was going to ask him to lower the driver's license age to 16."

"Well. We certainly wouldn't want to stand in the way of new regulation, would we? How about the following weekend? Who has a calendar?"

Spade Harmon said, from the other end of the davenport, "I've got the Post calendar." He slipped it from a loose leaf notebook. "October 3 is Friday." He spoke with his head at a slight angle as usual.

Doc Foss was consulting his own note book. He said, still reading it, "Yes. Yes. One second. I confess I'm the monkey wrench there. I'll be away that weekend."

Spade said, "The next weekend is October 10. That's the Get Acquainted Dance at the school?" He said it as a question, as Bobby looked up.

Doc looked up himself. "And that's a wildly attended social event?"

"Too wild for little me," Bobby announced. "I don't go to dances. Only burlesque shows. Did I tell you about that show at the Empire in Newark, called 'Back to Back' starring Willie Turner?"

Pete said, "I'm just going to the Halloween Dance."

Bobby survived the rest of the meeting, taking persecution like a prisoner of war and justifying his silence by feeling his huge, fiery throat. They needed no comment from him to decide on a one-night hike October 11. He survived the tales of Philmont, too, without much good to say about the place and the memories fading into the gloom of his former self. Mostly, Bobby recalled Pete's comment on the way home.

Their bikes were rolling by twos on Nassau. Just before Pete would swing right into Linden Lane, Bobby asked him, "You're really going to the Halloween Dance?"

Pete said, "Sure. Everybody's going."

"Yeah. Everybody but me. I can't dance anyway."

"I can't either."

He watched Pete swing away toward home. Young Bobby rolled on toward Moore, thinking about camp Billy Mills, Charles Atlas on the back of comic books, helping Einstein pull his sail boat into shallow water. But mostly Bobby thought about, "Everybody's going." They would. They would actually go whether Bobby went or not.

It was only nine when Bobby rolled into the garage, his throat feeling as if were in a clamp. Mother was reading in the living room. All he wanted was warmth and bed, but he went into the sun room and called Pete.

"Listen, if a bunch is going, maybe I'll come, too. The Halloween dance."

"I thought you would."

Chapter 6

Fineshriber

The gentleman took them all in as he looked around the table. "What I want you all to know first is how pleased everybody has been this last year. And that definitely includes Ronson."

Bobby was lining up his fork and spoon end to end, preparing to flip the spoon into his water tumbler. He felt himself above censure. Impervious. The better the restaurant, the more likely he was to try it. But he didn't have the urge right then. Maybe he'd never get that urge, that ultimate sense of *power*. As a talented and cheeky young man, Bobby had never quite learned to appreciate the charms of power.

Bobby: As a talented and sneaky young man, I appreciated the charms of Honey Winderlick.

The phrase *power lunch* didn't enter Webster until late in the century.

Webster: I had 'power play' in by 1975.

George said, from his own huddle, "I have heard from Cecil and Presbry that they are very happy with the show."

Dad nodded. "All right."

Fineshriber nodded, too. "So let's get right to the point."

Bobby had a horror of being forced to submit to listening to a judgment from someone who was clearly his superior. He thought at first that he would try to avoid the bind by pretending that he was in some sort of stupor, his eyes half closed, staring at forks and napkins and other things on the table. But then he said, kidding, "I knew a point there was likely to be." He was trying to cooperate but nobody seemed to take it that way.

Fineshriber looked at him. "There usually is at serious meetings." He looked up. "Oh." The tray had come. A waiter carried it. Drinks were upon it. "Thank you. Nothing for you, Bobby?"

"No thanks. I've been on the wagon since Ray Milland." You only had to be eighteen to drink in New York in those days but Bobby didn't look twelve.

"Okay." The host looked to the waiter. "We'll order in a few minutes." Then back to them. "And what I have is hardly a pejorative." He paused. "Let me ask the family as a whole what your opinion is…" He looked from side to side. "… of the guests." Pause for effect. "The guests."

Bobby found himself interested almost against his will and had to accept the purely serious expression on Fineshriber's face as genuine. But he still had to shrug. Guests were guests. Some had been awesome to a high school kid. Many had been totally unknown. He said, "As a whole they've been pleasant, stimulating, and able to put the audience into a deep sleep."

Mother smiled. "They've been very nice."

Dad said, "I think what Bill is thinking of here is their effectiveness as part of the show."

Fineshriber nodded. "That's exactly what I was thinking of, yes. And have been for a year or more."

Bobby said, "Their presence illuminates the margins of the show. Gary gets them. Right? Celebrity Service. People in town to plug their stuff? They're not exactly Bing Crosby. But…"

"No, no. Not that, Bobby. Not the guests themselves. Let's get this straight at the outset." His hands were wringing things clear, in front of him. "We're talking about how using a guest affects the pace of the show. Their impact on the show."

Bobby said slowly, ready to display his cooperation, "It would be stimulating, tuning in to hear a famous person talking, thereby affecting the pace of the show."

Fineshriber nodded. "Some do. But therein lies the problem. Are they disappointed when the guest can't play the game as well as you people can?"

Mother said, "Some do participate more than others."

Bobby frowned. Now there was some profound statement. She should have worked at the UN.

The gentleman leaned back, martini glass in hand, and sipped from it. "Anyway, we've had some discussion about it with the agency, the sponsor, and the network. And we've been looking at a few ideas."

Bobby went alert. "Ideas for changing the show?" His entire head lunged forward. "The agency, sponsor, and network have determined that the show is broken and needs repair?"

"No. But under the theory that anything can be improved upon, let me toss one your way and see what you think."

Bobby was poised to spring. He couldn't let people think he took *Twenty Questions* seriously, but he sometimes wanted to defend it a little. He said, "Do we accept a theory that a need to change the show has appeared?"

Dad said, his hand up halfway, a shield flat and holding, "Now, wait a minute, Bob. Let's hear this."

"Okay." He leaned back, daring the world and all the jerks therein. "Start tossing."

Fineshriber grimaced, as if he were overcoming a nuisance. "I toss this. Instead of sitting on the panel, the guest sits with Slater. He has brought his own subject for the panel to guess and answers the panel's questions with Slater."

Bobby smiled and said, "The guest, full of arresting stimulation, sits with Slater? A proposal almost as senseless as I am in Latin class."

"Bobby!" That was mother.

Dad had tried to explain what was coming as they drove toward New York that afternoon in that new blue Cadillac, with the red wheels. Although the family had known that some discussion was coming for some weeks, Fineshriber had kept putting it off. But this Saturday, October 4, Dad assured them, the die was cast with the fat in the fire. He had received a phone call that morning from Bob Limon, Fineshriber's assistant. Right after that night's show — cartoonist Ham Fisher was guest panelist — they would all sit down and thrash things out. It was a little bewildering. To Bobby this was turning Fineshriber into an enemy. Which was pretty dumb if not impossible. If it weren't for him, they wouldn't have a show. They were passing New Brunswick, with the ultramodern Ethicon Sutures building on their left, and Dad was saying, "I'm not sure what Fineshriber will bring up."

Bobby frowned. "It can't be good or we wouldn't be meeting." He wore a drippy suit he'd bought at a shop in New Brunswick. It was that long forgotten style that featured front panels of plaid, the rest gabardine.

"Not necessarily, Lamp Black. It's got to be something we care about. And that includes you."

It was sunny and warm, and in those days the traffic on US 1 was bearable. Traffic circles flowed free. They cruised around the Route 18 circle, past the Howard Johnson's and the Edgewater Diner. A tractor-trailer chugged around with them.

Straight and clear again, Bobby said, "Reflecting my new tolerance and expansive interest, I'll try to care about whatever he brings up. Gerard Darrow gave me that word in 1940, which he uttered in the famous sentence, 'Tolerance is what I need,' in response to Joe Kelly's query, 'What is your biggest need, Kids?'"

Mother was remonstrating. "After all, Jinky Bob, our new house, this car, your movie camera — all came thanks to the show." Although radio fame suited her better than anybody else, she was aware of its potential for corrosion.

Dad looked in the mirror. "So, let's be receptive tonight."

"All right." Bobby was speaking to the back of the seat.

Dad's eyes were still in the mirror. "Receptive, courteous, and professional."

"All right."

Mother said, smiling, "I think diplomatic is the word."

"All *right*."

He said it lightly, but maybe not lightly enough. No one spoke again until they swung up onto the Pulaski Skyway.

Dad said, "Who wants to practice? We're already at the Skyway. We haven't got much time. I've got one that's mineral."

"Fineshriber's gold?"

It was somewhere up there in North Jersey that Bobby sometimes felt in his bones a transformation from one person to another. Up there around Tonnele Avenue he could almost feel some hunk of festered flesh that reduced his whole image to pulp drop away. He could see it lying along the Lincoln Tunnel approach cut and growing smaller in the rear view mirror. You know what it was? Fear. Worry. What corporate America now insists on calling *stress*. Which is why he felt cool lining up his teaspoon, something he'd never dare in the PHS cafeteria.

When Mother had said, "Bobby!" Fineshriber seemed perplexed. His eyes swept the fast walking waiters all around, the nicely dressed people at other tables, the Broadway window of garish neon with the automobile lights sweeping it. Maybe they rolled a little, too, those eyes. Anyway they finally got back to them. "Now, let's give it a chance."

Fineshriber had been at the theatre, waiting for them like a spider. After the show, they had piled in a cab that smelled of dried dirt and headed for Dunhall's at 1440 Broadway. The building's upper floors contained WOR/Mutual studios and offices. Dad still had his 11:00 news show to do, an elevator ride away.

Now, Dad said smoothly, "I think it's interesting."

Bobby's chest went hollow at this betrayal. He felt pressure and a sudden throatful of fright. He had to recover. "If you give it a chance, you may find it interesting. But I don't see how it will work, which is what I meant by senseless." He smiled brightly. "Wasn't it?" He needed more than this to help himself off the floor. He flipped the hinged lid of a sugar bowl. "But how will the listener — the listener who sent in the guest's subject — get his Ronson?"

Fineshriber paused to consider it. "Good point. Hadn't thought of that. But I do think it's a detail."

Dad repeated, probably because his pronouncement was not acquiring the attention it demanded, "I think it's interesting." There was a subtle elan in his voice, a vote for the future. He seemed to be acknowledging an idea whose time had come.

Mother said sweetly, "Maybe the guest would choose a subject somehow associated with the guest."

Bobby said, "Bing Crosby would choose the bells of St. Mary's. Jimmy Stewart would choose the town of Bottleneck."

Sharp nod from Fineshriber. "That's it. That's precisely it."

George said, still from his hunched huddle, "Don't forget, Bill, a lot of the spontaneity of the show comes from the guest not — that's not — participating much or participating well. Audiences like to see the famous stumble. I've heard that from several sources."

Fineshriber said, "Yes, but from several more I've heard that many guests are very uneasy about coming on the show at all."

Dad said, "It's an idea to think about. The guest has always been both an asset and a liability."

Mother said, "Did you say you had another idea?"

Bobby grinned brightly. "I feel better already with assets and liabilities at hand. I thought we came here because you were going to make me agree to quit the Scouts and go to Princeton."

Fineshriber nodded like a hyena in recognition of the dilemma. "We'll worry about that sometime later. Scout camp's only in the summer. Right?"

"Overnight hikes are in the fall, mainly during blizzards."

Mother said, "Bobby means that he has one coming up, but he won't have to miss the show."

"Well. I should hope not."

Dad dismissed the great problem with, "We'll take care of it. What's the other idea on the guest?"

But Bobby went on, "There's the Halloween Dance, too, but that's Friday night and I'm going as more of a hayseed than I already am."

The man smiled. "Good luck."

Mother said, "You're going to a Halloween Dance?" Her hands gently closed the big menu she was reading.

"Sure. Everybody's going. Even little Bobby." He saw a great cloud of blue gas erupt from Mother's pipes.

Dad said, slightly impatient, "All right. All right. Go ahead, Bill."

Fineshriber's brow wrinkled. "You won't like it. But let me ask that you at least consider it. We like to call it *control*. With the guest still on the panel, we control the show so the guest always gets one subject."

Bobby blurted, "You mean tell him the subject ahead of time?"

"No." He paused for effect and got some. "We tell *you* one of the subjects ahead of time. And you lead the guest to get it."

Bobby made a face. "Remember Lederer?"

George actually sat up, wagging his head side to side like a polar bear at the zoo. "That really didn't work, Bill."

Bill Fineshriber sat up with slight astonishment. "What's this?"

They explained. During the show's first season, the European movie star Francis Lederer had been the guest. He was plugging his latest movie, *The Madonna's Secret*, with Ann Rutherford. Somebody thought it would help just oodles if one of the subjects to be identified that night was Miss Rutherford, and somebody also thought it would be just super if the guest panelist got that subject. Without *control* this would have been very doubtful, so Dad and Bobby were primed. They were broadcasting then from the theatre of the Barbizon Plaza Hotel which had almost no backstage spaces. Bobby remembered how hard it had been for the "controller" to find a private space to set up the fix.

Bobby said, "They told Dad and me that the fourth subject would be Ann Rutherford and Dad and I were supposed to lead Lederer to ascertain the subject as if he had done so on his own."

Dad said, "It was awkward."

Bobby said, "He barely got Miss Rutherford even after we led him there."

Mother silent with her eyes wide said, "I was never told about this."

Fineshriber was frowning. He said, "Would you agree to try something like it once more?"

Bobby said. "Pretty soon we'd all be Alex Groza and Wawa Jones, getting subjects in sixteen questions instead of twelve. The new question-shaving game they'll call it in the *Daily News* and the PHS *Chronicle*. Frank Hogan will start the probe and we all end up on Riker's Island."

Mother said, "Bobby!"

Bobby said, "Pardon me, but my hero, Sergeant Preston of the Yukon, wouldn't think it's right. It didn't work with Lederer. Really, when we were leading him by the cerebrum, I felt more like an actor than a player."

Fineshriber's hands became twin hatchets, "Well, what's wrong with that? That's what we're putting on. A show."

George was nodding away his naivete. "Bobby means it isn't playing fair with the audience — as a game. As a show, it might be different."

Bobby said subtly, "I wonder how Mr. Harris would like it."

"He hasn't been consulted. That's why he hires an agency. But I think he'd go for it. The president of Ronson is a businessman."

Dad said, making a large, very large, exhale, "Bob, you said you'd cooperate."

Mother more closely defined it. "You did promise."

Bobby smiled wildly. "Me? Cooperate? You must be recalling my grammar school days, when I was a twig easily bent."

Fineshriber was all diplomat. "Apparently you didn't complain before. With Francis Lederer."

"Me? Complain? When all I have to look forward to is life as an adult?" He chuckled in his false way. He swallowed. "I said I'd cooperate. I'll cooperate."

But for the rest of the evening Bobby froze. If he said another word between spooning his soup and crawling into bed that night, at one in the morning, with the late revel traffic on 206 swishing tire sounds through his open bedroom windows, it came from a plain flinch. Bobby was mad. He would take decisive action. See Al Nathan, Ronson's liaison man with the show. Mr. Harris himself. He would refuse to play the game. It was unclear how he was going to work this campaign into his schedule of alternative needs and drives, such as finding a girl, asking her out, getting a night off the show, and learning how to dance.

By Monday, with his ire cooled to the boiling point, word came that the fix would occur the following week and his fever rose again. But word came Tuesday that the fix was off. Some great power, probably Fineshriber's boss, nixed the fix, at least for now. Bobby would be spending the night at Camp Buck free of remorse if not flies.

The overnight hike weekend went all right. They met him at the Clinton Point traffic circle, where U.S. 22 crossed Route 30, mid afternoon on Saturday and drove to New York on US 22. The guest was screen writer Robert Riskin, who was there to plug a Jimmy Stewart movie he'd written called *Magic Town*. Dad took the train home after his news show and mother brought Bobby back to Clinton Point, where Mr. Foss met him at 10:30. The circle and the woods were pitch black. Bobby was hardly a happy camper. A lot of trouble for smoke, cold food, and a hard bunk.

The following week Bobby sold ads for the yearbook after school with McFarland, went to band drill for the coming PHS game, ran two miles and more with the cross country team, tried during English to pretend plump Mary Sue was thinner, and actually did some homework. Saturday, October 18, he sold programs for the Princeton University game and made seven dollars. "Hey. Hey. Get your pro -gram. Names, numbers and salaries of all players." He left at halftime for New York on the 4:17. Wendy Barrie was guest.

Fred Finklehoff, the screenwriter and producer, who had just laid *The Egg and I*, was guest the 25th. Nobody said a word about any "control." November 1 would be Rise Stevens, the night after the Halloween dance, in preparation for which Young Bobby was totally lost.

Chapter 7

Witches' Sabbath

Above the thunderous beats of the band, Jack said, "Come on. We'll look over the merchandise."

They weaved across the gym through the knots of the crowd, dodging bodies. With polite nods, they sidled right by Mary Sue's circle, as if they had to get somewhere else.

At a safe distance Jack shouted behind his hand, "Did you see that?"

Bobby said, "All I saw was my future in serious doubt."

"That new girl was really giving you the eye."

The saxes were groaning like a cow at milking time. Drums and cymbals made a climax.

"Oh, please. The last girl who gave me an eye wanted me to thread it."

"She was giving you the eye. You should ask her to dance."

"Me? Little me ask little her to dance?"

"Look, that's all girls can do, give you the eye. Girls don't ask boys to dance. Except during the Sadie Hawkins number."

"A name not in my memory, Sadie."

"That's when the girls ask the boys to dance. Very embarrassing."

"Why worry when I'd never get asked?"

"Sure you would. Some girls are desperate. Look. We'll both go. Make this a joint operation. I'll ask Jenny, you ask Mary Sue."

"A decision against my better judgment, or any judgment." He took a deep breath. "Lead on, O Custer."

The truth was Bobby wanted to ask her so much it crawled. He wanted to touch her. Hold her. Close his eyes in ecstasy. But even approaching her was so dangerous.

They eased that way. He felt like he was in one of those bumper scooter cars at an amusement park.

Pete was saying, "I'll ask Kimberly."

Jack was ahead of him, Pete behind, as they re-approached the magic circle. He saw Jack ask Jenny and she smiled. It looked easy. He went up to Mary Sue and said, "I approach with confidence, lean down, and whisper lightly in your ear, pardon my Armenian, but uh, would you like to dance?" The die was cast.

As he had approached the gym that night, Bobby knew that there would be no Emma Bovarys or Eliza Doolittles at PHS in the fall of 1947 to dance the night away. Instead they had Dolly Wright and Mary Marjorie Poole who would be jitterbugging all over the gym. That was okay with Young Bobby, except that it just prompted all the other babes to want to do the same thing. So they'd need partners, wouldn't they, which could be very frightening. Going to the Halloween Dance at all made jitters. Mingling with women would be like mingling with a pack of creatures from the cave. He steeled every nerve, tightened every synapse.

Bobby: I steeled every nerve and entered the gym scared stiff.

You could feel some sympathy for poor Mary Sue Hurley, too, the designated receiver. After all, when Mr. Chesterton had moved Bobby into her sphere, and Bobby became eager to get to school every day on account of it, you would think he would at least give her a tumble.

Mary Sue: You would think Bobby would at least be friendly.

Of course, Bobby never figured in Sue's plans.

Mary Sue: I was never the wily, scheming type.

But at least Bobby's interest in *Macbeth* grew and grew.

Bobby: You can take that to the Banquo.

So, when the big deal night finally arrived on an unusually warm October 31, with Fred Darkly, Pete, and Bobby approaching the gym's outdoor entrance through the drift of blowing leaves, Bobby was buoyed by his mother's parting words.

Mother: Dancing? There's nothing to it.

He was also buoyed by Mrs. Polesie's surprising comment one recent evening after the show.

Mrs. Polesie: You really look older with that new haircut.

And Bobby recalled the classic words long ago of his buddy Dick Weinert that afternoon they had stumbled through the forest upon a pair of prone lovers.

Dick: Boy, she must really like him.

Fifty feet to go. No turning back. He felt a sense of Columbus at San Salvador, Balboa at Darien, and Mickey Rooney at Ava Gardner.

Just before the door, Bobby said, looking aside, "Who are all those guys out there in the bushes looking in the gym? In the windows there?" Bobby saw thirty or forty boys, girls, and men.

Pete said, "I've heard about them."

Fred said as he pulled open the door, "Getting an eyeful, I guess."

Bobby said, "Creeps getting an eyeful. Peepers in the gym. Jeest."

So, in they went, passing from the silken silence of an October night into Mr. McConnel saying, "Tickets, please." Mr. McConnel looked at him as if surprised. "Nice to see you here."

"Nice to be here."

So far. He had handed over his ticket, followed Fred in, and was almost stopped by all he saw. He couldn't believe it. He had passed into the throbbing pulse of jungle drums. Vibrant music right out of the native thatch. They'd transformed the place into an eerie grotto, all dark, electric, and full of echoes. Black and orange streamers, dimmed lights, and the cavernous reverberation of the band had recast the blunt athletic room into something exotic. Wasn't this fine?

Mr. McConnel was reaching for tickets behind them as he said, "Take your jackets on to the boys locker room."

It was weird, this familiar space Bobby didn't know. They had thousands of chairs making margins. Couches lined the far end for the chaperones. Half teachers and half parents. Maybe they'd break into an impromptu PTA meeting after intermission.

Bobby floated along through the crowd of flannel shirts and peasant blouses, feeling a strange, wonderful crawling in his stomach — little thrills spreading northward. All the guys were there. Just great. There was Buzz with Frank Cottman and some girl. Frank was tall and distinguished. Buzz was about Bobby's build, maybe an inch taller and earnestly interested in the things he saw. He was calm and well dressed in proper blue jeans and a bright blue flannel shirt. "Hi ya, Buzz."

"Bob. What the hell you doing here?"

"Slumming."

Engulfed in drum beats and sprinkles of dainty laughter, they eased on through the double locker room doors. Bobby could see that the great change did not extend inside. It still smelled of wintergreen, floor granules, and jock straps.

Pete said, "Use your own locker."

Bobby headed down the narrow aisle between locker banks, straddling the single bench in between. The chamber had its own gloom of pale light. McFarland was emerging from one of the aisles, heading for the dance floor. As a varsity basketball player, he was used to this space. John had dressed as a hayseed, town style, with a tattersall vest over a striped dress shirt and khaki pants above his dirty white bucks. Preppie, hiker, student.

Bobby said to him, "It's John and he's confused. There's no game tonight."

McFarland waved one hand. "I was half dressed for basketball before I remembered that tonight's ball has a dif-fer-ent bounce."

Bobby felt lurking a hint of envy. This kid was top athlete and top student. Now he was social lion as well.

Bobby quipped, "McFarland, ready for basketball, learns the meaning of the Jersey Bounce. With crowd's on the floor instead of in the stands. Who you come with?"

"Kahn. Did you bring a date?"

"Me?" he said with a slight giggle. "Little me? I'm too young to die, being an individual who hardly knows what to do."

McFarland turned toward the door to the gym. "Employ the fund-a-mentals of the game." He left wearing his grin of clenched teeth.

In a moment, Bobby followed him out into the happy field and waited for Fred and Pete. Beneath the permanent backboard to his right was a file of corn stalks braced against the end wall. They seemed to shiver in the gym as they had in the field. Fred came out and went off to the right. Pete and Bobby followed the out-of-bounds line next to the stands toward where Buzz and Frank Cottman had been milling. They were still there, now joined by Phil Stillbrouck.

Bobby said loudly over the band, "I didn't mean it when I said I was slumming and hope you took it as the jest it was."

Buzz turned. "How do you like the band?"

"Very festive."

"Loud too."

The reverberation was so intense that even the deep beats of the bass drum seemed without edge or shape. Suddenly, it all stopped for an instant. Roland Sloan, one of the school's bigger wheels, was making an announcement on the band's tall microphone. "Good evening, ladies and gentlemen. This is the second part — of the first dance."

The band broke into "Near You." Bobby mumbled along, substituting other, risque prepositions for *near*.

Bobby asked Buzz, "Do they announce every part of every dance? Or do we acquire confusion as we go along?"

"Not usually. Maybe half the time. Why?"

"Why not? How many dances are there? After the habanera and the gavotte, I suspect newer numbers in newer modes."

"Usually twelve dances, three parts each, but who can tell? After the first couple, things gets mixed up."

Buzz, who had a semi-preppie background with connections to the town's west-end elite, knew all about dances.

They moved on. Pete led the way. Near the stands a couple of hay bales lay broken open. Real stuff that was soft and intimidating, reminiscent of farm and fantasy. Near the far jump circle, Jenny Crown, Kimberly Manners, and Mary Sue Hurley were gabbing in their own circle. Seeing those girls actually there, not protected by the rituals of classes and teachers, was thrilling. He was reminded of the first time he had climbed onto the garage roof, had looked over the edge, and was afraid to jump.

The boys' circle approached the girls' like a curling stone. The drum beats made it hard to hear. He shouted to Mary Sue, "Good evening. Fancy meeting you outside of Dunsinane." He had to admit she looked good, both appealing as a siren and approachable as a maiden.

She wore her party smile. "You don't know it, but I put you up to it." She wore a man's shirt above her jeans. Saddle shoes. Her hair wore red flowers. Not white. He was amazed that this was the same person he knew in class. Here she was free in the field like a wild deer, or rabbit.

"Uh huh. Blood all over," he shouted toward her ear. "I faint in five." Kimberly Manners leaned his way and shouted, "I thought I would die before I ever saw you at a dance."

"Why didn't you?"

Then, oddly perhaps, they moved on, as if they were not permitted to linger. Ma, he's hogging the drinking fountain. Jack Harnessall was near the outside door. He'd been talking to Chick Chuckerson, a big football player and school wheel. Chick was moving off.

Jack was Bobby's height but much wider. He was from Plainsboro, the farm community that contained the Walker-Gordon Rotolactor and the remains of Elsie, the Borden Cow. His early days in barn and pasture had generated about him an aura both earthy and bawdy. He wore jeans like the rest of them, but his had probably been worn to work that day.

Jack raised a hand.

"Ho, there, Robert. Vegetable."

Bob:	Show subject?
Jack:	Uh, no.
Bob:	Is it in the gym?
Jack:	Rats. Yes.
Bob:	All those corn stalks.
Jack:	Rats. Fodder in the gym and you got it in three.

Bobby bubbled, "Happy Hal of ween. And here I am at a school dance. My mother's warning came too late."

"Right. How many times have you danced?"

"I'm feeling my way. You know, like Einstein's sister Vitty, his last known relative."

Jack said, "Very funny."

Bobby said, "In an effort to lighten the evening, I made a jest from a local play on words and was greeted with derision."

Pete said, "He left Mary Sue guessing." Pete was smiling. His voice was always hoarse and seemed to smile on its own.

"Don't tell Miss Riggs," Jack said. "She'll call him to the office Monday for abusing a female student."

"Seriously, Jack," Bobby said, trying to grin at his inexperience, "Here I am in the Princeton High School gym carefully dressed like a facsimile farmer and ready to ask the obvious question, which is, what do I do now?"

"You just go up to some girl and say would you like to dance."

Bobby grinned grotesquely. "Uh huh. Which leads me to another problem."

"You don't know how to dance."

"I sort of know. But then Mrs. O'Leary sort of knew how to milk a cow."

So, Jack had mentioned merchandise, they had moved, he had asked, and she had smiled and said, "I'd love to."

Only the gods knew it, but that was Catastrophe's first act. It surpassed anything Mrs. O'Leary ever imagined.

Now, many have heard this phrase: If you want to learn to swim, dive right into the deep end? How many tried it and drowned? Bobby dived. He took hold of her as he might take hold of his Sunday School teacher. "If I get off on the wrong foot, which will probably be one of yours, don't scream too loud." He swore she flinched.

She was turning practical. "You won't. Except... No. You're supposed to... Hold my hand like this."

"Okay. Like this?" His voice was smiling but he was trying to grab hold of a fluttering sparrow.

"And your right hand goes around me ... on my back, not on my ribs."

"Like this? I apply my hands and feet in position for dancing and proceed with care." Bobby applied a grip, as if she were a rubber balloon and his fingers were razor blades. He hoped he was doing it right. But his grasp was barely a touch here, a slide there, a probe somewhere else.

She held him off and said, "What's the matter? Am I poison?"

Bobby gasped. "My goodly, no. Poison? No. You're not even caffeine. I just seem to be all toes and elbows."

The trouble was, he was afraid he was going to molest her. He didn't know anything about a female's body, about what parts were no touch. And his stomach was in his throat because of it. He might slide his hand too far, not knowing where too far was. He might press too hard, giving some wrong signal. She was all hot stove.

They danced, more fending than touching. He held his breath as if he were swimming underwater. He believed that they must have been the absolute worst dancers in the entire history of the Princeton High School gym. They would step and sway like shivering timbers. He would step sideways and she would step sideways, too, only in the other direction. He would step on her foot and, in trying to recover, step on her other one. At least nobody in the bleachers was watching. After a very long struggle, somebody tapped him on the shoulder. He knew what that meant. They parted or, more accurately, they released each other. They were going to be changing partners. Jack would be dancing with Mary Sue, Bobby with Jenny.

He spoke with a struggling smile. "Oh, hello. Another victim, by swan." Bobby was trying to sound game for anything. "But don't worry. Tomorrow I'll take you to the chiropodist."

Jenny was short and although thin she was also rounded. She wore blue cornflowers in her brown hair a shade lighter than her jeans. Jenny's best feature was calmness and patience. She was rather pretty, too. Her only real burden was a voice like a blue jay. Jenny tended to cock her head when she squawked. "You'll be just fine."

He was fine, although it wasn't his doing. When Bobby took her hand and slid his arm around her, she melted right into him. The drum beats became more etched, or maybe that was his heart beating in a new rhythm. He had to admit it was very different dancing with Jenny and he was frankly frightened. Her front was touching his from knee to chest. It didn't seem to matter how he stepped. Jenny was just glued on. Wherever Bobby went, her whole self was riding along on him like an x-ray apron.

After about six minutes of this frightening paradise, his young shoulder felt a tap. It was Kimberly's turn. The turn was about one hundred eighty degrees. They moved at arms length. Their feet moved very little. They just swayed and bobbed while facing each other, about a yard between them. What a change this is, he thought. Cotton candy to sliced liver.

Kimberly said, "I was serious when I said I was so surprised."

"She was serious and surprised, by goodly. And do you admit, by goodly, that we all lose our sense of shame sometime."

"Where did you learn to dance?"

"In New York mainly. Fred and Arthur both had a hand or foot in my training. I offered to show Fred a few new steps — very gingerly, of course."

"You don't dance badly at all."

"Uh huh. Now if I could just remember the difference between fingers and toes."

Jolly Kimberly was bigger and thicker than the others and Bobby wondered if any boy would ever be able to approach her as a serious romantic attraction. In some ways, she reflected the nature of this whole event, in his humble opinion. Lots of fun, but was it really worth the anguish and dread?

When the number ended, she said, "Now, you take me back to my group and say thank you for the dance."

He had to grin. She would probably be a teacher someday. They coalesced with Jenny and Mary Sue in another part of the field.

Bobby said, "Thank you for the dance and the raw emotion that went with it."

So, they had danced, and then the three young gentlemen retreated. Fred had been dancing with Audrey Sharmanns and joined them to make a circle of four. Then Frank Cottman joined.

Fred Darkly, dressed in light gray jeans and a plaid shirt of reds and blues, asked Bobby, "Who've you danced with?"

"They come and go, you know. So many. Kimberly. Jenny."

"And Mary Sue. I saw you dancing with Mary Sue."

"I seem to remember her skin tone, just one number being all I had time for. Something of a real pity."

"How'd you do?"

It hadn't occurred to Bobby that there was a gauge or meter attached.

"I wasn't asked to make relative judgments since who can tell with these pushy females? I suppose, to keep them all from fighting, I'll have to cut in on Ned Duckworth."

Ned was one of the school's star athletes, a senior, and was dancing with his girl friend, Marian Wiggin. She was dynamite and the prettiest girl in the school.

Pete said, "I dare you to try it."

Bobby expanded his dare. "Or Boyd perhaps, if I get bored with Marian."

Steve Boyd, another athlete, was dancing with a cheerleader named Sally.

Jack said, "I've known Sally Wren since kindergarten. She grew up near Cranbury."

"I wish I knew her," Pete said.

Bobby said to Pete, "You phoney baloney, Pete. You wouldn't ask her to dance if she took the mike over there and said the dance couldn't continue unless you did."

Pete said, "You cut in on Duckworth, I'll cut in on Boyd."

Their scene of dare and double dare was cut short by sharp blasts from the band and their launching into "Little Brown Jug." Almost instantly Winnie Marjorie Poole, in ballet slippers, was zipping around with Closter in an instantly formed forty-foot circle. Where was Dolly Wright? Ah. There. Shoes off. Jitterbugging with Don Poole in an adjacent circle. Bobby eased up to an arc. After a minute or so, he felt warmth at his elbow. It was Mary Sue, also joining the arc. He was afraid she was going to prod him into trying to form a circle of their own.

Bobby shrugged her off a little and said, "And here we are again."

Minutes and steps passed. "I was waiting for the jitterbug to either end or crash into an orgy."

Eventually it was over, to thunderous relief, and they were standing there more or less alone. The temperature of the gym felt higher by several degrees Kelvin. Bobby couldn't just walk away, and didn't want to anyway. When the band resumed, a slow number, Bobby said, oh so suavely, "Shall we? I'm game, and a little gun shy. But why waste a beautiful moment when we could be stumbling along together?"

She said, "Let's try it this way."

They faced each other as if they were going to try on the same overcoat.

"Just follow me. Later we'll try to dip." She was very earnest.

But nothing worked. At first she copied Jenny, her own version of a full court press. But, where Jenny had pressed her head against his shoulder, Mary Sue held hers away which must have been very awkward for her. So, they gradually slipped further away from touching and, when they finally tried to spin around in a circle and almost fell down, she said, "I give up."

They made their way to a circle of Dolly Wright, Kimberly, and Doris Black, which is where Bobby left her. It felt like halftime. But Bobby had no idea of time. Time passes quickly when you're feeling doom.

Shattered, failed, alone, Bobby wanted relief at any cost. He wanted to step out into the air, which was forbidden. He wanted to soar up through the grid, but there wasn't one. He moved toward the couches at the gym's far end. The principal, Mr. O'dell, was seated on the end. Bobby spoke to him first. Then, "Hello, Miss Riggs." She was dean of girls.

"Is this your first school dance?" Miss Riggs inquired.

"Yes, ma'am." He chuckled. "As anyone can plainly see."

"I hope it won't be your last."

Bobby smiled and moved off, stepping in rhythm to the drum beats as if he were reveling. He saw McFarland dancing with a cute sophomore named Marianne O'Keefe. There was Duckworth, still glued to Marian. Spade and Jeanne were dancing properly, although Jeanne's gaze was quite improperly sweeping. She had an eye for everything, that girl. Kimberly had wangled a dance with Tom Herman. He was a bigger athlete than Duckworth. Jack in the far corner was dancing with a blonde named Peggy Spivey. Platinum blondes always suggested sluttery, probably because of the movies — Lana Turner, Jean Harlow — but Peggy was a very nice girl.

Past the center jump circle, Bobby saw Spade Harmon and his group. Spade turned with a big grin. So did Fensher and Itchy.

"Congratulations," Spade shouted. "I told you you'd make it."

"Hold it, Spade. I haven't made anything yet, being about to jump my burro over a cliff." Their inside connection was pronunciation of the word burro. Boo roe.

"I'll watch till you hit the rocks."

Eons later Bobby found Mary Sue again. She had just made her own obeisance to the chaperons. He wasn't giving up. "You want to try one more time? I ask knowing the old saying, Once wounded, twice killed."

"I was going to sit this one out."

"In that case…You were what?" He welcomed the chance to do anything with her.

"Sit this one out. Come on."

The band was between numbers. She led him through the loud silence to the side chairs and they sat down with their backs to the big gym windows, which were protected from balls and bodies by heavy screens. He sensed the peepers' eyes from the bushes outside on the back of his neck.

Bobby said, "I'm better at sitting them out anyway, with long experience in bench warming and water fetching."

"Would you like to get me some punch?"

"Punch? Without Judy? I mention water fetching and she, without pause, cashes in on my experience." He rose. "Thy cup shall runneth over."

Bobby made his way to the refreshment table. Punch and cookies some mother had baked.

He returned and slid a cup of punch across the space between them. "Here's looking at you, kid." He saluted with a cookie. "And now, I have to ask you something."

"Ask me what?"

"Something of vital, personal importance." Bobby had his dance program out. It was in the shape of a barn. He opened it up and folded it shut. "I speak of your father. When he was in the FBI. Did he have anything to do with the atomic bomb or anything like that? I mean in occupied Europe?"

"He wasn't out catching spies, if that's what you mean."

"In Detroit, we all knew that they were making Norden bombsights right down the road at Burroughs, prompting me to ask if you knew what they were doing in Knoxville?"

"Yes. But they made us swear we'd never tell."
"To guarantee silence they extracted from you an oath to never tell. Uh huh. Tell what? I mean … oh." He wagged his head in defeat. "I was serious for the second time in my life. I mean, was your father always in the FBI?"
"He worked for them during the war."
"But, I mean, why?"
"Because he could keep a secret."
"I'm almost beginning to catch on. Or fall off."
Bobby also was beginning to feel a little irritated. Not at her but at not knowing what he was doing. Why was talking with a girl any different from talking with anyone? He did not know. Who does? Who ever did?
She smiled slightly, giving him something at least. Maybe she almost looked upon him as a friend. He had won her over. "Not that I have any secrets. The whole city looked gloomy."
"Did you live right in Knoxville?"
"Part of the time. How come you're so curious? You aren't a German spy, are you?"
"Achtung! In an eighth grade play I was a Nazi saboteur, wearing a light straw hat and a monocle. I was so good I spent half the school year in Alcatraz."
"I'm sure you were very convincing."
"You should have heard my accent. Miss Shinkle thought I spoke better in German than I wrote in English."
"Are you going to be in plays in Princeton High?"
"Total lack of talent. Saying yes is my mother. While in sports, I claim good reasons for not making the team."
"But what team?"
"I was actually out for football last year, with the likes of Pete and Fred and Jack."
"They're all in your group, aren't they?"
"So long as they pay their dues. Pete was in that play in eighth grade by the way, being the good guy, of course. Looks but no imagination. He's also in Explorer Scouts."
"Scouts? Still?"
"It's debatable. Explorers have parties and dances, which makes the idea debatable. They also have the usual overnight hikes. So far, we can

bring girls only to the parties and dances." He thought that was very witty but she didn't bat an eye.

"Kimberly is having a Christmas party."

There was no point in asking about a Christmas party, since he would have to find some conflict to cover up that he wasn't likely to be asked. He also sensed she had blundered in mentioning it, since she went right on.

"Athletes make good dancers."

After a drum roll, the music started again.

"Come on," she said. "This time hold me a little closer for better rhythm."

"Okay, while pretending I'm not afraid to."

"Why? I don't bite."

"With your vampire lineage?"

At that point Bobby was ready to retreat to the world of model airplanes, where he didn't have to worry about violating something. The trouble with that reasoning was that he'd never been any good at making model airplanes either. He had neither the dexterity nor the patience required.

They danced better this try but not by much. Afterward, Mary Sue and Jenny departed to the girls locker room. He was happy enough to see them disappear through the sacred doors, which seemed to part and swallow up whatever was thrust into them.

Bobby bummed around the gym. He always loved the sight of light reflected from band instruments. He decided he ought to say hello to the band leader, a heavy set man about forty. The sad thing was, Bobby had been weaned on band marches and Nelson Eddy. Pop music was low down and crass.

"Very good on 'Little Brown Jug.'"

"Thanks, kid. You play in a band?"

"Not seriously. School marching band."

"What piece?"

"B-flat trumpet."

"Want to sit in?"

"Thanks, but no thanks. Petrillo might object. I'm not that good."

The maestro turned then and said, "Heart Aches."

Bobby wandered. He found Jack again with Fred. They made some ribald comments on various flannel shirts on display, what was in them and varied suggestions. Then the band beats sounded louder than ever.

Jack said, "One more and then the Virginia reel."

With those words Bobby sensed a bomb about to explode beneath his left foot and felt ready to run for it.

"Okay. A name that conjugates things rural with things romantic. Tobacco Road comes to Moore Street?"

Jack was all serious. "Is Mary Sue going to be your partner?"

Bobby shrugged.

"Aren't you going to ask her? She's right over there waiting."

"Her heart no doubt thoroughly eaten out by my callous indifference. But, we face the reality that I don't know how to dance to start with, let alone this Virginia reel stuff."

"It's all right. Fred already asked her."

"Okay."

As they made the two lines, Bobby retreated to the locker room. The janitor on duty in one corner had a portable radio turned on. He was listening to Don Dunphy describe a prize fight. McFarland came in. He'd been dancing with the very elegant Leslie Luce. Bobby had to ask himself, what more could this guy possibly want? Maybe my job on the radio? He would very likely get it if he tried. Bobby caught one or two of Dunphy's rights to the head, when he heard McFarland inquire, "Have you been making peace with the opposite gender?"

"Not well."

John:	Mineral.
Bob:	Show subject?
John:	Not tonight.
Bob:	Does it belong to you or me?
John:	No.
Bob:	Is it in this building?
John:	No
Bob:	Is it in Princeton?
John:	Yes. Probably.
Bob:	Is it in or around your house or my house.
John:	Yes.
Bob:	Your house?
John:	No
Bob:	Is it in the living room, dining room, or kitchen?
John:	No

Bob:	Bedroom or bathroom?
John:	No
Bob:	In the basement?
John:	No
Bob:	Well, heck. In the garage?
John:	Yes
Bob:	One of the cars?
John:	No, not one of the cars
Bob:	Oh. The Cadillac's red wheels.
John:	That is it.

"Speaking of which, I was dancing like a hyena. How did you learn?"

"By invoking — the fundamentals of the game."

"Seriously. I get nowhere."

"Neither do I." He grinned. "Who cares, is the appropriate query."

Bobby had to go out and watch the reel. Ironically, he saw it was easy, just a lot of skipping, a dance Bobby could have accomplished. Fred sure had no trouble.

When it broke up, Jack came up. "Last dance. Want to head up to Renwicks afterward?"

Bobby wanted to head up to the moon. He couldn't dance. He would never be able to dance. He felt like an empty shoe. "Can you leave any time?"

The gym seemed to stand in an aftermath of sounds now. The noise still around sounded stale.

"Any time after eleven. And it's eleven."

"Does everybody usually stay till the last dance?"

"Either way. Why? You want to ask Mary Sue again?"

"Fred probably will."

"He will if you don't."

"Okay." Bobby didn't know why Jack had to be so logical, the jerk. Let Fred ask her anything. Let them shack up, whatever that meant (Bobby was pretty sure he knew). If he showed interest in Mary Sue, or any girl, people would laugh at him.

"Let's get out of here."

Outside, the air was cool. The peepers were gone.

Chapter 8

Bait and Switch

Next evening, November 1, this young man without a clue surveyed the guest, Rise Stevens, as if she were invisible. She was a lovely and talented guest, too, though Mother was somewhat restrained, and it was a good show. He identified four subjects and one quickie. But this was minor stuff, a mere network radio program, and his success during those thirty minutes had no effect upon his mooning all over the Mutual Guild Theatre. Only Bill Slater's very chic wife made something of it.

Mrs. Slater: Keep that hair combed, Bobby. You'll be dating before you know it.

Bobby carried this notion of hope, fantasy, and fear all the way home and held onto it all night and all Sunday morning. He thought that if only she — Mary Sue, not Mrs. Slater — would touch him, even accidentally, he would rise toward paradise.

Bobby: I would rise toward the moon and fly over it.

But he had no clue what to do next. What? Just call her up? You jest, Charlie. He could no more call her up than he could grow a beard. Sunday afternoon, mooning in the sun room, he sensed that maybe he needed a *plan*. He was about to grab for this atom when the phone rang.

He answered and heard Doc Foss saying, "It's time to schedule another event."

Burning oak and birch swept aside the newer scents of perfume and shampoo in his mind's nose. The plan shriveled down to a point. "Un huh."

Foss said, "Weekend at Camp Pahaquarra. I have it cleared with the Council for December 14."

"Sounds really fine."

"I haven't been to Camp Pahaquarra, but you were described to me as a denizen of the place."

"Like a Leni-Lenape. Referring to those paths on the Kittatiny Ridge that hide sprained ankles, nervous exhaustion, and diamondback rattlers. We can look for them all the way to Skyline or Sunfish."

They talked on, and later that afternoon Bobby received another call, this one from his great friend, Fred Darkly.

Fred said, "So, we're going to Pahaquarra."

"With bug juice and pork roll in fond memory."

Fred said, very straight, "Did Foss give you any details I didn't give him?"

"No. Oh, he said he'd checked with the school to make sure there was no conflicting dance."

"Yeah. There isn't."

Bobby reached for Dad's desk calendar. He saw that certain December dates were circled for some reason, which was suspicious. The fourteenth's circle was double, with a B alongside. Likely one of Mother's bridge groups.

Bobby said, "You're going, the post may assume?"

"I couldn't say."

Fred's voice had suddenly changed somehow. He was not quite challenging but there was no trace of camaraderie either.

After several seconds of pregnant silence, Bobby inquired, "Freddy, are you holding something back, behind your left galosh?"

"I didn't say I wasn't going."

"It might be chilly?"

"That's the night Kimberly is having her Christmas party, you know."

Flashes swirled. "I heard." The flashes were of grade school parties he had not heard about until the following Monday.

"Are you going?" Fred almost blurted the query.

The sun had swung around to the right, squashing the window patterns into parallelograms.

"I couldn't say either."

Bobby used to watch kids in the school yard playing marbles. If you played, you could lose them, so he never wanted to play. But all the others played. So Bobby played, too, and lost all his marbles.

"Just wondered." Then Fred said quietly, "I also heard that somebody is interested. If you are."

"Me?" That woke up his hearing. "What? Who?"
"Honey Winderlick."
"Who? Honey Winderlick?" The name was confirmed. "That's silly, Fred. Know her I hardly do."
"What I heard was she said you were the only kid in the school at all interesting."
"She's nuts, Fred."
"She certainly is. But that's what I heard. And she used to go with Duckworth, you know."
"She's finally showing good taste." But there must be denial here. "She's crazed. She's headed for Skillman." That was short for the New Jersey Psychiatric Institute.

On Monday, with Mary Sue unreasonably not in class to distract him, Bobby started mooning all over again. The epiphany re-emerged. But now he must make a different plan, with a new moon in a different orbit. And this moonscape was full of craters, one of them named Duckworth. Young Bobby was afraid to look across the room.

Of course, Honey herself did not understand his fear.

Honey: I didn't understand why Bobby didn't respond like some normal kid.

He was trying to. Plan B. After school Bobby walked uptown trying to figure out some casual way to bump into her.

Honey: I walked uptown after cheerleading practice, trying to figure a way to call him up on some pretext.

Fate got them both. He was walking past Palmer Square just as she was bombing out of Skirm's Smoke Shoppe on the corner. Traffic was droning on Nassau Street. Shoppers were choking the Square. People were swarming the sidewalk. It was late in the day, damp and chilly. The sky was gray.

"Well, hello, Tiger," she said. She had stopped when she saw him and now took an additional step forward.

"Uh, hello." He stepped backward a step. Was Duckworth around the corner in front of Zavelle's? "Oh, it's you. The Shakespeare scholar and eraser borrower."

"Never thought you'd meet me outside of school. Did you?"

As they talked, Bobby sidestepped all the way around her. She turned with him.

"Me? Meet you? Would I dream of meeting Lana?" His hands slipped into his wind breaker's pockets. "Where you going?" He may have stuttered.

"Renwicks. Want to come along?" She shifted her purse strap neatly over her shoulder.

Renwicks was a local eatery two doors down Nassau. It was nicely colonial and reasonable, clean, and refined. PHS kids who wanted to be seen by other PHS kids went there, including Bobby, who liked local places. They made him feel a part of the town.

"Sure. What can I lose?" He tossed it off casually enough but was elated well beyond casual. He wondered if people were noticing them. As far back as he could remember, Bobby felt a warmth, a special blossom, when he thought that people in the street, in the room, or anywhere else, were watching him. It drove him onto stages, campfire programs, and radio stations.

A gravel truck chugged by on Nassau Street. On ahead at the corner of Chambers Street, a Public Service truck had thrust up a guy in a cherry picker to change a street lamp.

They entered and took one of the knotty pine booths near the back. He was known at Renwicks because Mr. Harry Renwick was a friend of the family.

Honey had shrugged off her leather jacket with the big brown buttons. Beneath was a white scarf draped across a light blue sweater. Across the sweater was some kind of cameo hanging on a thin chain. Bobby was afraid to notice such things too closely because of their, well, their context.

Menus stood between sugar and salt. He handed her one but she shook her head. Just a twitch of a quarter inch that radiated savvy.

"What are you having?"

Honey said, "Ice cream soda." She smiled across the table. "We'll pretend we're ordering real drinks. Sin by proxy. Like you probably do at all those fancy New York night clubs."

"Drinks? Cold sober Bob, who never orders a dry martini without a twist?"

Renwicks was all wood, light knotty pine on the walls, with a floor of tongue and groove hardwood that thumped as you crossed it. Up front it had a soda fountain in the vintage drug store style.

A waitress appeared almost instantly. "What's yours today?"

"Hamburger and Coke for me. Soda for her."

"What kind?"

"Coffee."

The waitress frowned, nodded, and left. He stacked the menus back, turning them inside out just to be smart. And he was wondering. Was this a date? Did this count as a date?

Honey smiled. "How are you coming with Shakespeare, now that you're on the other side of the room?"

"Not much different, forsooth."

Her hands made a megaphone. "I'll bet."

Bobby stuck his fingers in his ears, mockingly. "Seriously. We're in the last act and I'm still not sure who Malcomb is."

"I was going to ask you."

Was this a set-up? Had she run home and changed into her wonderful sweater right after school?

"With luck and Cliff notes from the U-store, maybe we'll figure it out before the test." He grinned.

She opened her pocket book, looked in, and started to reach. Bobby was betting she would produce a pack of cigarettes, but she thought better of it and snapped shut the purse. Cigarettes to Bobby and his peers were worldly and slightly risque. Sex, liquor, and cigarettes were graduated levels of sin.

She smiled with finesse. "Why don't you ask your new friend across the room?"

"New friend? Could you be referring to Miss Hurley, that very casual acquaintance of mine?" His silly grin became a frown. "I doubt if she'd tell me the right time."

She stashed her purse on the booth's bench beside her and looked right at him. "You don't go out much, do you?"

He stared, stopped by a blunt object. "Not that I remember. Maybe I should."

"It's surprising, you know."

His ear was beginning to throb. "Un huh. Surprising?"

"Because of your *Twenty Questions* thing, silly."

"Oh." He frowned. Everybody seemed to think the show made him something he wasn't.

She added, "People think you must be very swinging and sophisticated."

"And conceited?"

"You have something to be conceited about."

Bobby always had trouble looking at people. He thought they didn't want him staring at them. But right then, he tied his eyes right onto hers. "Mother thinks so. But she's still dreaming. It's just a lucky break."

"Even so." She grinned.

It was pushing five o'clock. In this restaurant customer traffic was sparse but always moving. Businessmen came for lunch. Students after school. Supper people were yet to arrive.

Bobby said, letting out a little breath, "To be half way honest, I've always been scared of the whole thing. Going out."

"You don't give that impression, you know."

He grunted. "I doubt if I give off much of any impression at all."

"Oh yes you do." She leaned forward, chin on hand, and smiled into his eyes. "Shall I tell you?"

This was fiery stuff. Something called an *experience*. He swallowed and put his own chin in his own hand. "Sure."

Her eyes shifted from their frolicsome setting to a steady seriousness that Bobby hardly expected. "Well, you're very kind." Those eyes then lifted to another shelf. "Very serious. Very concerned about doing the right thing." She smiled as if to erase this wanton seriousness. "And you're always squinting."

He nodded in resignation. "Bad eyes." He shook off the bad eyes, "I'm just a dumb kid off the farm."

"Is that what you tell Mary Sue?"

"We don't talk that much."

"Like fun. Mr. Chesterton's always shutting you up."

He closed his eyes and rested a full second. "I'm the friendly type. My most serious thoughts are like milkweed flying out the pod, and carry about the same weight." He knew she was years ahead of him in every measurement but was so excited it didn't matter.

She leaned back against the high back of the booth. Her long fingers folded on the table in front of her. "My spies tell me she's the only one you danced with Halloween."

"They missed the true facts of the case."

"You'll wind up going steady."

"I'm steady only in my sober moments."

She leaned forward again, over her folded hands. "Do you ever take girls to your show in New York?"

Boing! The entire pinball machine erupted in flashing zig zag.

"Not very often. The parents probably wouldn't like it, which has strongly limited my plans for such events."

Her head cocked in a saucy way. "You mean they wouldn't let their daughter go to New York with you?"

"Maybe some would. I hadn't thought about it that much, to tell you the truth, being more concentrated on the trials of Malcomb and Banquo."

"My parents couldn't care less, what's left of them."

Outside it was getting dark. The suburban Transit line's orange and black busses would thunder by, passing Trenton Transit's bigger cream monsters going the other way.

"Speaking of dances, I didn't see you there."

"I don't go to dances unless somebody takes me."

Bobby, facing the front, saw Kimberly entering with a friend named Patty Carey. They would likely have taken a booth near the front but Honey was facing the rear and they could not see who was with Bobby. So they came back to their booth. Patty stood by bemused, but Kimberly was gawking.

"Well, hello." Jolly Kimberly wore a long straight skirt and a long corduroy jacket. She loomed large above their booth, like Margaret Dumont without the pearls. "Fancy meeting you here."

"It's fancy just being here."

The waitress brought their orders just then and their table hopping friends moved on and took a booth near the back of the house.

Honey said, "Now it will be all over." Deft fingers stripped the paper from the long straw. "Mr. Radio swings uptown."

"Just because we're sitting here?" He was applying ketchup to the hamburger, coolly both embracing and scorning the situation. Was the thrill of riding a horse at full gallop partly in the possibility of falling off? A mix of other metaphors swirled for choice.

Her lips took the straw now sticking up from the sweet depths of the soda. They circled it and clung to it. Her eyes watched him watching. Then the whole pointillism scene released itself and she said, "Maybe we'll make the *Chronicle*."

Bobby got home floating-on-air. Bobby, the smitten. The newly discovered social force of PHS. He looked up Winderlick in the phone book and made nebulous plans to ride by her house on his bike just accidently. Maybe he'd call her Saturday from New York on some pretext. He soared like a lovebird. He went to bed seeking a plan. Ah. A plan.

Chapter 9

The Best Laid

The scandal did not quite rock the school to its pedagogic foundations. Only Benny, the furnace man deep in the bowels of the boiler room, might have felt a slight shift.

Mary Sue: To me the entire earth had fallen in. Oh, yes.

Tuesday morning Bobby could see that she was at great pains to pretend nothing in orbit had shifted at all.

"Oh." She was looking downward. "Hello." She wore her purple sweater with a spread of beads. Her hair was empty and her eyes came up to look past his.

Bobby said with his pastel smile, "Where were you yesterday? Switching to journalism again?"

"I had a two-hankie cold. If you want to know." She was listing toward snippy.

He sensed that something was going to drop through a hole in his pocket. He sniffed slightly on his own cold. "You missed the big Macbeth finale."

"I don't miss much." She was erasing something from her notebook. Probably his name.

"That maybe means more than it means?"

Still erasing. "It means I seem to miss everything."

He could smell the shavings from her pencil left behind in some lucky sharpener.

Bobby said, "Little Miss Riddle today, says the young lady, the same young lady who missed the demise of King Macbeth, who lost his head. What's a pike?"

"He wasn't very nice, was he?"

"It's open to interpretation, Lady Macbeth's interpretation differing substantially from Lady Macduff's."

"Not exactly your kind of woman, was she?"

She was brushing away the crumbs his name had been rubbed into, looking down as she did so, afraid, he thought, of looking at him. Then she did look up and laughed slightly, probably at what she was doing and planning, showing her white teeth and the tip of her tongue, which was redder than usual. Her eyes were bluer than usual, too, he noticed.

Bobby started to swing to the front. "Nuh uh. Not being king of Scotland. Next we're going to read *Our Town*. McFarland described it to me as like Macbeth only wilder?"

"That will be very nice." She flipped over a notebook page. It crackled as it turned.

He felt like grabbing that pencil and dipping it in her ink well. Bobby asked, "Who you doing your science project on?"

"Enrico Fermi."

Bobby sat up, his forehead wrinkling. "So am I."

Then she almost smiled. "We better be quiet or he'll move us apart."

He grunted.

"Or maybe you'd feel better if he did."

Mr. Chesterton looked right at him. "Shshsh."

She closed the notebook. Bobby knew he was no longer in. He turned to face the front, then swung back and whispered, "What time did you get home after the dance?"

"That would be telling, would it not?" She folded her hands. Her fingers were not as long as those Bobby had seen folded in Renwicks.

"A firm answer was the hope of the question."

"Actually, Kimberly's father took us up to Renwicks and we walked home."

"Sounds exciting. We went to the Balt."

"Oh? I thought you were always going to Renwicks."

Bobby's brow wrinkled. "Me?"

"I heard it's one of your favorite places."

They both heard, "Hey, you two."

That night this scandalous ball of social excitement, feeling flutters like a social butterfly, called Fred, using the phone on his parents' night table. Fred was saying, "So, I give you an opening and you charge right through."

"Charge? Opening? What's upsetting you besides Miss Hight? What opening?"

"Honey Winderlick. Half the school, if not half the town, is talking about McGuire and Winderlick laughing it up at Renwicks."

Bobby was standing straight, staring around the room at wrinkled beds or his father's underwear on the floor.

"Come on."

"McGuire, you're so full of luck it isn't even funny."

"I was uptown heading serenely for the Music Shoppe and there she was coming serenely out of Skirm's, probably buying cigarettes."

"Okay, that's luck. That part could have been luck. But that's not what I mean."

"I wasn't following her and I know, by goodly, she definitely wasn't following me."

"I was referring to who it's gotta be. It couldn't be Marguerite Bogapopolous. Oh, no. It has to be one of the toughest girls in the whole high school. Used to go with one of the toughest guys. It had to be this jumping babe who's been out with university students."

"Polly Madden was out with students when she was in eighth grade."

"You know what I mean. You are Mr. Luck."

That same Thursday afternoon luck arrived in the mail, a square card hand addressed to him. He read it and read it again, assigning it an importance on a level with college admission. In a few moments he entered the sun room and made sure nobody was likely to enter. He reached for the phone.

Kimberly's little sister answered.

"Is Kimberly there, please? This is Bob McGuire."

"Yes. Just a minute, please."

"Hello, Bob. This is Kimberly."

"Thanks for the invite, to which one wonders if I may RSVP by phone."

"Sure you can. I'll mark you down."

"Coat and tie? I was planning on one but I thought I should ask."

He found a pencil on the leather desk top and looked for the date on his father's calendar.

"Yes. No tuxedo required."

"Oh. Then I won't send it out to the cleaners."

"And you probably have one. But just a tie, preferably without a spot on it."

When they hung up, he leaned back to consider things. In the back of comic books one always found ads from Charles Atlas and Vacutex blackhead removers. But they also had ads for How To Dance. Graphics showed basic steps. He would try them at home, locked in some room.

Friday afternoon at his desk for English, *Our Town* open before him, he heard, "Hello, you." She wore a white blouse today with a wide ribbon in her hair. Her eyes flipped to his with a great sauce of tease.

Bobby threw off, "Good like sin. How's things?"

"Last night. That's how's things." She leaned forward. One hand reached across the space between their desks and gently pushed his shoulder. This was real, actual, physical contact.

Bobby asked in a gulp, "Last night?"

"I had a dream, and you were in it."

Ah, fate. What sweet ambrosia. And across the room Honey was probably cursing because her fountain pen had gone dry. He could almost smell the green ink she always used.

At home that evening, he turned to scheduling. He had responded to Kimberly by phone but there was still the matter of clearance at home. To secure his coming Nirvana, Bobby asked his mother about those circles around December fourteenth on his father's calendar. One of your bridge clubs. Right?

"Now, Bob. It's been marked on the calendar for weeks. You know it's your *National Scholastic Magazine* interview in New York. At five-thirty."

Bobby had to admit he'd forgotten all about the interview. Kimberly's party started at eight. All the world was a conflict.

Chapter 10

Pix Trick Fixes Hick

He'd handle this. Just brush through this interview. What the heck was *National Scholastic* anyway, *Esquire*? He might hold still for a Varga Girl, but some education rag? Please. He'd squeeze it into fifteen minutes. Get the seven o'clock train with ease. Princeton by eight. Bike to Kimberly's by 8:15. Well laid plans.

So, over a month later, Thanksgiving eaten, snow flurries melted, Bobby asked the hostess at Dunhall's for Mrs. Doodle or some other name he'd forgotten. He was led through the same room where Fineshriber had held court to a table in front near the big Broadway windows, with the sweeping car lights beyond. He saw seated there a lady and a girl beside her.

Bobby: I saw seated there this lady and this sensational girl beside her.

The lady was smoking a cigarette in one of those holders. Bobby couldn't stand that kind of affectation, and it was going to enlarge his head, already beginning to make pain. But he went on, stopped, and she looked up. The girl just stared at the far edge of the table.

"I'm Carrie Dumont and this is Angela Rhome. You must be Bobby."

"I must be."

All right, nix the banter and hit the road. Fifteen minutes.

Books, clips and cups were spread all over the table. Angela Rhome was throttling a frosted glass and lifting it to sip. She eyed him over the frost.

Carrie Dumont was energetic and all business.

Carrie: I was all business and tired as hell after four interviews and a business lunch that day.

Bobby got the idea from her brief look at him that she didn't like interviewing young people very much.

Carrie: Eisenhower's in town and they give me this kid.
In fact, Bobby suspected she would really rather call him names.
Carrie: Snot.
He had no idea why the girl was there. Not even a guess. He couldn't guess her age either.
Angela: If anybody says I'm fifteen going on thirty, I'll kill him.
Without looking across the table, Carrie Dumont said, "Angela is in New York for the first time. She's just signed a Powers contract."
Angela: I just signed a Powers contract as my ticket to MGM.
Bobby never appreciated models very much. What did they ever *do*?
He slid out a big chair of wood and leather. The afternoon held little promise, which was all the more reason to start sprinting through this thing. Well, Bobby had warned them. He had tried to get out of it, but they all insisted. And it was the night of Kimberly's party and Bobby's entire persona was focused upon that.
Bobby: My whole persona was focused on sheer fright.
Dad knew about the party, of course, and also knew how Bobby felt about interviews.
Dad: I knew about the party and also knew how Bobby felt about anything having to do with his bread and butter.
Riding in to New York that afternoon, they had sat together in the smoker. The trains of the Pennsylvania Railroad in those days rode on a scale of decay, depending on the time of day. Cars for some of the self-propelled locals had been built before 1910. Clockers and *name* trains, however, were pretty grand. They made you think you were in a movie. In between were clunkers like Dad's daily preference, the 4:17, with older, smellier cars. Their seats were of faded, prickly, corduroyed plush. The backs could flip back and forth. Walls and curves at the car's corners carried ads, usually for cigarettes.

By the time the cows of Walker-Gordon had lowed by on the left, the trainman had punched Dad's ticket and taken Bobby's. Round trip was about three dollars. Dad's commuter ticket cost over twenty dollars a month.

Bobby said, some time after Walker-Gordon, "Uh, why am I here?"

He said calmly, "Because it's a valuable piece of publicity. You should certainly know the value of publicity." He eased his body around to find the best fit. Dad hated to discuss anything with him, probably because Bobby always wanted to argue about it.

They roared over the high bridge over the Raritan and slashed by Stelton and Camp Kilmer. The train's roar kept changing pitch.

"Just remember," he said slowly, "with the right publicity the ratings go up. With the wrong publicity the ratings still go up."

Things Dad said sounded weighty and certain, partly because of his voice. Its edge varied between saber and scimitar. And partly because of his dress. Dad always wore fine suits, but, no matter how much he paid, no matter how many times he returned them to the tailor for adjustment, he still looked portly. Distinguished but portly.

He went on, "Remember, George is working up an extended publicity tour for next summer."

He had spoken with piercing seriousness

"Uh huh. Contract George. Did you say out west, where I left most of my blood?"

"California. Your mother wants to include Colorado."

Bobby saw red rocks and gray peaks with marks of snow. "Would be my second trip West. The image of publicity looms again, now extended to include Colorado and California."

The train tilted as they entered the sweeping curve that would chase them through Metuchen. On the curve Bobby could see ahead the proud GG-1 leading the pack.

"Any publicity is good. Bad is good. Good is good. You'll find that to be a major truth of show business. Just make sure they spell the names right." His hand rose, palm up, to make a brief recapitulation. "Smile for the photos. Answer their questions. Give them the answers you'd want if you were asking. Frank Knox in Chicago one time came in and put his feet up on my desk and said, 'always give the answers you'd want from them.'"

By the time they dived into the *hole*, the tunnel beneath the Hudson, Bobby was feeling stuffy from all the smoke. He knew he'd have a headache within the hour.

He was delivered on time to the island of Manhattan. By then it was dark. He duly left Dad at the elevator of 1440 Broadway and duly sauntered down the lobby to Dunhall's and its glitz in the garment district mode. Inside he saw trickles of blue smoke hanging in the room like confetti.

Now Carrie Dumont was looking down at papers as she said, "Can we order you something?" Her glasses were on a cord. They were pushed up over her forehead into her hair. He had never seen such a thing before. He thought it was totally neat.

Bobby sat down across the banquette from the lady. The girl sat on the third side of the table to his left. In the spirit of friendliness and cooperation Bobby tossed her a polite and delighted smile right over his pulsating forehead. She flinched her lips in response and sipped her glass. His hands instinctively smoothed the wrinkled table cloth. He was a professional. This was an interview. Bobby would head toward his doom professionally and very quickly.

"No thanks. I actually have a train to catch sooner than later and would be amenable to proceeding without delay." He glanced at the Lusserna he'd been given for eighth grade graduation, then across at her. Carrie Dumont wore a navy jacket over a slightly stained white blouse. The whole works looked like she'd either slept in it or been born in it.

She said, still looking down, "Tom collins? Beer. Wine. Coffee?"

"No. Thanks. One can cite the premise, fall off the wagon, fall into the gutter."

"Oaksie doaksie. Then we'll move right along." She had notes on a clipboard which she raised. As she looked it over, Bobby cast his eyes across the ornate room, afraid to look to his left. "Tell us about Bobby McGuire."

This tired question asked in a tired manner displeased him. After all, here he was just a kid asked to a major media interview. But treatment like this, strictly routine to the questioner, irritated him.

Bobby smiled. Time for some gay, nonchalant material. After all, he wasn't just any slob. He was the reason they were all there. "Uh huh. I was born in Silver Creek Colorado, being left on the steps of two old miners."

Her pencil's eraser bounced around among her teeth. "Am I wrong, or did I hear *Our Gal Sunday*?"

Bobby lowered his voice beyond childhood. "Harkening back to school days home ill, when I ate up soap operas, I'm embarrassed to say."

Angela said with unneeded energy, "I did, too. I really did."

That gave him a chance to take this in. She was a model, all right. Those he'd seen inevitably stretched very tight skin across their faces and it was usually flawless, as if it wasn't real. And their eyes always looked bigger than they were. This one filled all those blanks. Her lips were wide and rather full. Her hair was a grayish blonde, strangely loose and straight in an age when most girls thought they needed tight curls. Models were always either carefully made up or scrubbed down to the bone. This one was made up as if she were on a job. Bobby decided that she was a kid without doubt. Maybe fifteen.

"All right, all right, kids. Let's get some nuts and bolts out of the way. Starting with school, which is what we're supposed to concentrate upon."

"Surely. For nuts, bolts, and washers, I go to high school in Princeton, New Jersey. Several times a week. I'm a junior there. Very junior."

Angela said, "I know a girl in Princeton, New Jersey. Is that a coincidence or not? I think it really is." She was leaning far back, her collins glass still wrapped in her long narrow fingers.

"So do I. What's her name?"

She looked down toward memory's lane and said, "I know it. I know it." Angela was a compact little girl, glowingly healthy and glaringly confident, the antithesis of a china doll. Smoky babes slinking out of night clubs would take one look at Angela and say, "Who's the picture of health." Her face was a mixture of things Bobby liked to see and things Bobby had no idea what they might mean. She looked up and her eyes grew huge. "I know. Lucy Lowe."

Bobby wrinkled his brow to dissipate some of the throbbing. "Oh yes. Lucy. Very nice girl."

She sat up, put down the glass, and got serious. "No drip? I mean you know her?" Her last word came out more like "huh." Her careful tones had disappeared and she was blurting like any girl. Maybe her only flaw. Her voice was shrill.

"Who doesn't? She being very popular."

"She ought to be. Especially with boys." She sank slowly back. He watched her dimples. They materialized and then vanished somehow.

"Why, Angela." Carrie Dumont smirked and sipped some coffee. It was cream loaded like Mother's.

"I mean it. I really do. I mean, if you ever saw her at all." Her luscious lips made a small pout. "I suppose you've taken her out."

"Not many times, since my dates are few, being rather selective." He waved down the experience.

The facts were somewhat different. He knew who Lucy Lowe was. She was a preppie he'd seen once at a Community Players meeting and one of the smokiest nymphs he'd ever met. He was about as close to dating her as he was to joining the Marines.

Carrie Dumont put down her cup. "Well, troops, let's get away from old home week and get to the questions I got written down here on this little pad." She smiled. Then to him, "We have you in school and now we want you in your radio show. How did you happen to be chosen to be on the panel?" She asked it and, having asked it, looked away.

"We have several prepared answers, my favorite being because I was home when it happened."

She nodded her eyes upward to the ceiling. "I'm not too clear on the nepotism angle. I understand your family always played the animal, vegetable, mineral game."

"Not really always." He detected the edge of his normal hostility creeping in. He often felt like pounding down the show's whole history just to show that everybody was wrong. But this time Bobby caught himself. He had responsibility. But keep it short. "We definitely were that Sunday."

"What Sunday?"

Angela was forming a faceful of determination. "I'm going to get a hold of that Lucy. I met her on a yacht."

She was examining her entire career to come and all the alliances that might come with it.

Bobby smiled and asked gallantly, "Are you actually from New Jersey?"

She said, "No, I'm not actually from New Jersey."

Somehow, Bobby wanted to take her name off the party list. He ignored her, very casually, and said, "Dad was a newscaster, being upstairs right now, getting his six-thirty show ready for broadcast. His announcer at the time was one Charles Stark, who came down one Sunday to play golf. I was so quiet at dinner that both parents had glanced at me to see if I was breaking out in red or black spots."

Dimples on, Angela said, "I had measles a few seasons ago. I thought the spots were going to end everything."

Bobby wanted to look at her, right in the eyes, and slam her down with a topper. In New York Bobby had the courage he wouldn't feel at all in Princeton. "Mere measles? When I had pneumonia and scarlet fever at the same time?" So there. He turned back to Carrie Dumont and continued. "Continuing. Mr. Stark says to me, 'How do you like school in New Jersey compared with school in the Midwest?'"

Carrie Dumont said, "So, you were actually born in the Midwest?"

"Kernels right off the cob. We're all Hoosiers, whatever that means."

She nodded. "Very good good."

He waved a professional, cooperative hand. "I've been over this before, as you can guess."

"All right, back to Sunday dinner."

As Bobby began the oft told story, Angela said in a whine, "Can I order another collins?" She rose, stepped back, and sat down again. Quite a show. Her dress was one of those parachute affairs, designed to billow when she turned. The top was buttoned high. She'd probably had trouble with some of the buttons.

Carrie Dumont leaned back and placed her pencil in the crease of the notebook. "Why not? Let's do a break. Waiter?"

He came and she ordered more coffee and Angela ordered a weak tom collins, then murmured at him, "You want one, too?" Some temptress she.

But Bobby was immune. "Too early in the day. I always wait until blood begins to flow."

The waiter departed, Angela slumped back, Carrie Dumont's pencil returned to its grip, and Bobby continued, past the morning of golf, the Sunday dinner, and the casual mention that they oft played parlor games including animal, vegetable, mineral, and they wound up playing a subject.

Bobby said, "I have this history on a piece of paper with a lot more detail than I have time for now. It's called *Birth of a Quiz Show*." He reached into his inside jacket pocket and produced the history he had brought along. This alone would save twenty minutes.

Carrie Dumont took a copy and scanned it for a few seconds. "Yes. Good, good. But just take me through the scene you'd started in a cursory way."

"Okay. Mother asked, 'Is it animal, vegetable, or mineral?'"

"You remember that very subject?" Carrie showed real surprise.

"Routine. Dad said, 'It's mainly mineral. With some animal and some vegetable.' Mother asked if it was around the house here? And Dad said it was. Mother asked, 'Downstairs?' Dad assumed his judicial manner. 'I would have to say no to that.' Mother asked, 'Is it upstairs?' 'No.' Of course, I knew what it was."

Carrie Dumont said, "You knew what it was right then?" The pencil was quivering. "I'm damn sure I wouldn't have."

"You would though. Mother asked if it was in the basement? And Dad said no and I guess I made a face, as only idiot adolescents can, and said,

'All right. Is it outside?' and he said yes and I said, 'I know what it is. Mr. Stark's golf clubs.'"

She stopped everything and considered it. "Oh. Very good good. I can see what you mean."

"Then, later on, Mr. Stark, still grinning, still leaning his chair back against the doorway to the hall, turned the key." Bobby looked to both, one then the other. "Verily and historically, Charles Starr in his next words sent us on our way. No, look here, he says. I can see it. What we have is a *panel of experts. They* play the game. Our new Clifton Fadiman has the subject, like my golf clubs, for instance, and the panel guesses it."

She finished a note, then looked up. "Well, oh, good good."

"But what I remember most was a great wind sweeping around me."

Angela glanced his way, a small sop. "I don't know what any wind's got to do with it."

Bobby said to her, "I refer to a sort of warm wind on your face that makes everything seem pleasant and fine."

"Oh, please. Spare me."

Carrie Dumont ignored her. "He's speaking emotionally, I think. And let's use it to swing into some questions about Bobby McGuire himself."

Angela waved off any swinging. "When are we going to have the setups?"

Carrie Dumont said, "When the photographer comes."

Bobby glanced at her, his rolling smile changed to a flat frown. "What's this? Nobody said there'd be pictures." He was calculating the delay they would cause and a later time of arrival at Kimberly's party.

"Oh, but yes." Carrie Dumont was protesting his words. "It's all right isn't it? That's why they booked Angela."

Angela sipped. Angela was consent to sip and get it done.

"Nobody told me." He swallowed down any complaint that might interfere with cooperation.

"We do need them."

Angela said, "I think the whole idea would be drippy without Pix."

Drippy, huh? This kid needed discipline. "In a manner of speaking, how can one deny that you're right. *Twenty Questions* is just another show."

Angela wound up and swung a thundering smash, "I never even heard of it before."

Carrie Dumont tried to cover it. "Why, Angela."

Bobby said, "One understands." Her smash lay there but he wasn't going to let it win the point. No, sir. No cute kid was going to belittle them. Sometimes he wanted to defend it a little. "One thing personal." He looked for heavenly guidance over near the lobby entrance. "I ought to start any personal stuff with Uncle Harry, since he gave us the idea for the screen test."

Carrie Dumont said, "Screen test?"

Bobby nodded in bored acceptance. "They're already thinking about television, if a little distantly, and it's natural, they believe, to make a *Twenty Questions* movie and, when your uncle's a movie producer, you can bet he's going to get first shot at it." His brows rose.

Carrie Dumont looked down as her eye brows went up. She had a piece of useful stuff. "Well good and good. I hadn't heard about this angle."

Bobby tossed in a standard disclaimer. "Making sure you realize that nothing's signed, and many a slip twixt cup and actual production."

And Bobby heard from his left, "Screen test?"

Bobby forged onward. "While it is true that I haven't seen Uncle Harry for a few years, he's been out there in Hollywood cranking out the flicks. Specializes in young stuff, you know. The Wanda Hendrix and Peggy Ann Garner stuff. He would have given Elizabeth Taylor her start but got beat to it."

Bobby didn't have the heart to tell her that Uncle Harry, his father's older brother, had worked all his life as a truck dispatcher in Indianapolis.

The waiter arrived to deliver a tom collins and a silver pot of coffee. He poured a cup and departed.

Carrie Dumont sipped anew and said, "Forgive me but why haven't I heard of Harry McGuire?"

Bobby said apologetically, "The reason why being perhaps that he's not immensely well known here, but pretty well known on the other coast."

Angela was suddenly leaning forward. A hint of a professional smile was beginning to emerge. "Look, have you talked to him about when's this screen test? I mean when it's going to happen?"

"I've got to meet him tonight to get things started, being why I have only a short time left." He looked away.

A light hand of narrow fingers caressed his left forearm. "Well, I mean, do you know if it's an open call or if they need ... Look, you know me. I mean, keep my face in mind will you? And my name."

Bobby condescended to glance at that face. "Uh huh."

"Here. Let me give you my number, where I'm staying. Come to think of it, maybe my agent ought to … No. Not on this one." She dug hard into a small purse. He was shocked to see it matched her dress. Her smooth hand came out with a large card, like a miniature composite, her picture on one side, her vital statistics on the other. He took it with suave casualness and stuck it inside his jacket without looking at it.

Carrie Dumont said, "Kids, don't forget me. Let's see, I need to know what you do in your spare time."

Bobby tried to talk above the drama in the air. "My primary activities of leisure moments would tend to include kites, model airplanes, roller skating." He went on for a minute or two.

Carrie Dumont looked over her shoulder. "Oh. Here he is now. Alan Richards, I think it is."

He was tall, angular, and slightly elderly. Looked and sounded very British. After introductions, Carrie Dumont got the check, gathered her piles into an immense briefcase, and they all adjourned down the hall to the ground floor studio 1A. This was the site of Bobby's great audition of over two years before. It presented the usual studio design of bright walls hung with wall units and inserts of sound proof paneling with thousands of little holes. A grand piano rested beneath the control room window. One wall had been hung with a large backdrop, a huge photo of the downtown New York skyline. As they got down to business, Bobby finally grasped Angela's role. One teenager was greeting another in Olde New York. He wasn't sure who was the greeter and who the greetee.

Mr. Richards posed them up. "Okay, Bobby, smile. Angela, good."

He shot fifty times, his Rolleiflex constantly winding, cranking, and clicking. The whole time Bobby was touching, releasing, and looking at Angela, which was beginning to have an effect.

Bobby looked at his Lusserna. "It's six fifteen. Can I still make it?"

Richards said, "One more with the skyline back drop." He frowned as he moved and ducked to new angles. "We need to emphasize a theme here."

Angela said rather loudly, "How about I give him a welcoming kiss."

Richards nodded, taking a second to consider this. "On the cheek."

She was demure now. "Of course."

Carrie Dumont, calmer now, sat on the piano bench, observing the action like a coach. "Don't scowl, Bobby. Your audience will think you still hate girls."

Bobby looked at her. "Uh huh."

Her head slanted. "I mean, if I were the show's agent, I'd want to emphasize the transition from marbles to make out."

Bobby almost did a double take. "To what?" He smiled his silly smile. "To what?" His headache was receding.

Richards interrupted. "Bobby, turn slightly and, Angela, you've been giving him a welcome hug and now you turn, still hugging and smile right at him. Got it?"

Angela put both arms around him. The two teenagers were roughly the same height. "Like this?" She molded herself into him so that Bobby had to stiffen. She said, "Hold still."

Bobby held still, still flinching. He now felt extra breaths coming on.

Richards was waving a hand. "Yes indeed. Now break apart slightly and Angela turn." She was on him to their chests and now she pried herself backward and turned her torso toward the camera. Richards said, "Good. One more."

Between them, Bobby glanced again at his watch. It was 6:20.

Carrie Dumont said, "I'll get you a cab." She rose and scurried out.

Angela, standing alongside now, said, "Where's this train that's so important?"

"Penn Station."

She froze and Bobby could see wheels turning. "Oh." She looked at him and smiled. "Say, can I ride along? That's where I was headed."

"Forsooth, it takes two to taxi."

So, the shoot was over. Richards packed his suitcase. Angela found her coat. They found Carrie Dumont across Broadway, catching the downtown cabs. He was careful but Angela dashed over, dodging traffic. She looked good doing it. She could actually run. Even on heels. Carrie Dumont held the door, smiled at him with a profuse thank you, and slammed them on their way.

Two blocks into the ride Angela was sitting close, in the middle, and turned to face him. "Listen, you. Look right in my eyes." She was positioned for an I-can-stare-you-down contest.

"Sure. Okay." He turned slightly. "What portends?"

Angela had marvelous eyes, both in their liquid surface and in their talent. They flipped this way and that both to catch everything and to let onlookers know that they were oh so shy. She had eyes. Oh yes.

"Hold still."

Bobby was mystified. He was holding his breath. What strange game was this? Maybe some kid ritual from where she came from. Her two hands came out and held his cheeks between them. She pulled herself forward and kissed him right on the lips. One of her hands dropped down, seized his index finger and gave it a squeeze.

She let him go and said, "I shouldn't have done that."

Bobby swallowed. He did not breath again.

Silent minutes passed and the driver swung into the Penn Station hole. Bobby wanted that last look at her to be the only one he'd remember. When the driver stopped at the deep curb, she said in her chirping voice, "Call me. I'll keep the cab. You better run for it."

Bobby did. He ran like hell. But Bobby had long since missed both the train and the bus.

Chapter 11

String Along

Kimberly said, coming down the stairs to her rec room, "Bob, why are you jumping up and down? That's not what you do with this number."

"This is a sock hop and I'm a kangaroo." He was still hopping.

"We don't allow pets in here, or wild animals from New Zealand." She was looking at him up and down as if his pants were wet.

"If the swagman comes, will his billy boil?" He was still hopping.

"Nobody here named Billy. Will you please stop that funny dance?"

Mary Sue said, "I'll bet I know what he means. In fact, I was expecting a visitor myself. And maybe Bobby knows about it." She brought on her widest grin. "Did your mother mention the scavenger hunt?"

"Uh huh. I never listen to mother to avoid bringing in the Civil War."

"That's funny." She did look a little mystified.

Kimberly said, "What's funny? What everybody talking about?"

Mary Sue said, "I think the hostess should inform the late guest that his first duty is contributing to the excitement of the party."

Kimberly nodded. "Right. Forget the kangaroo. If a visitor comes to the door, mother will probably let me know."

"I'd comply if it were my choice to make, but..."

Kimberly over rode his. "We're laying the law down. If I hear the word again I'll make you bob for apples."

Bobby stopped the hop.

Jenny said from the side, "Bob said he'd dance with me anyway."

Merriam-Webster says that a party is also a bacchanal, a debauch, and/or a *group grope*. It lists other synonyms, too, but they're downright salacious. It says salacious means...never mind. If either Merriam or

Webster really means group grope, they probably had a different group from Young Bobby's in mind.

Webster: We base our synonyms on the latest data available.

Bobby didn't have any data available on teenage parties. Mother, who met his train at the Junction just before nine, didn't help much.

Mother: Just be yourself.

Bobby could have told her that the warden probably said the same thing to John Dillinger and look where it got him — the warden, that is. But Bobby held his peace, probably because he didn't know how to be himself anyway. He didn't even know who himself was.

They had driven from Princeton Junction across town and out the other side. Kimberly lived nearby which meant he'd probably walk home. Mother said she would leave the door open and that Bobby should remember to leave it open for Dad if Bobby got home before one o'clock. She had other advice and admonitions, too numerous to mention.

Mother: Bobby never listened to me. He was a law unto himself.

She also had some quaint memories of parties she had once attended, which she had described as they drove through town toward Jefferson Road. "We used to have scavenger hunts, too, and all the rest, and rest our souls." Mother was wearing her glasses. She drove with her head up to see over the wheel.

"Uh huh. And I anticipate your expertise in pinning tales on donkeys and pulling taffy." He was slumped in the passenger seat to avoid being seen. Had he been spotted being driven to a party by his mother, the world would have erupted in calamity.

They dipped down toward Wiggins. A cat was crossing the street.

She said, "How come you missed the train?" She turned right. Then left onto Jefferson. They were rolling beneath the street lights.

"Forsooth, the interview went long because the pictures went long. Nobody told me Pix there would be."

"Mm." She looked fluffy in her fur jacket. "While I was getting calls and surprised to get them about... Well." She fluffed her lapel. "Never mind."

Bobby was sitting up. "Mrs. Livingstone, are we lost? The party being at Kimberly's and this passenger wondering if you know where she lives?"

"I know her mother from Present Day Club." She looked over the wheel. "I don't suppose you know somebody named Mary Hurley?"

The name spoken out loud actually gave him a shock. "Uh huh. We've met, you might say daily, since I sit next to her in English. We were discussing family crises when I divulged you had your appendix out."

Mother had often discussed the event as Lowell Thomas would discuss a trip to Tibet. Can I show you my slides? Bobby had felt sorry for her pain, but she carried on a little longer than anybody wanted to hear.

Bobby cried out suddenly, "Right here. Here!" She hit the brake. The big Cad's red wheels dipped to a stop. She turned in the driveway.

"Have a good time." He barely heard it, already out of the car.

She backed out, leaving him on Kimberly's card table of a front porch. Also on the front porch was Pete. He wore a dark blue suit. The porch was cold and Bobby was waving his arms. Before Bobby could greet Pete, the door opened.

Kimberly stood there. "Well, look who's here. We'd given up on both of you, and all the ice cream and cake are gone." She wore a peasant blouse and a swishy black skirt. She looked less jolly now and more in command.

He lifted his voice to its brightest level. "And breakfast I skipped in anticipation. But was detained. Didn't mother call?" He could see into the bright foyer. A stairway led up.

"Nobody called. Come on in. We can't heat the whole outdoors."

She held back the door and Bobby went in ahead of Pete. He buttoned his jacket.

Buzz was standing inside the door. "Bob's here. Pete's here." He wore a sport jacket similar to Bobby's. Tattersall and gabardine.

Kimberly said, "See why he's late and make a full report."

Buzz said, "Why were you late?"

"Military secret." He should be himself but nobody wanted that self.

Pete was shaking the cold out of his jacket. "I just got here, too."

Kimberly said, "What's your excuse?"

"My father had a flat and I had to change it."

Kimberly said, "What did you change? The flat or your shirt?"

"Both." He smirked.

"A likely story. Who's next?" They were awkwardly easing around the small foyer. Kimberly shut the door. "Bob, you had to go to New York."

His back was to the door. His hands shaped something while he was explaining, "A routine spy mission in which I met this gorgeous model, took her to the Stork Club, and wound up missing both the train and the microfilm."

She nodded. "That's the best one I've heard. We're all downstairs."

Buzz said, "What did she model?"

Kimberly said in passing, "Probably gloves." General snicker laughs.

Bobby felt a little defensive. He shrugged, still brightly. "Into detail I do not think she would want me to go."

Kimberly was turning toward the hall. A mirror hung above a side table. He took a step after her. She said over her shoulder, "Did your mother tell you about the scavenger hunt?"

Bobby stopped. "Indeed not. Scavenger hunt? Mother? We're having a scavenger hunt?"

"You weren't there when I called. Everybody had to bring something beginning with X."

Jenny Crown appeared behind him. She reached out a hand onto his shoulder. "Why don't you both come downstairs? It's almost time for the Balboa." Her voice squawked as much as ever.

Bobby turned to face her. "Balboa? Referring to the illustrious conquistador of Darien?"

Jenny said, "It's a dance where you jump from side to side like a tree about to fall down." She wore a tight skirt and a white sweater. Over the sweater was a string of pearls. Jenny was a pretty girl tonight.

"I'd probably fall down before I got started."

Jenny said, "You just hop back and forth. Look."

Bobby watched her put her body where her mouth was. He was impressed, as she put her hands on her low hips and tipped back and forth like a wooden soldier.

Kimberly turned back in the narrow hall. "Let's do it downstairs."

Jenny eased forward at him. "Haven't you ever done a Balboa?"

"I've ridden in a De Soto and driven through Columbus."

Nobody got it. He had long since learned that the wittier the crack, the leaner the audience.

They all crowded through the hall. It led to the kitchen in the back of the house. He glimpsed a refrigerator, closed doors, a sink, an open door to a pantry. The basement stairs had rubber treads. They jammed down. At the bottom was a Bakelite table covered with ruins of party favors and refreshments. The basement was full of kids. And full of webs, strange string he'd learn about later. It was strung all over everything. *Hawaiian War Chant* filled the room with sound. He stopped at the bottom of the steps, not exactly sure what to do. He saw a cement basement floor painted

dark red. He saw a phonograph on a table. He saw a couch, a ping pong table, a dart board. He saw Fred Darkly, Frank Cottman, Lon Carson, and Jack, among others in the room. He saw Joan and Polly and Norma. He saw some he barely knew. Most of all Bobby saw Mary Sue Hurley, who was standing nearby in the noise. She shouted, "The latecomers."
    Pete slid ahead of him. He said loudly, "I had a flat?"
    Bobby yelled. "I missed the train?"
    Mary Sue said, "Sure. Probably with some blond bombshell."
    While Bobby appreciated the compliment, all he could do was stand there before the altar, dumb like a boob. Maybe he was reprising his fourth grade horror, when he'd returned from the boys room with his polo shirt tucked into his undershorts with a crescent moon of white elastic for all to see. So, anyway, with no idea how to answer, all he could do was hop up and down on two feet to the music.
    After discussion of kangaroos, *Stardust* replaced the fast number. He didn't know what happened to Jenny, but Mary Sue sashayed up to him like a Hawaiian and they started to dance. Sort of a sashay itself. He kept his feet moving in very short steps. If Bobby was a lousy dancer, he at least wanted to do something neutral where he wouldn't make a bad gaffe. Safe ground.
    After they danced in his shuffle a while, she whispered in his ear to try to take exactly half as many steps. He tried it and got into it a little. But he would hardly remember it. Bobby was crazy for the moment. Call his thoughts what dreams are made of, such as that the girl was his, however short the interval. She was dancing almost as close as Jenny had, bless her, and Bobby realized well enough that his hands were feeling warm cloth. He probably had a notion that, if this was what *woman* was all about, Bobby was ready for the next lesson.
    Then she leaned away and talked with a bright eyed smile. "Are you sure you didn't hear about the scavenger hunt?"
    He was still in his smile mode. "Cross my heart, coming as I did right from the train."
    "Didn't your mother bring you?"
    "In truth. Full of wisdom about what to do at a party."
    "Your mother is a very smart lady."
    "Uh huh. We hear it all the time."
    Mary Sue said, suddenly pulling him tighter as if for attention, "I think somebody's coming with a big surprise."

"Who?"

"You'd die if you knew. Let's just say a messenger."

They had danced up to Kimberly and she heard Mary Sue's last words. "What's going on here? Phone calls in the middle of the night. Secret messengers arriving. I'm beginning to think somebody spiked the punch. And it wasn't me."

Mary Sue looked very good tonight, with her hair in some kind of a hanging clump and wearing a floppy light blue sweater and ballet slippers that made her an inch shorter than Bobby, and a foot shorter than Fred. He was thinking of ways to make things a little more secure, such as gabbing about movie stars he'd met, when Fred cut in. Bobby managed to bow as he yielded.

Bobby moved to other sections of the basement. After throwing a dart, losing a game of ping pong, and inspecting the phonograph, he got Jack Harnessall aside.

"How does it go, harness leather?" Bobby inquired.

"Good."

"We apparently face kite night, this personage never having seen so much string since my last yo-yo party." String was everywhere. Twenty tasseled ends were stapled to a bookcase on the far wall.

"Everybody gets an end is all I know. And they're labeled. Yours is right there. So's mine."

Bobby nodded as he took the tag. He was standing to the side, chest out, surveying the scene. So this was a party. He still felt unsure, almost queasy. He wondered if he could maintain his giddy mood. Why not? Parties seemed like fun.

An idea flashed. Bobby said, "Take mine until I get back."

Jack nodded.

Bobby sidled away through the maelstrom and eased upstairs, where he found Mrs. Manners in the livingroom. It was a traditional room with a small grand piano in one corner. She was reading a magazine.

"Hello. You're Bobby."

"Who ought to be downstairs but was thinking I might get a phone call."

"If it rings, I'll let Kimberly know." She was wearing whatever grown-ups wear. Bobby didn't notice.

"Uh huh."

Of course, Bobby wasn't expecting any phone call. When you don't know what you're doing, you might say anything.

"Are you ready for the big string along excitement?" she inquired with a gentle smile.

"I plan to be. I asked Jack Harnessall to take mine, since somebody has a scavenger item and I don't, so I've been thinking of something. I figure somebody's bringing a xylophone and I can't let Mary Sue get ahead of me."

"Well, I don't know what you're talking about, but good luck."

"You wouldn't know where there's a dictionary."

"Why, yes. I think it's in the bookcase right there." She leaned forward and pointed. "You open the glass door and, maybe, down near the bottom shelf."

Bobby found it easily enough. It was an ancient Funk & Wagnalls, college level, and Bobby left the room thumbing it to impress Mrs. Manners. He stopped in the kitchen, which was empty but too public for what he had in mind. A closed door led to a pantry. He entered, closed the door, did his work, and left a few seconds later.

At the bottom of the stairs, Bobby saw bedlam. All the kids were moving like crazies. They were crawling on the floor. They were moving furniture. They were squeezing behind the furnace. Kimberly was screaming, "Slowly. Slowly!"

They had started without him. He said, "Did I miss something?"

"Bob. Where have you been? Wait a minute, everybody. Bob, where's your string?"

"My … Jack was keeping it for me."

"Keeping it?" She couldn't believe it.

"I had to go upstairs for a minute."

"You can't *do* that. Jack, you must have two strings."

Jack was heard behind the couch. It had been swung out. "Right. One in each button hole."

"All right. Bob, you have to be in this. You aren't supposed to go bounding off when the big thing … Jack, give Bob one of them. In case you didn't know, there's a girl at the end. But which girl? All right. I had it all figured and every…"

Jack was clawing at string. "Which one does Bob get?"

"The one that's labeled BOB, silly."

"I had to bend the labels off to get them through his button hole. Holes."

Kimberly's hands were on her hips. "You had to … I never … "

Mary Sue, who was in the doorway to the furnace room, said, "I think we ought to start over."

"How can we start over? Half of you are half way, or … Jack, give him either one. And if Bobby winds up with Lon or Buzz, too bad."

Bobby could figure out the operation. You had to follow the string while you slid it through a button hole, balling the gathered string as you went. His wound all over the basement, of course, and at one point he was snarled with Jenny and they had to hand their strings back and forth a moment to keep going. It went on for several minutes. On the end of Bobby's string was Jack Harnessall.

Kimberly imploded. "It can't be. It just can't be. Bob, did you … "

Bobby swung around from Jack to offer a defense. "So solly please." He chuckled. "I asked Jenny to hold mine a second and when she gave it back to me, I handed it to Jack."

"You handed it to Jack? You must have got the wrong one back from Jenny. But then …"

Jack said, "I had to put mine down a minute. One went one way and the other one went the other."

Kimberly concluded, "All right, then two girls must have wound up with each other."

Mary Sue, now beneath the phonograph table, said, "I know it. Jenny and I saw it coming over the couch, so I traded off with Fred." Bobby stared. Even in chaos this angel spoke with bright light.

While confusion begot more confusion, Bobby remembered what he had left in the pantry. This was as good a time as any. With the string-along sort of over, Bobby figured scavenger hunt would come soon. He went up, opened the pantry door, stepped inside, and shut the door. The dictionary was still there, between the Campbells ox-tail soup and the fruit punch. He had to suck in his gut and take a deep breath to go ahead with this plan. It would take a minute or two. He had started along when, suddenly, he went stiff. He gulped. Voices were coming through the pantry door. The soft one belonged to Betsy Baldwin. The deeper one belonged to Betty Jane. Then Bobby heard a third voice. It was Lon Carson. The voices were embarrassingly near, as if there were no door at all.

Betsy was saying, "I told him the only thing we could do was break up." She was new in the school. Very pretty and very mature. She had a slight southern accent which was very seductive.

Lon said, "I guess so. But, I mean to tell you, Larry put it a little differently." Lon was a confidant with a smile in his voice.

Betty Jane said, "Differently how?"

Betsy said, "I wanted to go to the shore. I told him that."

Lon said cordially, "But you wanted to go dancing and he wanted to go swimming."

Betsy said, "Swimming in the ocean at night didn't appeal to me . . . with or without suits."

By now, Bobby was frozen in icy panic. Trapped. Caught. He had a torn book in his hands and hot stuff in his ears.

Betty Jane was outraged. "He suggested that?"

"He suggested a lot of things."

Bobby gently stashed the book in a trash basket, but, when he straightened up, he accidently nudged a can of chicken noodle. It thumped to the floor.

Bobby heard Betty Jane say, "What was that?"

Lon said, "I don't think we're alone."

Betty Jane said, "Maybe Kimberly's mother's in the pantry."

Bobby opened the door, holding the jar of fruit punch high. They were seated around the Bakelite kitchen table. He pretended he knew they were there.

"This being the one they're looking for?" He held up the jar.

Lon said, smiling, very cordial, "Well, it's something."

Betty Jane said with a frown, "How'd you get in there?"

Bobby was calm and confident. "Me? In there? Not being a matter of how. I thought I'd spike the punch."

Lon said, grinning, "I think we better continue our discussion, uh, someplace else."

"All I heard was mumbles." He turned and shut the pantry behind him. It was awful but all he could think of.

Betty Jane said, "Well, what are you doing up here anyway? The party's downstairs."

"I know, but you know what they say. No? I'm not sure either, and besides, I had to come up for a phone call." Very casually as he spoke he slid the jar across the kitchen counter.

"In the pantry? I think you'll enjoy life more downstairs," Lon said.

"It was stuffy in the pantry. I got my string messed up downstairs, so I didn't know where to go." He moved past them to the top of the stairs.

Betty Jane said, "I'd take a chance on the basement."
Bobby skipped down, free, dumb, and slightly lucky.

Some kids he knew slightly had been talking to Pete and Jack. One was Skip Hanson and another Carl Lowe, both in the class ahead. They turned from Jack and came over to Bobby at the foot of the stairs.

Skip said, "Hey, McGuire, we got one for you."

Jack said from behind the group that was forming, "It's a good one. A legitimate one."

Bobby said, "A show subject."

They nodded as Jack said that indeed it was.

He added, "Animal."

Bob:	Is it a whole animal?
Skip:	Well. No. It is not a whole animal.
Bob:	Is it part or product of an animal?
Skip:	Hun uh. No.
Bob:	It's not a whole animal and it's not part of an animal or the product of an animal. How can it be animal?
Jack:	Nope. They have it right.
Bob:	Oh. Are there more than one of this?
Skip:	Yes.
Bob:	We usually say *partly* if somebody asks if it's a whole animal. Okay. Is it a group of human beings?
Skip:	No.
Bob:	Is it a group of four-footed animals?
Skip:	Yeah. I guess. Partly.
Bob:	Is the subject fictional?
Skip:	No. It's not fictional, is it, Jack.
Jack:	Not fictional is right.
Bob:	Does the subject exist?
Skip:	Uh. No. What do you mean. It's a subject I'm thinking about.
Bob:	Can I go somewhere right now and see it, hear it or smell it?
Skip:	No. I guess not.
Bob:	But they did exist at one time?
Skip:	Sure. Yeah. Right.
Bob:	Okay. Were these animals beasts of burden?

Skip:	Beasts of burden.
Bob:	Like horses, camels.
Skip:	Oh. Uh, well, partly.
Bob:	Were they all of the cat family?
Skip:	No.
Bob:	Were they all the dog family?
Skip:	No.
Bob:	Were they farm type animals?
Skip:	Uh, partly.
Bob:	Did they exist before 1900?
Skip:	No. I don't think so.
Bob:	Did they die after 1900?
Skip:	Yes.
Bob:	Were there more than two?
Skip:	Sure.
Bob:	More than twenty?
Skip:	Yes.
Bob:	When they were famous, were they in the United States?
Skip:	No.
Bob:	In Europe?
Skip:	No. That's eighteen questions.
Bob:	Eighteen!
Jack:	That's right. I kept count.
(Long pause)	
Bob:	Wait a minute. Did these animals die at the same time?
Skip:	Pretty much.
Bob:	All right. All the animals used at the Bikini atom tests.
Skip:	Shit.

Skip lunged away in disgust.

After they broke apart, Jack said, "They'd thought that up a long time. There were bets."

Downstairs, Kimberly was lining up a Virginia reel. He was determined to join it after seeing at the Halloween dance how easy it was.

Kimberly was saying, "All right, everybody. Let's have six boys to his right and six girls to his left."

Bobby wanted clarity. "To your right?"

"No, Bob. The other side. You're not a girl." She was pointing. "After this we'll have the big scavenger show down."

Bobby was opposite Mary Sue, of course. They would soon lock arms and rotate in glee and glue. The reel went all right. It was easy enough. A lot of skipping, which even Bobby could do. Some. He would never be really good at any dance.

After that, Bobby danced with Norma. She was a tall, proper girl. Dancing, for her, was an extract from Saturday morning dancing class. Then Jenny did her full court press again and finally Bobby jigged a bit with Kimberly, at arm's length. More ping pong. He lost badly to Jack. He tabled his paddle and returned to the dance floor, which was the main part of the basement. Mary Sue had just put down some punch. "Your turn," said Bobby. She glided into him. It became a time that almost passed and almost stood still. As pleasing an interval as the evening had provided.

They were dancing to *How Soon*, near its end, toe to toe and chest to chest, when she suddenly squeezed him hard. Just for a count of one. Whatever she meant to convey, it was so totally unexpected that he was dumbfounded. Over his years, he'd felt similar shocks coursing through his ganglia. In Miss B's class when she had called on him with a question he had utterly no answer for. In the school auditorium, sixth grade. "The judges have decided on Number Six," as he won a speech contest. He had swallowed, stood up, and stood there stupidly. He was just as stupid after the squeeze and release.

In the midst of this funk, they heard Mrs. Manners's voice. She was speaking from the top of the stairs. "Is Mary Sue there?"

Mary Sue withdrew from him. She said with a huge grin, "Hold on to your hat." And went up the steps.

Kimberly appeared. "Hold onto...Wait? What hat? Mother, what's going on?"

Mary Sue said from the top, "I'll be right back."

Kimberly said, "Bob, what's upstairs?"

"Speaking of the pantry, juicy stuff with Betsy and Betty Jane."

"Juicy..."

"I would have stayed upstairs to join the discussion, but it was over my head and under my skin."

"Discussion? What were they discussing?"

"I think it had something to do with wearing bathing suits in the ocean, or not."

"Or not? Juicy stuff! Surprise guests and late arrivals. What are parties coming to?"

When Mary Sue returned, Fred said to her, "Get it?"

Mary Sue nodded.

Kimberly was mystified again. "What are you two saying?"

"Well, we had a sort of bet," Fred said. "And I think I lost."

Kimberly was perplexed. "Lost what? What is everybody talking about?"

Fred said with a shrug, "I went to the Music Shoppe to borrow a xylophone for the hunt. I went but they were closed by the time I got there."

Mary Sue said, "That's just too bad."

Kimberly said, hands clapping together, "All right, let's do that right now. How many people got something beginning with X?" Her eyes swept the empty response. Nobody said a word.

Pete said with his smirk, "I move for adjournment."

Buzz said, "Second the motion."

Kimberly was fretting. "I knew it was too hard."

Mary Sue said, "No it wasn't. I have something beginning with X and Bob will kill me."

Bobby blurted, "Not on weekends or holidays."

"It's in my purse."

Kimberly was frantic. "Well, what is it.? What is it?"

"It's an x-ray."

Bobby frowned. "To see through everything. But why will I kill you?"

"It's an x-ray of your mother's appendix."

"My mother's!"

"She just brought it over."

General laughter, glee, and hand clapping.

Bobby said, "Okay. I guess that's one on me?"

Fred said, "Right out from under your nose."

They stared at him like his fly had been open the whole party. "Okay, gang. But I got something, too."

Kimberly said, "You do? Well, where is it?"

"Upstairs. Hold it."

Bobby took the stairs by twos to the kitchen. The discussion group had moved to the dining room. He fetched the dictionary from the pantry basket, arranged it the way he wanted, and went back down stairs.

Kimberly said, "What's this? That's my father's college dictionary."

"Ready to open."

"What? What's this page torn for?"

Buzz said, leaning for a look, "Let's see. Oh. Hey. Pretty good. The page beginning with the letter."

Pete said, "Clever, I admit."

Fred said, "Lucky again. But Sue's is better."

Mary Sue said, "I think I understand. But mine is better. Definitely."

Kimberly was staring at the book Bobby held open. "I don't. He's ripped a page out of my father's dictionary. He had that through five years at Rider."

Bobby said, "I doubt if he uses that page very much."

Kimberly went on, "I'm showing this to mother. I think Mary Sue gets the prize."

Buzz said, turning away, "Both are clever in their way."

Jenny Crown chirped to him, "Come on, clever one, this is my dance."

Chapter 12

Fear Strikes Out

A full month passed after Elie's party. Each day Bobby felt closer to getting a date. He was steeling up nerve to ask. Planning for all contingencies. As the winter moved on, Mary Sue taunted and teased him every school day just by being there, and during safe social duties without her Bobby mooned and moaned, probably dampening them for everybody else. Taffy Bobby pulled at a church function was judged a hint of a tint whiter than Lon's. Never mind. He moaned because Mary Sue wasn't there to taste it. Camp Buck tried again to freeze his gonads. He talked about her the whole weekend until Butch Ludden, the leader, told him to shut up.

Worst of all, his pining slopped into New York. He treated the guests as ciphers at best. Could Bobby care less about Ben Alexander who hadn't made a movie in six years.

Ben: I didn't become Officer Frank Smith for six more.

Or Spec Sanders, who was scoring touchdowns for the New York Yankees, while they still lived.

Spec: When they died, I graduated to Roller Derby, and skated hard until they died.

Or Buddy Rogers, who was pushing a flick called *Sleep My Love*.

Buddy: They really wanted Mary.

Or Al Capp born and bred in Dogpatch, who said about as much as Emmert Kelly had. Bobby didn't care. He was violently in love, or something.

The two weeks of Christmas featured choir sings, brass quartet recitals, and the famous 1947 Christmas blizzard. He saw her face in every snowflake. Throughout all this social commotion, the parents wondered whether this sick dog was going to drop dead or throw up on the rug.

Kay Summersby, the guest of the show January 1, didn't get famous for another thirty years.

Kay: I had a book to sell, Ike as I knew him, whatever that was supposed to mean. I remember there was a kid on the show. Maybe we were both pining.

But, as 1948 began, the whole mooning process was crushed by a single event. Fred Darkly was taking Mary Sue to the New Year's Eve dance. Bobby stayed up till one doing a jigsaw puzzle on the card table. Only next morning could he relax, when he knew Fred wasn't with her anymore.

Mother and Dad discussed the Bobby problem into the wee hours. What to do, they asked. Their answer emerged a week later at Toots Shore, that famous uptown bar and grill, where big guys met bigger guys and all of them made like they were giants.

Ronson had booked the place for a plush party after the show and no one knew why. Very mysterious. Johnny Desmond, the singer, who was guest that night, went along. In fact, who didn't? Even Mr. Slater and his wife, Marion. Publicity gal, Flo Cahn, was ecstatic with possibilities, layouts, and column mentions. Toots Shore was big stuff in those days.

Toots: I wasn't there days.

Fineshriber shook hands with Mr. Harris, president of Ronson. So did Dad. So did Bobby. And when the photographers came and set them all up to record the big event, whatever it was, out trotted Angela.

Bobby hadn't seen her, of course, since the cab ride, and she may have had other guys on her mind besides him, believe it or not, but Bobby didn't care. He was so enthralled he wished he'd worn his new suit. Young Bobby tried to show nothing but cool, even when she offered a hand and managed to shake his index finger.

"How'uv you been" she inquired, properly downcast but hardly inconspicuous in a white party dress she must have had help getting on.

"Afraid to climb into taxicabs."

He was smitten, of course. Who wouldn't be? But he was also a little too wildly optimistic. He allowed himself to feel a liking for her. He liked the way she greeted him as an old friend, with an upward flash of eyes just to show him she remembered everything.

"You didn't call, you traitor."As if this had crushed her.

"Uh huh. I should have, but didn't know you were serious and besides my insurance wasn't paid up."

During the pre-dinner mingling, Bobby blew a small portion of his cool in favor of sitting next to her at one of the round tables, which had probably been planned anyway.

"Listen, I know all about your show now." She was apologetic.

"Lucky you."

"No drip. I really do. Like for instance, mineral. I got a subject that's mineral."

"Your heart of gold."

"No."

"I give up."

"You can't give up."

"The Lone Ranger's horse."

"No."

"I still give up."

"Did you go out with Lucy Lowe, no kidding."

"I'll never tell."

She elbowed him.

Then came sliced filet and slick speeches. Toots said something very brawny, which apparently came with the booking. Then Harris, Fineshriber, and Al Nathan all wished to congratulate them "upon this"—they held their breath—"the second anniversary of *Twenty Questions*." What? Who? It didn't seem to matter to anybody that the show had premiered in February, still a month away. Wry glances circulated. Brows wrinkled. But, heck, maybe this was the only Saturday night Toots had open. So, everybody ignored the anachronism and smiled all around. Even Bobby entered into the spirit of the blunder. Now, said Mr. Harris, we'll have a few words. And here they came, elicited from everybody—from Slater, from Dad, from Mother, from Herb, and from Bobby. From Bobby! Aaaaaghghg!

He swallowed hard, rose quavering, and thanked everybody in sight: Mr. Harris, Mutual, Ronson, "and, of course, my parents. Without them I probably wouldn't be here." Slater thought that was awfully funny. Angela let her eyes roll upward.

The evening at Toots's was all very nice and silly, but explosive news came later that night, after Toot's.

Dad did his eleven o'clock news and they were in the Cad homeward on the Pulaski Skyway, when Dad was saying, "You know, Windshield, I had a thought." Highway light was wiping their faces. "You're going to start to have dates anyway, which has led me to suspect that it might be a good idea to start with that Angela." He flicked him a glance.

They were starting the plunge down the Skyway into Elizabeth.

"Oh, Dad." His brow wrinkled. "Me? Boy Scout Bobby? With Angela?" Bobby slid forward to lean over the seat. "With Angela. You are kidding."

They pulled up on US 1 at the long red light just beyond the brewery.

"No, I'm not kidding, Beer Mug." He nodded in agreement with himself. "She's very pretty, and publicity advantages might develop."

They started forward again across North Avenue's bright street lights. The restaurant with the black facade that advertised steak, chops and chow mein appeared and disappeared on their left.

Bobby hardly saw it or anything else. He knew it was silly but who was he to turn off a silly dream? He said over the seat, "Sire, she's light years ahead of me."

"I doubt if she is."

Bobby said with very unsure gravity, "Which might be true. She is a model," as if that explained all. What he wanted was to feel her hands on his cheeks again. "But, she's also really … what do they call those spiders that eat their mates?"

Dad nodded. "I know. She's on the make. But that's no problem."

If Bobby's shock showed, it was in little gasps he tried to keep low. "No problem? Dad, this is still little Bobby, often afraid to walk by the girl's locker room."

"Do you expect to be little Bobby forever?" His voice was oozing now to dull the adult edges of his thoughts.

Bobby leaned back a little. "Probably."

It was well past midnight but there was still traffic. US 1 was a low canyon here in Elizabeth. Soon they entered the Bayway traffic circle and its still brightly lighted Howard Johnsons.

"George can get her number through the agency."

That's when Bobby murmured, "I've got her number."

"Oh?" Dad was digesting this slowly. "Well." His eyes were turning like slot machine cams. "Congratulations."

Mother said, "Bobby." He heard quiet tremor in her voice, like a bass piano string held with the pedal. "How did you get her number?"

Dad said aside, "Does that matter, Chickadee? I think this might be a good idea, on all fronts."

"It might be, yes." She paused. Her eyes were concentrating on an image of wisdom out over the Cadillac's hood. "But shouldn't we wait?" Her voice became throaty. "I think we have many things to consider. Render unto Caesar."

Bobby said, "While you're rendering, I wonder if I would have anything to say about it."

Mother said with parental solidness, "Of course you do. We'll be home soon. Maybe we should sleep on it."

But Bobby, already encouraged by Dad's attempt at partnership, lifted his attitude upward toward his wise adult level. "I judge that at least half of me wants to sleep on it. What's the big objection that we should sleep on?"

Mother said, looking into an imaginary book of notes in her lap, "What was all that about Mary Sue Hurley last fall?"

"Mary Sue Hurley? She's just…"

"She's a very nice girl, I thought."

"Nice girls finish last, but who cares is the appropriate query. I'll take both of them out."

"She's a very nice girl and she's from your own school and your own community. When you all live in the same community, you're more likely to have the same set of values."

Dad abandoned his camaraderie to plead. "Now isn't that a little provincial, Flossie? New York and show business are bread and butter right now."

"I suppose they are but I'm a very provincial person and I happen to believe in down home values, the kind you don't find in New York show business."

One of Dad's hands waved aside, palm up. "I believe in down home values, too. But I don't see how Bobby's escorting that model somewhere is going to ruin him. And it might help in the ratings department."

They passed the White Castle at South Park Avenue, with the memory that went with it of six lean years before, when they would each get five of them for a dime with newspaper coupons and make a feast on the cheap.

"Maybe." She nodded. "But haven't we always agreed that Bobby and the show are two separate things?"

"That agreement was reached when Bobby was fourteen."

"And now he's an adult at sixteen?"

Bobby couldn't argue with that. If Bobby were an adult, there wouldn't be anything to discuss.

So, Dad retreated a little. "I just think it's a possibility. I also think we ought to ask Flo about it at the very least. She might think it's a bad idea." But he didn't stop there. "And at the same time might want to push the idea of your own contribution. Remember, we had thought very strongly about exploiting your piano from the very beginning."

Mother as a musician would call this a modulation, a change of key. Her voice changed with it, losing righteousness and taking on the tone of the realist. "We never did."

"Nobody thought of a way to go about it. This might be a good time to ask Flo to work on that, too. Book you into recital halls, colleges, and clubs."

Bobby said, "Flo's going to need a night shift."

Dad was speaking with great seriousness as he thought things over. "She ought to for the hundred and fifty a week we pay her."

Mother said, her eyes right on his, "All right, if you insist on it, I won't wet the blanket. Will you ask George to call her?"

"I'll call her myself."

She turned to face the glove compartment, chin tucked into a new pose. "Still, it will mean practicing. I'll have to dust off that Grieg sonata."

Bobby sat all the way back. "I'll have to dust off my tuxedo."

The following Friday evening Bobby went to the Playhouse with the gang. This was the town's premier movie palace, so steeped in dignity that it had no balcony, just a loge, which cost you more, not less, and no candy counter, so gauche.

After the movie, they rode bikes to Bobby's on Mansgrove Road, an easy couple of miles down Bayard Lane and State Road. Lon, Jack, Frank, and Pete. The basement was paneled in knotty pine. Asphalt tile covered the floor. A brick fireplace angled off a corner. They played ping pong, shot darts, and started a game of Monopoly.

After trading Marvin Gardens and Atlantic to Jack for New York Avenue, Bobby said, "Silly as it seems, the parents want me to do something that sounds pretty silly."

Jack said, "If you're going to do it, it probably is." Jack, short, strong, and blunt, was counting his money and arranging his corners. Bobby's announcement was ancillary to the real estate problem and Jack had the casual capacity to handle both on equal footings.

"May corn silk fill your navel, O Harnessall. There's this model Dad wants me to take out. Publicity strikes again."

Lon said with a glint, "Model? Like in cover girl?" He had the enlightened grin of one who knows from the inside. Bobby glanced at Lon's face. If Angela kissed Bobby, what would she have done to Lon?

"Tough work," Jack said. He could shrug off envy.

"Sounds great to me," Frank said. "Assuming you don't sign anything first." Frank's dark good looks contained big grins that he used to cover problems.

"How soon?" Pete asked. "Meaning what about next Friday?" Pete's voice was smooth but intense, able to switch the conversation's tone from the jaunty flippance of the others to the pragmatic.

"Friday? The loneliest day in the week? What about Friday?"

"We're all going out."

Pete's smile looked aside for support and got it from Jack, who said to Bobby, "Including you, we thought."

Bobby may have gulped. "That you would have thought such as that is enlightening but ... me? Girl? Take out? Who would I take out?"

Pete said, "Mary Sue. We're going to the movies and Kimberly's afterward." He extended some money to Lon. "Two hotels, please." Pete was building hotels on Park Place and Boardwalk.

"You refer to Mary Sue Hurley? Me?"

"I'm asking Jenny Crown tomorrow," Jack said.

"I already asked Alma Grunyon," Pete said. "She's going." When Pete was pleased, try as he might, he just couldn't suppress his smirk.

Lon said, "And, believe it or not, I'm taking Kimberly." He grinned. "That seems to leave you either out or in." Lon was always pleasantly neutral.

"I could ask her, I guess."

Jack said, "You guess?"

"Guessing goes with the job. If I ask her, she probably can't go."

Jack was nodding, "You just better ask her. Call her up right now."

"By goodly, not on the phone. I'm not ready to breath in her ear."

"First thing Monday then." This was an order. Jack felt impelled to give orders all his life.

"Sure. First things first. If she says no, I'll ask Miss Hight."

All right, this was it. He would be destroyed if she said no. And, if she said yes and something came of it, something like a sense of, well, possession, then he would just have something more to be lost.

"But, lads, what about this model? Our publicity agent might hate it if I went out with Hurley."

Frank said, "Why so?"

"Probably thinks I'm pretty young. With some reason."

"The model's probably pretty young," Jack said.

Frank said, "You're not going to marry her, so what the hell."

"Yeah but what'll Mary Sue say when she hears I'm going out with some dame in New York?"

That mystified them. "What difference will that make?" Lon asked.

"Difference! Lads? Does Garbo tell Dietrich? I should go out with two girls at once?"

Pete said, "Look, dating is just dating. You're not going steady."

Jack said with finality, "And you never will either."

"So, I guess we just leave loyalty out of it."

Lon was still grinning. How could a compeer be as uninformed as Bobby seemed to be? "Loyalty hasn't got a thing to do with it."

"I don't mean loyalty exactly, in the sense of Benedict Arnold."

Lon said, "Maybe you're being too serious about it. Dating in general."

Jack said, all knowing, "Yeah. When you get serious you get clobbered."

Frank said, "Hell, yes. You haven't even asked anybody out yet. Getting clobbered comes later."

Next day, Saturday, Bobby went in on the 12:49 and took the subway up to see Flo Cahn. She booked acts into a supper club on the upper east side, when she wasn't dropping *Twenty Questions* lore and *Twenty Questions* names into newspaper columns. By now, with his mind at ease and ready for Angela, Bobby was eager for the deal.

Flo came forward from the back of the haunt. It was very ornate with lots of red leather showing, dark paneling and acres of white linen, silver, and crystal. It was open for lunch but few patrons were there. She led him back to a banquette, seated herself behind and motioned him to a facing chair.

"A drink? Coffee? Milk?" She had a breathy smile and always seemed dressed for a party. The look of her was all New York, all Broadway. Her body was big and friendly but maybe contrived somehow to look that way. He couldn't guess how old she was. All grown ups were the same age.

"I'm not exactly drinking at this point. You talked to Dad?"

"Of course." She lit a cigarette and leaned forward on her elbows. This was her private domain. She worked for her clients, including them, but in this haunt she was queen.

Bobby said, swallowing with uncertainty, "He suggested an idea, I guess you'd call it, for some publicity." He had trouble talking on the grownup level when he didn't know the grownup.

She inhaled, clouded the sky, and tried hard to take him seriously. "Are you willing to swing some publicity deals, Bobby?" She had brownish grayish hair that angled every which way. Her face looked very dark and very lined, with the lines somehow filled in.

"Uh huh. I'm willing to get my picture in the paper or my name in the paper is all."

He was speaking breathlessly, almost defensively, especially as Flo kept staring at him, sizing him up.

She stared as she might at an open window. "Yes, as I say. He mentioned Angela Rhome. She's a Powers model with a good future and Ronson's been using her." Her thoughts tilted upward. Problems and ideas began to flow. Her eyes narrowed to sort them. "But we'll have to find a gimmick that matches you up." Then straight to him. Apparently he deserved some explanation. "You see, Bobby, when I break stuff, the columns eat it up. The columns are the boffo wherein we catch the conscience of the burbs. Which column did your father have in mind?"

"Probably the minus column."

"No. No. You don't understand. I mean the society columns. The showbiz columns. Wilson. Winchell. Walker. Gardiner. Do you read the columns on a daily basis? Ed Sullivan."

"I've heard of them. In the paper. Right?"

She leaned across the table, suddenly aware that educating this kid would take some time. "Bobby, the whole pulse of society and show business can be measured in the columns. How old are you?"

"How old. How does that matter?"

"Very simple. If you're eighteen, you can get into a night club."

"Uh huh. I'm sixteen. Angela looks about fifteen."

"She does." She nodded, thinking it over. "And they're keeping her right there. That's her shtick." She looked across the room for her next thought, then casually tossed off a bomb. "She's eighteen, of course. Her agent craps whenever I tell him she can't hold onto the kid stuff much longer. But Lordy how it pays."

"Eighteen, by goodly. I'm not sure I want to go out with a girl who's eighteen."

But she wasn't going to be nudged off her trail. "Something in the young romantic line. You both looked good in the *Scholastic* spread. The welcome-to-Gotham bit. Expand on that. Doesn't have to be Stork Club with cleavage. Though God knows she's got it. That might smell like a bribe anyway. In fact…" Her eyes flashed about the ceiling, then circled in on Bobby's and held them in a serious lock. "Bobby, what's your contract situation with the show?"

"Dad says I have one. In fact, it was a sore point a couple of months ago. But he means my union contract. I've never signed anything regarding the show itself."

"No. You wouldn't have. Your parents have the contract and agree to provide you. That it?"

"Except when I have Scout stuff and when I go to college."

"College!" She smiled.

"In the distant future. I'm just a junior in school."

She was nodding slowly. "It's interesting. I'll need to talk to Al Nathan." She sat up. "Meanwhile, maybe — I know. Circle Line tour. Night passage. Lighted skyline in the background."

Bobby was losing his way. "But how would I go about asking her to go for a Circle Line tour."

She paused in mid word, whatever it might have been. "Oh, no, Bobby. Not a real date, if that's what you're thinking."

"I wasn't really thinking at all. I've never dated much, being merely Young Bobby."

"When you do, please promise me you'll forget the entire model/actress species. Oh, please do. They'll kill you. They'll dry you out because, you see, they can never stop selling. They simply can't afford to stop, with never more than a few years of work ahead. No, no. Forget it's a date. This is business. I mean, after all, Angela's shacked up with some hockey player last I heard and he can't even speak English."

Bobby crashed out of there with a headache. A tooth ache. Maybe some other organ was aching, too. Disgust mixed with disappointment and, sure, devastation. He moped up and down Times Square all afternoon. He brooded through the amusement arcade at Broadway and 52nd Street, looked at flip-card movies, played a pinball machine. Then he shambled down the block, head down, to the Guild Theatre.

Jean Parker was guest that evening. He hardly saw her.

Jean: I was pushing a little film called Rolling Home for Monogram. B movie queen on a B quiz show.

Just before the warmup, Bobby got Dad aside. They'd finished training Miss Parker and were standing back near a pin rail. By then the pang of disappointment Bobby felt had become a nagging ache. He told all.

Dad nodded at his great idea. "Maybe other ideas have been better. But it still might work."

"Dad, she's going with a pro athlete and I was thinking about buying her an ice cream soda."

His brows wrinkled. "That's show business." He paused to digest it all. "And this can be a lesson to you, too."

His tone was not father-to-son but strictly business. He almost seemed to be speaking right by Bobby to some other person nearby.

"What lesson to me, too?"

"Don't mix businesses. If this harbor tour comes off, go at it like a pro. Nothing personal. Ever. "

So, who was he? Bobby, the kid in show business? Or Bob, the kid with mooning on his mind?

He got many subjects that night.

This is Ronson's mystery Voice again, hidden from view in a soundproof booth. This time Bill is asking the panel to identify that ship of legend, The Flying Dutchman.

Bill Slater:	All right, let's get going on this tough subject. Who'll start.
Dad:	Is it manufactured?
Bill Slater:	Yes, in a sense.
Herb:	Does it belong to one person?
Bill Slater:	No. Not really.
Bob:	Does it exist?
Bill Slater:	No.
Dad:	Is it a structure?
Bill Slater:	No. Not what you'd call a structure.
Mother:	Is it a place?

Bill Slater: No
Bob: Is it fictional?
Bill Slater: Yes. It's fictional.
Dad: Is it in prose fiction?
Bill Slater: Yes.
Dad: Is it in American fiction?
Bill Slater: No. Not American. I don't think I've ever seen it in prose either. Make that no to prose.
Bob: Is it in English fiction?
Bill Slater: Yes. Partly.
Dad: Is it a conveyance of any sort?
Bill Slater: Yes.
Bob: Is it in Shakespeare?
Bill Slater: No. That's eleven questions used. You've got nine to go.
Mother: Does it have wheels?
Bill Slater: No.
Herb: Well, is it a boat of any kind?
Bill Slater: Yes.
Herb: The houseboat on the River Styx.
Bill Slater: What a grim thought. No, Herb. Not that.
Dad: Is it Cleopatra's barge?
Bill Slater: No. Not Cleopatra's barge.
Bob: Is it in musical fiction?
Bill Slater: Yes, Bob.
Bob: Was it in Gilbert and Sullivan?
Bill Slater: No. That's eighteen questions. Just two to go.
Dad: Is the word ship used in the title?
Bill Slater: Not in the title. Now, you got just one question to go. Okay, who'll try it?
Bob: Okay, well, I'll say the Flying Dutchman.
Bill Slater: Bobby McGuire! (Applause)

 Jean Parker was impressed as most guests were. Showbiz Bobby. Home, of course, Bobby was the kid afraid to ask a sixteen year old for a date.
 He sat in the sunroom most of Sunday listening to records and mooning about the lost Angela, even more attractive now that she was gone forever, at least on a personal basis. Mother, never one to let a full moon go by, came in as Bobby was passing into his half moon phase. The library

was in the room and she had come in to fetch her Grieg Sonata from the stack.

Monday afternoon, Bobby entered Mr. Chesterton's room of English. He was absolutely certain he would be absolutely unable to do what he knew he had to do. The tooth ached. Dr. Majarian would see to it, but not until next day. She was smiling at him, actually smiling at him, as she arranged her pads, books, and pencils.

"You were especially good Saturday."

He turned, throwing the tooth's ache like a hot coal all around his mouth. "I was?"

"What did Miss Jean Parker look like?"

"I'll let you know when I cool down."

Mr. Chesterton struck again. "Hey, you two."

After the bell, Bobby rose, took a big breath, and said, "Oh, one thing I forgot to mention several years ago. A bunch of us are going to the movies and then to Kimberly's Friday and I wanted to ask you to go."

She paused for a killing instant. Sure. It was the pause of deathly suspension. You've all had those little pieces of time too short to even measure in which, short or not, your whole life went up like the tank under Cagney.

She cocked her head saucily and said, "I guess all things considered I can say yes."

"You will? You'll go? Okay, I'll let you know how we're gonna do it. I mean get there and arrangements. To the movies."

"Good."

"Don't mind my stuttering. It comes with the phases of the moon."

Chapter 13

A Very Nice Time

When Mother let him out in front of the Playhouse at six-forty-five that Friday night in January, and Bobby walked past the poster in the window that told passers by on Hulfish Street that the movie they would see should they buy a ticket and enter was *Gallant Bess* with Marshall Thompson, he looked around and saw who he was longing to see. She looked a little shorter than she did in school that day, maybe because she was wearing a heavy camel coat that made her look bulky. Her smile was a little wider than it was in English, too. But that was probably because all the other kids were already there. There had been calls among Jack, Pete, Lon and him, and surely more among the girls involved — Kimberly, Jenny, Alberta, and Mary Sue — that arranged the whole shebang, so he knew the schedule, and he was right on time, but they ribbed him anyway.

"Two in the loge, please. Preferably side by side."

"One sixty."

The arrangements had been simple enough, with Kimberly's cellar reserved, Renwick's planned, and cars promised. That had all been done before Tuesday, when she had said yes, and Bobby had been ready to swell and fly through the two whole days of waiting.

But no. Wednesday he was hauled to New York. Some radio workshop had asked for a *Twenty Questions* session, one of the public service duties show business required. So they all went to Town Hall on 43rd Street and played the game for an hour and a half. They got home at 9:30. What a bore. Jaunts like this were turning the show into a burden. And the only comment he heard regarding his performance was, "Doesn't Bobby ever smile?"

They crossed the lobby carpet, pushed through the red swinging doors at far left and, at the back of the theatre, took a hard right where they would find the silent carpeted steps up to the loge. He showed their loge stubs to Bitsy, the usher, and they were allowed to mount. Lon and Kimberly, who were first, chose the second row. The eight made a long line overlooking the whole theatre.

When she was ready, she gave him a glance, another big smile, waved her hand to take in the whole place, and by the time he had turned to follow her gaze, was saying, "Who do we know?"

He murmured, "Spade Harmon and Jeanne. They're the couple who look like one."

"Where?" Her head slid toward him for a better view. He automatically shied away an inch or two.

"Halfway down, left hand aisle."

She looked at him. "He's a friend of yours?"

"Definitely on my gift list, having gone out west with him to New Mexico."

She said, "I have an aunt who lives in Denver." She sat back.

"This was New Mexico. The rock and desert place, representing the first time I was ever west of Indiana."

Bobby turned and said to her, "Have you been to New York, the city east of Hoboken?"

"No. What's it like?" It was a breathy tone she used, as if the whole question were awesome to her.

"Very dirty but very exciting. Especially on Saturdays. One deduces that when you're there every day, like my father, it isn't so exciting."

"My sister wants to go to New York for a birthday present someday."

He didn't even know she had a sister. "Sister? Like a female brother? Is she older than you, or younger?"

"Two years older."

"When's your birthday? So I can mark it in my master file."

She paused just a second, then said, "March 15. Which will make me old enough to know better."

"You're probably old enough to know better already."

"No, I'm not. I'm just an innocent sprite." She looked at him as an imp. "Looking for wild excitement."

When the news was over, she said, "I hope it's a Tom and Jerry." She was so darn enthusiastic. She hoped it was a Tom and Jerry. Who cared?

Rumors suggested her sweetness was compensation for a troubled family, and Bobby was totally dumb in such things. No grasp at all. His parents had argued and threatened each other years before, but not since *Twenty Questions* went on the air. The concept of divorce and separation were utterly outside his range.

Tom and Jerry it was and Bobby found himself smiling in spite of himself. He was slumped way down by the time it was half over, giggling like a little kid. At one point a sight gag made her turn in a wild howl and both her hands grabbed his arm. He sat up then, all right. Actual physical contact.

By the time the feature began, her left hand was right there, white on the end of her seat's arm. He noticed it. He couldn't just pretend he didn't see it. That white hand said that she was willing and so was Bobby. But he wasn't sure. If he took her hand, how long was he suppose to hold it? Would letting it go mean something bad? He sat there, knowing he had to do something. She was his date, after all, and if he wanted to date her again holding her hand might be required.

Anyway, for better or worse, Bobby did it. His covered hers. Well, you might have thought he'd hit a switch. Her hand turned. Fingers intertwined. It went on and on. They maneuvered them with new and exotic grips and squeezes for eighty-six minutes, until Marshall Thompson's horse Bess was suitably rescued and made safe for democracy.

When the lights came up and the other six rose and filed out to head for Renwick's, they were still holding hands.

Lon said, side stepping by in front of them, "All right. Show's over." Lon was always joyous, full of wisdom and humor. Here he was with Kimberly, the jolly girl Bobby saw nothing in at all. And Lon was handsome and very popular.

Kimberly said, "Yes. No double feature here."

They didn't move until the lights went down for the second show. That delay, that great sign of self-assurance, made them the prime couple in his book, yards ahead of the others.

Finally, she said, "Maybe we'd better," withdrawing her hand.

"Right. They'll charge me double."

It was night on the Square with street lights and window lights giving it a cool, classy texture. Imagine a courthouse square with a colonial-styled hotel in the middle instead of the courthouse. Around it were rather colonial apartment buildings of three or four floors with shoppes, chic or quaint, at the sidewalk. By the time the lingering ones were passing the Silver Shop, the other six kids were already wending around Claytons (dry goods) and past Zavelles (books, records, gifts). Jack turned back and, though many other strollers were on the Square, shouted, "Speed it up there, love birds." Oh yes. He loved him for it, Jack, who would become something of a psychological rival in later years but then was a leader of the pack, smart and raucous.

At 9:30 they were spread along Renwick's back wall, with the girls on one side and boys across from them. Lon was beside Bobby and Pete beside him. Jenny, who was three tables down across from Jack, was squawking her order.

"Coke and grilled cheese."

"Large Coke and grilled cheese," Jack said.

Bobby wanted to wow everybody by ordering something wild, such as a banana split, but he knew that, if he did, Jack would feel required to try to top him with something wilder, such as a malted float. So, Bobby ordered a hamburger and Coke and so did Mary Sue.

Renwick's was darker at night. This was the after-movie crowd, dressed in a different mode from kids in the afternoon. Back their way it was a gay scene and everybody was smiling, even him. He may have begun to forget he had to be different, better, and that maybe it would be okay to be nice and happy, because, oh no, they couldn't take that away from him, meaning Mary Sue, who was right there, at his table. His date. He felt something warm in his spine

Pete, looking at him with more than a smirk, said, "I guess you liked the cartoon." He was a great ally, Pete, who would count neutral in beefs and arguments. He was so good at everything you didn't have to worry about keeping him even.

Bobby didn't get it. "I'll try to remember."

Alberta, across from Pete, added, "You were laughing so hard you had me laughing."

He smiled wanly. "Plead guilty. Was I sober?" He didn't know Alberta very well and had nothing on her as the basis of a retort.

Kimberly, beside Alberta, said, "If you want to laugh really hard, go to the movies with Bob."

Jack said, at the opposite end, "You should have heard him with Bugs Honey and the Australian Bush Man."

He could see Sue's eyes askance at him with a touch of both wonder and, maybe, pride, when he responded, "Pleading guilty, I confess being on the floor only half the time."

At 10:15 Kimberly went to the phone and called for transport. This turned out to be the Manners's 1939 Chevrolet and his mother in their Cad.

"Mother's taxi service," she said as he opened the front door at Renwick's curb. Mary Sue slid in. Jack and Jenny slid in back.

They eased from the curb.

Bobby said to Mother, "You may know Mary Sue as well as she knows your appendix."

Mary Sue laughed. "I won't let him forget it."

"And," he said, "in back with Jack is Jenny Crown, the well known ball room dancer."

"Now Bob!"

Jack said, "Bob had the whole theatre laughing in the Tom and Jerry."

Mother said, "Is Eileen behind me?"

That was Kimberly's mother and she was and the wheels delivered them to Kimberly's red-floor basement. This was old territory now, darker and thankfully free of string. He saw a couch against a wall not there before.

Kimberly, who had led Lon down first, said from below, "Turn the light on when you want to play ping pong only."

At the bottom of the stairs his date, his lady, leaned up and, very close, said, "I never road in a Cadillac before."

They moved to the phonograph table. He picked up a stack of records.

"Our car has a missing fender."

"Call Mr. Kean, Tracer of Lost Fenders."

"It got a dent in Tennessee and they couldn't get a new one because of the war. I'll bet you never road in a Studebaker." She was setting up the little portable phonograph, flicking her finger over the hot needle. It made a loud rip.

"I've tried to. My uncle had one, maybe two. I'd like to see your car sometime."

"My father's picking me up later."

"A long way home for you."

She said, "How about 'Moonlight Serenade?'"

The record crackled into its groove and up came Glenn Miller. They flowed together. Her puffy light blue sweater felt silky. He plodded ahead and then behind and then to the side, not quite dancing, but almost.

"Is he still in the FBI, your father?"

"He's with the University now." She swung away. "Now we walk."

He followed. Three steps forward, one step back. Then together anew.

"What department, meaning what does he teach?"

"No. He's head proctor. He runs the security operation there."

"Never heard the word, proctor."

"Like campus police, but no uniforms."

"Have to watch my step all over again."

"I don't think he'll bite."

With dates at parties, cutting in was rare. But Lon suggested it and Bobby was maybe a half step that night toward becoming a gentleman, so he bowed. Dancing now with Kimberly he felt a nibble of vexation that some of his dollar and sixty cents was being wasted.

Bobby said, "This place begins to resemble a high school hang out. If we had Mickey and Judy we could put on a show."

She nodded. "Yes and it isn't fair. You'll have a party in your cellar."

"That's an idea. I'll take it up with my appointments secretary."

"What did you think of the movie. Seriously."

All this activity blended into a game of doubles ping pong. He joined Kimberly taking on Pete and Jenny, who won easily. He blamed Kimberly for always getting in the way when it was his shot.

Mary Sue greeted him at the end of the game with arms spread invitingly. Steps, steps. Phonographs had little bass in those days. "Stardust" was on. "Stardust" was always on.

Mary Sue said, "Bob, I want you to know I was kidding you Tuesday, or was it Monday, about Miss Parker."

"Miss Parker Pen. Do I get the point?"

"You don't mind if I kid you, do you? It's interesting sitting next to you in class."

They were dancing into the corner where the darkened cellar was even darker. The others were dancing, too, but Bobby didn't see them.

"Wondering if you say that to all the guys."

"No. I really don't, and you shouldn't suspect me of such a thing. I would hate it if you didn't like sitting next to me."

Bobby said, "Mr. Chesterton's to blame, putting me there, and all. And you're so new and everything and I can almost understand what you're saying, which is new, with girls."

"We're both new, in a way. Each of us finds a sympathetic ear from the other, like people traveling in foreign countries."

"In class we talk to each other and risk getting good grades. Of course, I risk it just showing up."

"But it's fun," she said smiling, and sort of pushing him away.

But it was okay. She left him standing there, because it was time for refreshments and she moved to help Kimberly set out the stuff.

Bobby said to Jack, "Hey thanks for the big call on Palmer Square. I'd have gone incognito if I'd had one in my pocket."

"Any time. You know — if the shoe fits."

"I'll have to watch it."

"I think she likes you, boy."

"It's in her genes. And I'm not."

Much punch and pretzels and Coke and Seven-up. Small sandwiches. Nothing spilled. Mary Sue and Bobby sat in a corner behind the ping pong table. She balanced things neatly in her lap.

"I wonder if talking in class does have any effect on our grades," she said.

Bobby waved a pretzel. "Not yours. Girls, have that extra thing, able to get away with talking in class. Teachers are never going to crack down. Or crack up, for that matter."

She smiled. "Sometimes." She thought it over as she chewed a small sandwich. "Maybe sometimes."

"One is tempted to inquire if you ever had a man teacher you couldn't get away with things with? I'll bet you didn't."

She washed that down with a sip of Seven-up. "Most of them have a human side." She set the glass down on the red cement floor beside her. "But Mr. Chesterton is very smart."

Bobby stared. It never occurred to him that teachers could be anything but smart. "A true appraisal not before noticed. He may be human but he doesn't let anybody fool around, even girls. Even good looking ones."

"Even girls my foot."

Bobby nodded like a horse. "Oh yes, even girls. You being what I call at night a sorceress, attracting like a bright light. You get me talking like an idiot, about me and my thoughts and ideas, and what do I get in return?"

"My undivided attention."

Kimberly had scheduled one game. No Xs in sight. Charades, amplified into something coming to be called The Game. Girls against boys. He had to act out "Tea for Two", which was a cinch. Lon got it within a minute. It went on for an hour, all charged against his one sixty in time away from Mary Sue, so he was very thankful when it was over and somebody put on "How Soon" for the last dance. It was one o'clock.

As they began to dance, he found himself holding her now more naturally. He had not apparently touched anything forbidden. He said in a low key, "You really do get me talking about things I never talk about, especially the show."

"I like to hear about it. Who wouldn't?"

"The danger appears since I feel like I'm bragging when I talk about the show and that it's really nothing to brag about."

She paused before she said, "I think I know what you mean." She leaned away and looked at him. "I think I do. But boys are always bragging, until they stop being boys. And what difference does it make whether they're bragging about running on the football field or bragging about getting hard *Twenty Questions* subjects."

They stepped. They stepped. They bumped knees a little.

He mumbled, "They're both games is about all that's the same."

"So, as I began, I hope sitting next to me isn't a bad influence."

"It's not a bad influence at all." Step, step. "And I'll try to stop bragging."

"Oh no. Don't stop. I like to hear you." She began to hum with the song. They were sort of dancing, sort of rocking from foot to foot like a card table on a tossing deck. "And I like to dance with you."

"That's you. Mary Sue, the sorceress."

"Oh yes." She hummed. "I just flick an arm and turn all boys into pigs or something."

"Slaves."

"Like this?" A squeeze again. A copy of December's, but legato rather than the previous staccato. She was wild. Ravishing.

"Yes. Like that."

She stopped humming. The silence somehow told him she was considering things. She murmured, "I hope nobody misunderstands."

"The normal reaction is very, uh, fundamental. And by the way, what will Fred say?"

"A ha. I hope you're very jealous."

"That'll be the day. If you add me to your trophy bag, I'll find poor Fred already in it."

"You know I haven't said anything to Fred. We never talked like this…like I do with you."

"He moons around and hates me."

"Now, Bob, please listen. I know you are very intelligent in most things. But in some things you need lessons."

"I do not. I mean, of course I do. In most things I'm an idiot."

"Things I've learned the hard way, I mean."

Then they heard the voice of doom. Mrs. Manners was calling down the stairs."Mary Sue, your father just pulled in."

"Walk me up."

The other five were making exit prep. They found coats and stuff. They found good night's to their hostess and her mother. They opened the front door to the cold, clear night, and Mary Sue took his hand and pulled him out after her.

She stopped and turned to him on the porch. Her hair flashed silvery glints beneath the porch light.

Bobby said, "Sometimes I wish I knew what the hard way was."

"No you don't."

"I better shut up before I say something intelligent."

Bobby saw a dark shape sixty feet away in the driveway. It had one headlight.

She said, "What's hard for some is easy for … well, you don't want the hard way anyway."

"I was going to ask you something else."

"What?"

The one headlight blinked. "Well, uh, can I ask you to go out with me again?"

She looked ahead, probably going over her schedule. "I think, yes. You can ask."

"Well, what's the answer?"

She grinned like a coquette. "What's the question?"

"Uh…Will you go out with me again?"

"Now, Bob, you know that's not the way. You really are supposed to be a little more specific."

A horn tooted every lightly, but it tooted. "Being more specific then, I wanted to ask you if you could go to *Twenty Questions* with me sometime. I refer to that little circus in New York."

She looked startled. "In New York? I don't know. I'd certainly like to, but I don't know what the powers that be would say. When would it be?"

"Being specific, I refer to March 15? Your birthday."
"Wouldn't that be nice."
Another toot. A fraction longer.
"You can beat out your sister."
She moved off the porch. "Yes. That might be a small problem, you know."
"Let me know. Please. Pretty please."
She broke off and ran to the car. He waved then headed home, a half mile or so in the crisp night air. Bobby had a girl friend. He was sure he had a girl friend.

Chapter 14

Elsewhere

Their guest that January 25 may have been columnist Henry J. Taylor, a friend of Dad from their cub reporter days in Indiana, but Bobby was in no position to be sure. Sure of anything. He did the show through the fog, with her face swimming around inside it.

Bill Slater: All right, this next subject was submitted by Mrs. John Newsome of Toronto, Ontario, Canada, and it is animal. This is Ronson's Mystery Voice, letting you in on the secret. Bill's subject is the Dionne Quintuplets.
Bill Slater: All right, let's begin this animal subject.
Dad: Is it a living American man?
Bill Slater: No. Not this time.
Bob: Is it a whole animal?
Bill Slater: Partly.
Mother: Is it a group of men?
Bill Slater: No.
Herb: Is it one man and one woman?
Bill Slater: What a romantic thought. But no, Herb. Not one man and one woman.
Bob: Is it a group of four-footed animals?
Bill Slater: No.
Mother: Is the subject human at all?
Bill Slater: Yes. Sure. Who's next?
Bob: Is it a group of women?
Bill Slater: Uh, no.
Dad: Let's review. You said it's human, but it's not a group of men or women, or one man and one woman?

Bill Slater:	That's right.
Dad:	Well is it a group of mixed men and women.
Bill Slater:	No.
Bob:	Oh, well, is it a group of children?
Bill Slater:	Yes. Now that's nine questions.
Dad:	All they all boys?
Bill Slater:	No.
Mother:	Is this a group of girls?
Bill Slater:	Yes.
Bob:	Is it five little girls? (Applause)

At school all week he was of her by her and for her. When the week was over, and he faced another Saturday, February 2, and the guest was a rising model named Candy Jones, he hated her, because she stood between him and another week of euphoria.

There was a catch, of course. Euphoria always comes with a catch. He had no idea what to do next. Two weeks had passed. February 9 brought Guy Lombardo, who was always their anniversary guest, because he had been their first guest, two extenuated years before. Never mind Guy. Her birthday was coming and he had said nothing.

Emptier days passed, then a fuller Saturday, as a memorable guest cut loose with a slapstick explosion. This was burlesque comic Zero Mostel, who stalked onto the Mutual Guild Theatre's stage and did a perfect fall, full length. He continued doing prat and making weird sounds the whole show. Mr. Slater said afterward, "Did you ever ride a bucking bronco?"

Somebody else's worry. Zero could be a real cipher, for all Bobby cared. Fineshriber could fire him, for all Bobby cared. He could skip the western tour, for all Bobby cared. Mr. Harris be damned. Over a month now had passed since his first date. He needed help.

Bobby dined in winter months in 203, an oversized room of one-arm desk chairs. He would buy sandwiches in the cafeteria and take them upstairs. The gang made a group against the window wall, sort of a wee Algonquin roundtable of higher discussion, ripostes, and ribald thought. When Elaine Setter entered, dominating the far wall and the whole room, it was mostly ribald thought.

That Monday in late February, as Jack, Lon, Pete, and Bobby watched, Jack was saying, "If she takes off that Jacket, I won't be able to eat my lunch."

Pete smirked, "Yes. It's quite a sight to see."

Bobby said, "I suggest it's a sight you'd like to see."

The mammary culture of 1948 differed from that of fifty years later. Most girls then dressed like pupas, not butterflies. Elaine was an early Monarch.

Midday in 203 was relaxing and warm. Snow was blowing horizontal outside the windows but the radiators sizzled inside.

Bobby paused for an opening before he got serious. "The question is, for all you Miss Dorothy Dixen, who do I go with?" He bit into the sandwich, one of two. The other was a tangy paste of wonder food.

Jack brought his lunch from home in a brown paper bag. Opening it, he said, "It's your own fault if you don't go with anybody." Jack chewed a bite to extinction before he swallowed and said, "You take 'em out and don't ask em out again and they think you're not really interested."

Bobby sat back and considered it. "I still get scared asking."

Pete offered, "Ask her out while you're already out."

Bobby lowered the half sandwich. "I should try it for your own better knowledge."

"For the better knowledge of boykind." Pete was almost serious.

Jack said, "Then, you soon know when and if you're going with her."

Bobby wanted clarification. "When do I know that?"

Lon said as he brandished a banana, "Two or three times."

"Two or three dates and I'm going with her? Let me get that in writing." He could see great disaster coming from assuming too much.

Jack said, "Maybe three or four. Maybe two or three."

The working phrase in those years was "Sure of her." He either sensed or knew that you could never be really sure of any girl, but the condition was certainly something to seek, to strive for, although he was still not sure why. A sense of contentment? Of triumph? Of peace?

Bobby pressed on. "I know you're not talking about going steady because my hand isn't shaking."

Jack said, "That's not going steady." Jack wadded the remains of the brown paper bag and shot it toward the big waste basket in the center of the room. It hit the rim and rolled before it dropped in.

Lon added, "Going steady's more a mutual agreement. Just going with her is what people see and think."

In English class that day, Young Bobby asked her to the Sophomore

Dance March 8. She said yes with an appropriate smile. Arrangements were made. They would meet at the Nassau Tavern. Her Dad would then take them to the school gym.

The dance went all right. Although his dancing was still pretty bad, she made up for it by steering him clear of a lot of stumbling and tripping and generally making an idiot show. They left the gym at eleven. His plan was to walk uptown to Veidt's or Renwick's and then take her home in a cab.

Outside, the crisp night air was cold for March and cold for walking uptown at night, maybe a mile, to Renwicks's through the town. But any worry was overpowered by the moon. It was dazzling and around it was the largest circle he would ever see, thirty or forty diameters of the moon in radius. He took it as a sign of something.

They walked briskly over to Moore and turned left toward Nassau, making Renwick's in a frigid trek. Their teeth were chattering as they ordered.

When the waitress left, Mary Sue said, "We've never been in here alone, have we?"

She had shrugged off her coat, a black and grey tweed of some kind, and he had hung his long camel on a post of the booth.

"Nuh uh. Not that I remember. And I would remember."

"Would you?"

It was a taunting question. He looked up to see her eyes on his and it gave him a dandy feeling. She was there and she would stay there with him. The dark lights of the restaurant made her a prize, a presence there with him that he savored. It never occurred to him what her feeling might be or that she really had any.

He said, "Cause I wanted to ask you something. Almost important." He smiled.

Her eyes rose. "Uh oh." She gripped the table knife in her fist.

Bobby smiled away her worry, or tried to. "Not a pristine subject. I already did ask you about it. About New York next Saturday, on your birthday."

"Oh. I don't know. My parents weren't too happy about the idea." Her smile had become a frown of concern.

"Were you happy about the idea?"

"I'm excited about it." Her eyes opened on him.

The food came at that moment and they got it organized.

Brandishing his hamburger, he said, "Well, heck, I know my away around New York and have for two years." He waved the bun in support of his great experience.

"Yes, but it's still New York." She almost pouted

He pressed his lips together. "Mary Sue, I could get from Penn Station to the Radio City Music Hall by subway without looking. I mean that actually. Take the Seventh Avenue to Times Square. Cross along Forty-Second Street past Vim's and Wurlitzer to the Sixth Avenue, then off into the Music Hall's basement, and there's a ticket booth right there."

She hadn't bothered to follow his directions. "I'm sure you know your way around. I'll ask. It's just that I don't want any trouble about anything." She sipped her Coke. "Who's the guest going to be?"

"Uncle Remus. Seriously, does that matter?"

When they left Renwicks's, the night was even crisper. Across Nassau Street they could see the Doric columns of the First Presbyterian Church with its deep porch and facade. In front of it and down a few paces taxis were lined up at the curb in the night. He knew some of the drivers. When he would come home alone Saturday on the nine o'clock train, he'd take a cab home from the railroad station. He approached one he knew, who recognized Bobby and opened the door of the Dodge.

"This will be quite a trip, Johnny," Bobby said, feeling something dashingly romantic about riding through the countryside late at night to see his girl friend home. They held hands the whole way. He would recall forever those freezing fingers. Mainly his. The trip cost him two dollars. He could hardly wait to get to bed to swim through Paradise.

Then, next morning, *elsewhere* intervened again.

That Saturday morning at ten he saw Explorer Post 60 crossing the back yard. Itchy, Rineheart, Spade, of course, Pete and Fred. Butch Leyden led the pack. Bobby answered the chime in pajamas, endured ribs, and departed a happy hiker in ten minutes. They crossed the front yard, ducked through their split rail fence designed to repel Indian war parties, and penetrated the deep woods and the northern frontier. They were seeking a place for a day hike campsite in this virgin forest, this climax woods.

Early spring woods were icky squishy. A few ground leaves of green were working their way out, but the trees were still bare. Explorer Post 60 rested once or twice in grassy clearings. They swigged water from olive drab canteens. They crossed ancient stone walls. Then, maybe an hour later, they broke out of the woods into a great clearing. Not just a clearing but a scene. Ahead they saw the weedy ruins of a quarter mile horse track. A low stone building, probably a stable, lay decrepit nearby. Everything in sight was closed, weathered, and empty. Not a sound.

To their right, toward where State Road must be, was a mansion of field stone. As they closed in, they could see the lower windows were boarded up. Upper windows were closed, sealed, dark. Never mind Mary Sue. This was top stuff.

Nothing in the Scout Law prohibited entering. The question was how and where. The answer was through a ripped screen porch where a kitchen door was actually standing open. They eased in, unsure of goblins even on a bright Saturday morning. The kitchen was old but not ancient, with Monel sinks, space for a dish washer, and modern ceiling fixtures. All were dead. A kitchen closet was empty except for fallen plaster and its stack of shelves. A breakfast nook awaited Wheaties. Other rooms awaited their wonder. They roamed the whole place, marveling at a ball room's inlaid plaster ceiling, careful not to damage but equally careful to leave no niche or closet unseen.

Bobby said to Pete, "Ghosts are probably upstairs."

Pete said, no smirk in sight, "I think it will be better to stay downstairs."

Fred said, "This must be the old Grimes place I've heard about."

They stood in the kitchen, hearing the others roaming and shrieking.

Bobby said, "Where are the zombies and who's Grimes?"

The scene seemed wrong for an abandoned mansion. It was all bright and quiet, a little dusty, but serene and hardly frightening. The only real decay in sight were chips of plaster on the hardwood floor. He picked one up and flipped it toward what was to have been the breakfast nook. A little cloud of dust rose like a baby ghost.

Fred said, "Some millionaire. He built it for his bride and then either she died on the honeymoon or left him for a bull fighter. Stories differ."

"How long ago?" Pete inquired.

"During the Depression sometime, I heard."

Bobby said, "Nice place for a depression. Whose is it now?"

"I think he lives in California." Fred moved toward the screen porch. "The thing is, nobody has ever lived in it. That's the story."

That afternoon Bobby asked Dad about it on the way in to New York. Dad had heard of it too. "Movie producer is what I heard."

"Such as Gary Stevens? Maybe he knows him. What gets me is that nobody has ever lived in it."

"So they say. Tied up in litigation."

Their guest that Saturday was Senator Harry Cain, a new bright face from the State of Washington. He later rose to heights in the political scale but as a guest was merely a freshman senator happy to meet people who knew people and had a radio show. They dined with him in Dunhalls.

Tuesday evening Bob and Mary Sue talked on the phone. It was past seven. *I Love a Mystery* was over.

She said almost apologetically, "Mother says I can go if somebody goes as chaperone."

"Which means in reality somebody as baby sitter."

Bobby was snuggled in the sun room's yellow leather chair. He had its sides pulled up as far as possible. This would be a discussion of incredible importance.

"I don't know about that, but I couldn't change her mind."

"Would it do any good if I talked to her? In my charming, boyish baritone?"

"I don't see how. It's not only the so-called danger they worry about but just in principle."

"Kids go to New York all the time."

"They can't see it, without somebody else along."

And then, almost with horror, he heard himself saying, "Like who?"

"Well…"

"Well, who. Your sister?"

"Yes. My sister."

It sounded more like a confession. Powers were conspiring to get him. He wanted to sit Mr. Hurley down and talk some sense into him.

"I know you're kidding from the tone of my teeth chattering."

Mary Sue rushed on. "I found her almost delirious when she heard you'd asked me, after she's wanted to go for so long. I don't even know if she'd do it."

Still, if her sister meant the difference between going and not going, was it an offer he couldn't refuse? He saw disaster. He saw chaos. But he also saw Mary Sue trotting out onto the stage beside him in full view of eighteen hundred people as he showed her to a seat in the front row.

Bobby murmured, "Why don't you ask her?"

"She might say yes, you know."

"Would you like it if she did?"

"It's the only way for me to go with you. So, I think I say yes."

"If you want to go on that basis ... that way, it's okay with me."

It was a deal, a contract. If Mary Sue went to *Twenty Questions* with him, met Mr. Slater, and maybe even dined with them at Dunhalls, Bobby would be going with her. For sure.

Chapter 15

On the Town

They left the Princeton Junction station on the 12:49. Luncheon in the diner over mild protests. Bobby had insisted. "My treat, by golly."

Danny Shea seated them. "Welcome again, Bobby. How are your parents?" The steward pulled a chair for Mary Sue by the window, into which she glided smoothly. Bobby eased toward her wake.

Alice said, "Hey, I sit with Mary Sue, Big Boy. You sit down over there."

From then on, Young Bobby's goal for the day was less ecstasy than survival, and survival might require an extreme measure, which might bring on total disaster. Sure, Charlie, and all sorts of metaphors come to mind. Say, you'll just play it by ear. Say, there may come a time to just bail out. Or maybe, Run. Ah, run. Run.

Roaring along the high iron, people staggering in the aisle, waiters balancing enormous trays on one palm, silver tinkling, people coughing, blue trails of tobacco smoke wafting upward—three kids at a table of silver and white linen each wondered if it was all true, for very different reasons.

Bobby had seen Alice first in the little parking lot next to the Princeton Junction station. Anybody would notice her. She emerged from the one-fender car to tower over it and over her sister. As the Cadillac alongside departed, as Bobby joined the Hurleys, and as the Studebaker pulled away, she had shouted, "Hey, lead on, Big Boy."

Even in the busy dining car she attracted attention. Waiters and adult travelers at the tables stared bemused. She shrugged off her long black coat and every male around had to approve. Mary Sue's eyes were downcast and seemed to be saying that, with Alice, this is what you get.

"Now we order," Alice said, easing forward and arranging her snow white napkin. "Luncheon in the diner on the way to old New York." She held a menu in two hands. Bobby casually slid his into sight.

Bobby said across the whiteness, "If you're Mary Sue's older sister, how come you're not in PHS? Or a similar institution of lower learning?"

"Cause I'm at Miss Fine's School, silly. Ma has a fixation about getting into college."

Seconds and power poles flashed past their window.

"Here. Give me that." This was Alice grabbing the order check that Danny Shea had initialed and placed by Bobby's hand. "I know all about it. You write down your choices, you know. I know all about everything on this trip. Just leave it to Alice and we'll have a fun day."

Mary Sue, directly across, said, "What do you recommend?"

"Hungry Bob always gets the hamburger steak with the diced-in-cream potatoes. It takes less time," he coughed, "and it's easier on my lower intestine."

"A sandwich is all we need," Alice said, scanning the menu. "Do they have a good club?"

"Only on the first tee."

"That okay with you, Sue?"

"I guess so. And a Coke?"

"Make it tea."

Bobby said, "I'll write my own down. Don't worry. I can spell." He extended his hand.

"I'll write it. You say it. What'll it be?"

He told her. In writing it down, her eyes were committed, providing him his first opportunity to look at his date. They exchanged brief smiles, roaring through New Brunswick.

She said, looking up and sliding the check aside for the waiter, "I have my own agenda for this trip, in case you didn't know."

The waiter came, smartly lifted the check, read the items aloud, and departed. Bobby found himself staring at the single rose in a silver vase.

Young Bobby said, "Your own agenda is fine with me. What?"

Mary Sue said, almost pleadingly, "Alice, you're not?"

"Why shouldn't I. We."

Bobby, obviously mystified, said, "Why shouldn't I, we, what?"

As Mary Sue's lips tightened, Alice said, "You ever go ice skating?"

"Like Abel, Lindsay, and Howe."

Mary Sue said, "All right, Alice, I'm going to pretend you didn't say what everybody in the diner must have heard."

Alice ignored her sister. "At that rink they have near Radio City?" She was bouncing on her chair with exuberance.

Bobby sat back. "Oh. Yes."

Mary Sue said, "Now listen, Alice. I'm warning you." She had turned her pretty, brown-curled head to talk straight talk to her older sister.

"We'll go right after the Music Hall. It can't be that far."

Bobby nodded, eyebrows high. "Right down the hall."

Mary Sue said, "Alice, listen. We are not going skating. Bob asked me to New York. Not you."

"You talked him into it just to get at me. You knew I've wanted to go to New York for years." Bobby stared at the rose. This was not his family. "You'd get to go while I have to be satisfied with the Playhouse, McCarter, and roller skating in Trenton. Well, I'm not satisfied with the Playhouse, McCarter and roller skating in Trenton." She looked hard ahead and growled, "I want to be Sonja Henie."

Power poles. Back doors of industry. Bobby stared as they wiped past.

Alice leaned back. "Now I'm going to the little girls room at the end of the car and, when I come back, I don't want to hear any more complaints." She scooted out and up and swerved down the moving aisle.

Mary Sue faced him across the table. "Fine date I'm going to make. We only have so much time before your show."

"At which point your parents meet us and take you home. I was planning the Music Hall and maybe a walk later in the park. Maybe a bite at Toffinetti's. Meet my father up at WOR. Now it looks more like chills and spills on ice."

Suddenly Mary Sue turned to him and snapped her fingers. "Wait a minute." She actually smiled. "Wait just one little minute!" She leaned an inch closer. "While she's skating, where will we be? If we happen to walk away somewhere, how is she coming after us on skates? She can't. While she's doing loops and whirls, we can grab that bite to eat, meet your father at WOR and still get to the theatre in time for the show."

Bobby smiled. "You have generated a plan of genius, which I heartily go along with, except for one little item. Isn't she likely to get a little sore and tell your parents about it?"

Young Bobby had met her father and could easily visualize her young body making itself cozy on his lap as she twisted him around her finger.

Mary Sue leaned back. "Let her tell my parents. Let her tell the whole world. She'll learn that little Mary Sue can take care of her big sister when she has to." She nodded to herself in the *so there* mode. "All we have to do is reluctantly agree and we're in."

In a few moments, the waiter arrived balancing a tray and Alice arrived balancing her considerable self. She reapplied her napkin and fingered the club sandwich in front of her. "Take my word for it, a train is no place to go to the bathroom." She raised the sandwich and attacked it.

Bobby said, "By golly, I think you'll have time to do some skating."

"I know I'll have time."

"We'll watch," Mary Sue contributed.

"Whaddya mean watch. You've both skated."

Bobby said, "I couldn't skate today. Problems in the contract, you know."

"Big Boy's contract? Come on."

"Something about day of show, unnecessary risks. I guess they think I might break a knee cap and not make it to the theatre."

"You'll break your kneecap, sure."

"Oh, and it reminds me," Bobby said. "You should have an address in case we get separated."

"We're not getting separated, Big Boy. I'll be on you two like glue."

"But even glue gets unstuck sometimes. Here, I wrote it down. Mutual Guild Theatre on Fifty-second Street between Seventh and Eighth. Here." He handed her a tear sheet from a scratch pad.

The route from Pennsylvania Station to the Radio City Music Hall began with a maze that included a dark, dirty platform, a cloud of people in the station, white tile corridors like an endless mens room, turnstiles that swallowed nickels, and the shuddering roar of the IRT local.

"One stop," he said over the roar.

They stood silent in the lurching car. Every other rider was a German spy, a local pick pocket, or a spastic begging for coins. Times Square supporting pillars soon flashed by like dominos. He led them off.

He waved like a tour guide. "Love the gum machines." There was one on each steel pillar. As they walked toward the stairs at the north end of the platform, he said, "Guy told Dad that in China they'd break the gum machine and steal the money. Which shows you the level of American honesty."

Above they walked briskly through the sidewalk crowds. "This would be the lower end of Times Square in and around which one always finds crowds. You wonder where everybody could be going."

It was past two o'clock, cold, damp, and bustling in the canyon of buildings that reached to heaven. The brightest lights were the neon signs in the windows of the stores they passed along Forty-second Street. The drug store on the corner of Broadway, VIM appliances and records halfway down to Sixth Avenue, Wurlitzer beyond that. All were in buildings that soared forever above them. Noise swarmed all over. Whining buses. Horns. Tires on brick and asphalt. Ahead, beyond Bryant Park and the library, Bobby noticed the modest tower of the Chanin Building looming a hello. They had done the broadcast for three weeks in its roof theatre long ago. Of course, he didn't know it, but it would end there, too.

Walking three wide was impossible and, since Alice led Mary Sue firmly by the elbow, he drifted behind them, marveling at their seams.

Alice looked back briefly, "You having trouble keeping up?"

"No. Enter the next subway entrance."

Down on their second platform, he said, "We take the D Train.

They emerged at Rockefeller Center. Through the big brass doors and they found their way up to Forty-ninth Street and entered the line for Music Hall tickets half way east to Rockefeller Plaza. They passed the newsreel theatre in their shuffle and then the entrance to NBC. They waited twenty minutes and saw a forgotten Hepburn-Tracy effort called *The Sea of Grass*. They saw the Rockettes and the ballet. They heard the orchestra and the organ. Bobby showed them how to illuminate the small lights on the back of the seats in front of them to read the program. When Bobby tentatively extended an arm around Mary Sue, from beyond her came, "There'll be none of that." Nearby people tittered. Bobby swallowed. He looked forward to the rink.

Afterward, in the Grand Foyer, Alice said, "We're going to the ladies."

He nodded, "Down in the grand lounge."

"You stay right here."

He stood watching them trip across the deep carpet until they turned down the broad steps. Although he had been in this immense lobby many times, he still thrilled to its size and its style. It was the grandest expression of the style of those movies he had seen when he was a little kid. The meaning of modern. Its enormous chandelier, eighty-foot ceiling and flat, polished brass were his for the price of a ticket.

He followed them down alone, entered the men's side, wondering if they had found the ladies side, and was soon back upstairs where he had been directed to wait, hoping nobody noticed that he had disobeyed. Hoping also that at least one of them would get lost. Hoping the plan for the rink would work. He thought of the little restaurant behind the rink. They could have a soda there while Alice tried her blades. A soda alone in New York with Mary Sue. Somehow the concept of being alone with her in a faraway place magnified the romance of it. Far away places. Strange sounding names.

"All right, girls," he said when they had returned, "indoors we could gain access to the rink's very threshold, but it's easier to walk it outside," which is what they did.

The stairway down to the rink was between the British and French buildings. The RCA Building loomed above them overawing. They skipped down to the area. The ice was crowded but not packed. The crowds moved and waited, sat on benches to put on skates, stumbled across the rubber mats to the ice, took tentative steps, fell or sailed. Old guys with suits. Little girls in skating skirts. Guards and attendants in brown uniforms. Bobby went up to the window only to be elbowed aside by Alice. "I'm paying for this." She made the exchange, admission and skate rental. "It's been on my *must do* list for years."

Mary Sue, coming down behind them, said, "Where can we watch?"

Bobby said, "Right behind the rink. A little restaurant with big windows between the English Grill and the French Café. It will provide us with delicious ice cream sodas."

It did. They were given a perfect table. Through the plate glass they watched Alice circle the rink in whirls and steady step. They looked at her and then at each other. Time passed but the thought did not. Mary Sue said, "Looks like fun."

They polished off the ice cream as compeers in a later age would polish off appropriate alcohol. But the treat was being overborne by the thought in the air. The focus was not their tulip soda glasses but the scene through the window. They tried to talk to each other as they would at Renwick's, but her eyes kept turning to the rink. Finally he said, "I give up."

She turned to him with great warmth. "Just a half hour?"

He shook his head in defeat. "You go ahead while I make a phone call."

"I'll meet you center ice."

"Oh, not me. I'll watch. And remember," he pleaded, "less than an hour."

"I understand." She was on the edge of her chair.

He said, "Go ahead. I want to see you do it."

"The people on the ice won't."

She moved away. He paid the check, wandered out into the vast terrazzo concourse, found a bank of phone booths and dialed Pennsylvania 6-8600. He left a message for his father that they would meet at the theatre. By the time he had returned to the admissions and skate rental booth, both Hurleys were on the ice. Alice, for the occasion, had worn a wide enough skirt to try spins in the center of the rink, which comprised most of her ice time. He saw her make one circuit of the rink with the counter-clockwise crowd, which was her last and she drifted to the center, where semi-pros in skating skirts and tights were dominating the scene. While guards in the flow limited the speed of faster skaters, Alice stood and tried to spin, stopping to watch the experts, and tried again. Mary Sue now wore a dazzling skating skirt she had rented and changed into within fourteen minutes. But she more or less stood waiting. She took a step here, a trip there, and, when Bobby showed up sitting on a bench near the entrance, glided up to him in a breathy smile. "You're afraid to skate."

"Contract."

Her face was blushed and awfully physical. "Come on," Mary Sue said. "We can skate like a couple."

"I dare not risk my patella."

Bobby had skated very little in the three winters he had spent in Princeton. As a kid in Michigan he had skated daily.

"Watch me." She sailed away with a flourish.

He watched her and, of course, that was it. He held out perhaps ten seconds. Bobby rented and laced skates in six minutes. They were black hollow blades, hockey style without the hard toes. He entered the ice with two steps of hesitation, silly worries such as if the ice here was as level as the rinks in suburban Detroit? Was it as vast and empty as Carnegie Lake? In two thrusts, worries forgotten, he was regressing to the age of ten. Bobby followed the crowd in slowed-down frustration, interrupting each circuit with a pause next to Mary Sue, who was his alone now with the chaperon otherwise occupied. She said once as he flashed by, "You're going too fast. They're going to have you arrested."

She skated behind unable to keep pace. After several minutes of her own frustration, beside a spinning Alice she complained. "How do we make him stop?"

She tried half-rink loops, cutting through the center. This way, they met twice per circuit. After two of these ice trysts, she actually grabbed his arm. "Aren't you going to skate with me at all?" Her face was positively glowing. Little beads of sweat were there for his polish.

"You go too slow."

"Try it with me. Please."

They tried it, hands grasped in front cross-armed as in a community pond tableau, all the way around in step to *Roses from the South*.

"I find this too inhibiting. I'd appreciate just a couple of freedom loops in the time remaining."

"Oh, okay."

Once around and it was Alice's turn to shout, now beside her sister as well as herself, "It's getting late."

Once more around and Mary Sue was trying a new approach, gamely keeping up with him stride for stride. He relented and they skated again. The ten-year-old grew toward adolescence and enjoyed minutes of wintertime bliss, flowing with his date, almost the girl he was going with.

Bobby murmured into her ear, "Maybe she's right. We'll be late."

"Oh, I suppose so."

"Go get your skates off and I'll take one more loop."

"You better hurry."

He did hurry. But real speed was impossible, and not because of the guards. Most of the flow consisted of toddlers towed by mothers, old men serene, and spraddling adolescents whose ankle bones seemed to scrape the ice with each frantic stride. He wove among them. Bobby's Lusserna indicated things very late. He tried a couple of loops, then a couple of revolutions of the rink always facing north all the way around, hands behind hips, so cool. Alice was shouting. Then, into it now, a couple of circuits rotating with each second step. Alice forgotten, he slalomed around without taking a stride. Sometime in this warp, he felt a hand on his shoulder. "You're going to be late for the show and they'll blame me for it." Both girls were in shoes now and he sailed on.

Alice was exclaiming, "I should never have wanted to come skating. Never." He could not hear this because he was gunning now on another loop. He could see them off ice, heading to the change bench as part of the wipe, part of the blur at the rink's margin. He would skate on forever, the present flowing back to the rinks of Detroit, flooded by the fire department, where everybody skated almost every day. Bobby was lost in his thin, little strength.

Chapter 16

Yes, Mr. Harris

The people from Ronson, who, after all, made the *Twenty Questions* radio program possible, included, of primary importance to many, especially to the stock holders, Mr. Samuel Harris, who was Ronson's president. He was also Mother's friend. Bobby looked upon the gentleman with mixed feelings.

Bobby: He was old, dumb, and thought he owned us.

Sometimes Bobby compared him to fictional personalities.

Bobby: Simon Legree!

Hardly justified, perhaps, but Mr. Harris did seem to look upon Bobby as a prized property.

Mr. Harris: I fed him well.

He lived for ratings that Bobby did not care about.

Mr. Harris: I lived for ratings whether Bobby cared about them or not.

So, he was naturally upset that Bobby looked upon the show as a nuisance and constantly wanted the night off.

Mr. Harris: Ingrate!

As for Ronson, known officially as Ronson Art Metal Works, Inc., it designed, manufactured, and sold a very elegant line of cigarette lighters.

Adonis: Press, it's lit. Release it's out.

Whirlwind: Safely out, the instant you lift your finger.

Bobby wouldn't have given either Ronson or Mr. Harris a thought except for the disturbing fact that Mother seemed to give him and them more than one. Her life's work seemed to consist of pleasing Ronson and/or Mr. Harris, so long as it kept the show on the air.

Mother: Why not?

Some might say with justification that she was a great fan of her own show and loved seeing her picture in fan magazines.

Mother: I loved seeing my picture in fan magazines.
She loved to join in pictures that featured the entire cast.
Mother: I loved seeing my picture in fan magazines.
That Saturday on stage before the show, as she was being gracious and welcoming to Mary Sue and the other Hurleys, and, as Bobby was explaining their lateness to Dad, she played her role of reigning theatre queen, seating the four of them in the front row, while Bobby had to seethe. He had lost the great anticipated vision of escorting Mary Sue from the wings to the front row in full view of fifteen hundred people.

Well, it hadn't been the best day in the world anyway, Bobby decided, as he went backstage to comb his hair, straighten his tie, and shake hands with guest Vincent Lopez. Bobby felt awkward after the show, too, when he had to say goodbye to his date and her leering family at the same time, and would still feel awkward the following Monday in class, unsure whether he should treat her as a prized possession, a casual friend, of a partner in social disaster. They had ridden trains, seen a movie, gotten some exercise. But there had been nothing, well, personal. Physical. Emotional.

That was on his mind that Monday morning at breakfast, too, so that he hardly noticed that his mother had on her mind something entirely different, as she was saying, "I told Sam Harris your thoughts were your own and outside our ability to control, which was what he did not want to hear."

Bobby at the black kitchen table was spooning hot cereal. Outside was pre-daylight- savings-time gloom. He pushed down the chrome toaster lever to start the raisin toast that would soon fill the room with delicious sweetness.

Bobby responded. "My thoughts not being on anyone's mind."

Mother went on. "So, by way of promising, I agreed to mention it and see where we got."

He spoke with calm excitement. "My more immediate thoughts being focused on what Miss Hurley will say when I confront her with further requests, the Ticket Dance this Friday first among them."

Mother's drone continued unswayed by dance arrangements. "I was thinking that, well, anything that might serve to continue the show on the air. It will pay for your coming college education. Ticket dance?"

Bobby extended a buttered slab of toast. "To which we agreed to go and meet not as a date but more as a liaison."

She allowed her eyes to see him. "Jinky Bob have you heard a word I've said."

"I certainly have."

Her eyes, satisfied, went away again. "I think we have a right to bring it up. It's the most serious decision you'll be making in a little while."

"Bring it up."

"Of course, the decision is yours, but we both know that Princeton is one of the leading colleges on anybody's list and one of the most sought after."

"I couldn't get into Princeton."

"That's when … Whatever do you mean?" Her drone had been jolted free of its program.

"I couldn't get into Princeton with my grades and academic position." He chewed toast.

"Now, Jinky. I know Mr. Harris would do whatever he could to open its doors to you." She let that set in before admitting, "But I know you're figuring on making your own decision and I told him so in no uncertain terms."

Bobby's impression of his mother did not extend beyond the next few days. "Would Mr. Harris want me to go to a college I didn't want to go to?"

"Well, he'd want you to want to." She sipped.

"A college I didn't want to go to and into which I probably could not get?"

"Which remains to be seen." Her cup went to rest. "Not that I'm taking sides, but I think it wouldn't hurt for you to march right into New York and talk to him about it."

"Saturday before the show?"

"Well, we were thinking Wednesday, when you're going in anyway to that basketball game with the Slaters and taking Johnny McFarland along."

So, Wednesday he and Johnny joined Dad on the 4:17. They sat by themselves to discuss Bobby's status as a social lion. Bobby said, after serious discussion, "So, I guess you'd say I'm going with her."

"To the exclusion of anybody else?"

"Yeah. Right now, yeah."

"And same with her?"

Bobby paused. "I guess so. Yeah. Nothing in writing."

He grinned. "Nothing in writing. Nothing in writing suggests a coming catastrophe."
"I take my chances."
"Animal."

Bob:	Is it a whole animal?
John:	No
Bob:	Is it part of a human being?
John:	Yes.
Bob:	Above the neck?
John:	Yes
Bob:	Is it hair?
John:	Yes
Bob:	A mustache?
John:	No
Bob:	Is it hair on the top of the head?
John:	No
Bob:	Is it somebody's beard?
John:	Yes
Bob:	Is this a show subject?
John:	Maybe yes. Possibly not.
Bob:	Well, is it a famous beard?
John:	Not as a beard.
Bob:	Is the owner of the beard famous?
John:	Somewhat.
Bob:	Well, is the owner of the beard famous for having a beard.
John:	For having a beard? Not exactly.
Bob:	I mean like Shaw or Rex Stout.
John:	Not in that sense. You might say this Beard is famous but the beard isn't.
Bob:	I quit.
John:	The subject is Ralph Beard's beard.
Bob:	Hm.

After Dad departed for 1440 Broadway, Bobby and Johnny separated in the bowels of Penn Station with Bobby directing, "Meet you at the Orange Room at 6:30. Sixth corner of Fortieth."

By 5:30 Bobby had cabbed to the apartment building on Fifth Avenue, alighted beneath the canopy, and allowed the doorman to escort him inside.

Bobby had heard that the ditsy Mrs. Harris manned the door upstairs.

Mrs. Harris: I manned the door upstairs . . . what?

She manned it that day, allowing him to enter the vast, stuffy suite and inquired if he would like a glass of sherry.

When Bobby declined, she looked at him with obvious mistrust and said, "You aren't the new milkman, are you?"

"Milkman? What milkman?"

"The one I hired to bring us Walker-Gordon. You can only get it at Fritz's and it's so difficult going down and coming up and going down all day."

She was, Bobby judged, a mixture of the rich, addled dame and the gracious, scatterbrain hostess. Both come with age, he thought, feeling warm and stuffy in the dark, upholstered room. He wondered why they had only a single dim lamp lit and also if the seven-foot grandfather clock against the far wall might stop, short, never to go again.

"Is, uh, Mr. Harris ready?"

She tossed her head like a horse. "He's been waiting for that boy." She suddenly stared as if he were truly before her. "That must be you. Are you at Princeton?"

"Yes. Princeton High School."

"Do you teach there?"

"Not quite. I'm a junior."

She wound away, thinking this over. "I'll see." She walked away, requiring more time to digest this news, to return in a moment. She flicked a thumb over her shoulder.

When he entered the next room he was somewhat shocked to see that it was a bedroom and that Mr. Harris was propped up in bed.

"Well, there you are. What's the idea keeping me waiting all day? Heh." He nodded to Mrs. Harris. "Go on out, Irma, and find that milkman."

Bobby sat down on a silken straight chair.

Sam Harris was not demonstrating hostility, certainly not at Young Bobby. It was more a state of grouchiness in general that he likely worked up each morning. With Irma out of the room, he seemed to relax without the need to forever show how much of a curmudgeon he could be.

"Well, how's the high school business?"

"Different every day."

"Ha." He picked up a small glass of tomato juice. "Well, we haven't seen each other too much, have we?"

Bobby nodded. "Each other we haven't seen at all beyond a couple of parties on the Astor Roof." He leaned forward. "Is that a college encyclopedia I see there on the bed?"

"Yes, it is." He drank and placed the juice on the lap tray. "Have you been going through one?"

Mr. Harris was finishing what appeared to be an egg salad sandwich. After each bight, he would wipe his full lips on the back of his hand. Bobby kept his hands at his sides or on his knees.

Bobby's forehead wrinkled. "No such luck. Look, Mr. Harris, Mother tells me you want me to go to Princeton so I can stay on the show, and that's a fine thought but one to which I cannot agree."

Sam Harris, president of Ronson, paused then summoned a short nod. "You're not surprising me. Just don't be hasty is all we ask. It isn't my idea, you know. It's the advertising department. Those dummies are even more ratings conscious than I am, if that's possible. They're planning a package from Mutual with an exposure cost ratio even higher than we have now. That would mean an even better contract for you and your parents."

With the final sandwich morsel being chewed, Bobby almost felt himself frowning to discover that the president of a big and famous company could also be a man in bed eating lunch.

"You mean, if I go to Princeton, you'll sell more lighters."

"The more we sell the better your compensation package."

"I still don't want to go."

"Yes, but just think about it. Always keep the door open, I've learned."

"I can't argue with that."

Presidents have white hair, he concluded. They wipe their mouths. They seem to weigh each word before saying it and look a little foreign. Books, movies and plays suggested that such powers could wave a hand and wipe out people, events, and even memories. Bobby McGuire? Fire him. Bobby winced.

"You think about it and we'll have a party on the Astor Roof you haven't even dreamed about."

Although Bobby was shaky enough here, he seemed in better control than Sam Harris, whose frustration at having to deal with this kid was becoming evident.

Bobby leaned his head to allow his thought to slide out. "A party on the Astor Roof I would dream about would just mean I'd have to say no, not only now but in the future."

"But, good Lord, young man, Princeton is a good and famous college."

"A good and famous college it surely is."

Mr. Harris raised both hands. "Bless me, that's the first positive thing I've heard. Let's leave it there for now."

"The trouble is, Mr. Harris, I probably couldn't get in anyway."

"We could see about that." He wiped his hands.

Twenty minutes later, Bobby alighted from the cab at the orange room and, after two hot dogs and orange each, he and Johnny hiked on to the Garden, two blocks west, nine blocks north, where they met the Slaters and watched Kentucky's Ralph Beard and company lose to Utah's Wat Misaka and company.

That Friday evening Bobby and Mary Sue went to the Ticket Dance separately, but left together with Fred and Jackie. The four walked to Renwicks's and then around the streets amongst the street lamps and the dark shadows of the town, singing songs of camps and colleges like carolers. They sat on the bus stop bench at the head of Palmer Square, the statue of the tiger behind them, and sang "Bull dog, bull dog, bow wow wow. E-li Yale." Then came a giddy game of hide and seek down Nassau toward Jugtown, once hiding in shrubbery beside an ancient mansion, where she glided into his arms as if they were dancing, without that excuse, and stayed there, cheek to cheek, or chin to tresses, and found warmth in the embrace.

Though she was surely his, if only for a moment, he still had to swallow before he murmured, "The Explorers are having a roller skating party at the Capitol Arena next Saturday. I hope you can go with me."

"Saturday?" She leaned back to ask it, then re-entered his embrace. "Saturday?"

The second show he would miss. "They'll get a substitute. Some kid from New York probably."

"Quite an honor. How could I say no?"

He felt the fiery urge to crush her against him and to stroke the silkiness of her dark hair. She was Miss Perfect, this calm, hesitant girl, who seemed to probe her way through life like a traveler through a fun house. Or, he suddenly worried, was he merely scaling a peak only to fall from the cliffs that came with it? Well, even if he did, the climb had been exhilarating. She was worth the work.

He whispered, "I worry though, thinking maybe they're letting me take a day off, expecting me to go to Princeton in return."

"I'm hoping to go either to Skidmore or Stanford. If you go here, we could meet in summers between is all. I heard you really wanted to go here, to dear old Nassau."

"Never. I never said that."

"Good." A little hug went with that word.

Next day, Mother and Bobby went in on the 5:49, one of the clockers with a white linen diner.

After penciling in their orders, she dropped the pencil into its silver slot and said, "It's not as if the college of your choice will turn out to be the one Mr. Harris chooses."

"I guess not, if that's my choice."

The soft table top and fleeting scene out the window were cleaner and more serene that they had appeared during the course of his more recent trip in this dining car.

She said, reaching into her purse, "So we knew you wouldn't mind looking this application to Princeton over, knowing that you won't be going there anyway."

He took what she handed across to him. "The only thing I lose by reading it is the time it takes."

So, Bobby read it through, between his Salisbury steak and his diced-in-cream potatoes.

It was an odd sensation to be sitting there in an upper middle class milieu on a footing equal to all the adults around. He would order food and it would come as easily to him as to his mother.

She said when he looked up from it, "What do you see?"

"It's an eastern school, it's beyond my ability, and Mary Sue is going to Skidmore or Stanford."

She pondered. "You father knows the real reason, so he said. Princeton's a little close to home."

She took up her menu again, seeking desert. He glanced at his and returned it to the slot.

"The why-I'm-not-going-to-Princeton list now seems long and secure."

"Okay, Jinky. Then do your mother a favor so I can do Mr. Harris one, by signing it up. He'll never know the difference."

"So long as nobody hears about it, why not? I'll affix my appropriate signature to this document that means nothing anyway." He cleaned up his plate, shoved it aside, took his mother's mother-of-pearl pen in hand, and jauntily signed.

After the show—the guest was Bennett Cerf—the little scene backstage near a harp case was bubbling with good humor as Bobby sidled up to it. He was in good humor himself. "Good show."

Mr. Harris was just departing the little circle with Mother and Dad. "Good show, yourself," he said. "And thanks for seeing things our way."

When he was gone, Bobby said, with an edge of suspicion, "What's he so jaunty about?"

"I tried, but he wouldn't listen," Mother said.

Bobby nodded. "You tried but he wouldn't listen is a quirk of his character."

Mother said, "He's booking '21' for next Saturday after the show to announce your decision."

Dad said, "We've been there before."

"To announce my what decision? That I signed a paper?"

"I told him it was just a paper but he wants to announce it to the world. Bobby's going to Princeton."

Bobby calmly exploded. "I haven't applied. I'm not accepted, and wouldn't go if I were. He enters me into a matriculation process which could constitute a black mark against any application I make anywhere else. And he books '21' to announce it."

Dad said, "It will boost the ratings."

Bobby moped out, "A sham and I'll suffer for it."

Mother said, "No you won't. I'll accept full responsibility at '21.'"

"Will Angela be there?"

Dad nodded. "Most likely, I suppose."

"Give her my best. I'll be roller skating in Trenton with my girl friend."

Dad's chin tucked in. "What? You didn't ask for a night off."

Mother said, "Bobby. You'll miss Robert Merrill."

"Call it a quid pro quo."

Chapter 17

Dawn and Dusk

Our subject for today is class. Or, how rumor, gossip and innuendo ruled the school.
Bobby: Mostly in the cafeteria.
To be "with it" at all, you had to know who was whom and who was going with whom.
Bobby: Which is a heck of a lot of whoms.
Little of this applied to Young Bobby until March after the ticket dance when Bobby and Mary Sue were seen together and after which they disappeared together. The following week, with their date secure for the following Saturday's roller party in Trenton, they became a minor item, at PHS level. The item was augmented by the widely circulated fact that, to skate, Bobby would miss a broadcast, a major sacrifice he was making for Mary Sue. Maybe it would make Winchell, if not the PHS *Chronicle*.

So, off they went that night in cars adults provided — the Fosses and others — to Lalor Street, Trenton, and into the vast, wood-floor Capitol Arena. Not a sleaze at all, but a closely monitored venue almost as chaste as Sunday school. Ties required. No speed skating. But it was fun. Wheels on tongue-in-groove rather than blades on ice. But similar music, similar laughs, similar cross-handed grips upon each other. The atmosphere had just enough of the carny about it to generate a sense of pleasant danger and maybe even a hint of the exotic.

The event officially ended with their deposit back at the curb in front of the First Presbyterian Church, seventy feet from the cab they had taken home after the Sophomore Dance two weeks earlier. But there would be no cab tonight. Mary Sue had her father standing by for the "come fetch" phone call. Midnight was the hour agreed upon, which left time for Renwicks, or, more likely, a walk in lieu of privacy. Bushes the week before somehow seemed inadequate now.

So, hands locked, they walked through the town, past Hinkson's Stationery, the Nassau Barber Shop, the Balt, the Balt Bakery, the newsstand, the First National Bank, Western Union, the Cummins Shoppe, Liggett's Drug Store, Nill's Bakery, Zinders Toys, Yeoman Liquors, Luttman's Luggage, The Flower Basket, Veidt's Chocolate Shoppe, Woolworths, the Annex, Kaserel Optometrists, Zapf's Hardware, Bellow's Dress Shop, Miss Chambers, the bowling alley, Farr Hardware, Hulit's Shoes, Clearose Studios, Leigh's Dresses, Borden-Castanea dairy bar, the library, the Garden Theatre, the Methodist Church, Nassau Interiors, Thorne Drug Store, the A&P, the Christian Science Reading Room, Nassau Liquors, Cox's news stand, Morris Maple paints, Gene Seal Flowers, Acme Supermarket, and, where they reversed, St. Paul's Roman Catholic Church. Across the street was Cleve's, long closed that night, who would halve a pint of Hershey's ice cream with a corn knife and serve each half with a wooden spoon sticking into the strawberry at ten cents the half. By the time they returned to the First Church it was just midnight and they had talked and hugged without notice of Bobby's Lusserna.

In those days the church was never locked. Through a side door they entered its dark office to make the call. Then, behind the front portico's immense Doric pillars they waited for the one-fender car. In an alcove there, Young Bobby, somehow, found out how to kiss the girl, or any girl, for the first time in his life. Her cool, slight lips seemed like foreign, forbidden dreams. Once, then twice, and, if his febrile mind contained any doubt of who was going with whom, the doubt evaporated as inexorably as the time.

Next evening, after assurance that his replacement in New York had offered little, Young Bobby more or less awoke to find himself with Jack in a side box at Baker Rink. Sunday evenings the gang often gathered where the Princeton Tigers played hockey. The scene was a frolicking mixture of adults, children, and kids in between, such as this night, the last session of the season, with Bobby and Mary Sue, Jenny Crown sort of with Jack, Pete, Fred, and Buzz. Bobby was on hand not only to skate, not only to continue his liaison with Mary Sue, who was on the ice with Jenny Crown, but to bathe in recognition by the gang that he had officially become a social tiger.

On the ice Bobby was alternating amongst fast rounds with the boys, slow rounds with Mary Sue to the Skater's Waltz, and sitting in the stands to discuss the meaning of it all, concerning which Jack was saying to Bobby, "When you can let her skate by herself, you're got it made. It's called confidence."

"Confidence I feel. I guess."

Jack was explaining. "Fred says it's just because you're on *Twenty Questions*. But what could you do about that anyway?"

"A burden more than a help."

In his new social situation, Bobby was not sure whether he was more relaxed or more tense. He sensed that some danger lay in wait somewhere but he could not identify it.

Jack was re-lacing his skates. He'd just had them sharpened in the booth beneath the end stands."Now the next social event of great scale is the Junior Prom." His eyes thought aside as his leg and foot rose with the final pull of the tightening laces.

"And to it Jenny Crown you will ask?"

Jack said, "Maybe yes. Maybe no." He thought that over, but a different thought emerged. "You know what? You'll be in the *Chronicle's* column of *Who's with Whom*. I'm called a stringer. I feed tidbits."

"That I didn't know. Sometime in the middle of next month? That dance."

Jenny Crown and Mary Sue came through the boards. Both were flushed and pink. Their skates clicked on wood up to the row where Jack and Bobby sat. Bobby had an insane urge to rise, take both her hands, and greet her like a grown-up as he'd seen grownups do in the movies. Happy, healthy, and his. Miss Passionate. Still, could he explain her odd habit of eyes each step seeking some hidden peril. He never saw any. But, could that worry a young man who was "going with" this girl, a condition that was, just then, as important to him as anything would be again. Ever.

Mary Sue said to him with a surely private smile, "Where do I find you? Taking it easy."

Bobby said, "I just heard about that column."

Mary Sue was showing a great grin full of health. "Okay. But what column?"

Jack said, "In the *Chronicle*. As soon as I call Kimberly. I feed her tidbits."

Jenny Crown asked, "You're a stringer, too?"

Jack said, "I feed her stuff from the boys side. I'm going to feed her something — and I think you know what — for *Who's With Whom*."

Jenny Crown looked back and forth between Mary Sue and Bobby. She said in her squawking voice, "You are not. I'm calling her with it."

"Not if I call her first."

Bobby said, "Could it matter?"

Jenny Crown said, "It's all in the rules Miss Hazard laid down and I'm playing by the rules. It can't go in unless it gets confirmed first and, second, comes from the girls side."

Bobby said, "But . . . "

Jack said, "We can bend the rules just once."

Jenny Crown said, "No, we can't."

Jack said, "I'll just give her a hint."

"You do and I'll file a grievance."

Mary Sue said, "Grievance about what?"

Jenny Crown turned to Mary Sue. "It's for journalism class. When you're a stringer, you get points for placing stuff in the columns. And the points affect your final grade. But everybody has to stay on their own beat, and all stuff for the *Who's With Whom* column is my beat with Kimberly."

Jack said, slightly petulant, but smiling, "You can also have scoops, you know."

Mary Sue frowned, ignoring both, thinking. "I'm not sure. Even if…"

Bobby said, "But…"

Jenny Crown said, "My guess is you ought to call Kimberly yourself."

Of all the teenagers there, the only one who seemed very serious was Mary Sue, for some reason. She alone seemed to want to get things straight.

Mary Sue said, "Maybe I better, all things considered. I'm not sure…"

Bobby said, "But…"

But there was little more to it that night or the next, or any night of the following week, because it was spring vacation and Young Bobby was in Indiana. It was a quick trip with Mother on the *Jeffersonian* to see the relatives on her side. George Adler had negotiated the tickets with the Pennsylvania Railroad, which sent a representative to Richmond to make sure the trip had been smooth. Even such a thin slice of show business generated such perks. Because of them Bobby felt a definite sensitivity, as if eyes upon him in the sleeper, in the diner, in the stations they passed.

He would almost strut and pose in response. He couldn't help it, possibly because the sensitivity had been in him long before *Twenty Questions* had let it show. At camp he had performed at campfire evenings, usually "Casey at the Bat." In auditorium class, fourth grade, Miss Lewis always called upon him to develop the climax of the class's sequential story. Even in pickup neighborhood games, softball to tennis to backyard croquet, he couldn't help adding little flourishes when he knew anyone at all was watching. The whole world was a stage.

The role he adopted on that trip was the mooning lover. The kid accepting the new responsibility of having a girl friend. He may have left her behind, but that was temporary. He compared it to hitting a golf ball to the apron of the green — something abandoned temporarily, but he could see it waiting for him right there in the center of things. He kept his anxious eye on the ball from Indiana through the rest of that week.

Dad met them at Princeton Junction about 8:30 Friday morning. The *Jeffersonian* did not usually stop there, but George Adler had negotiated that, too. Twenty minutes later, Young Bobby was deep in the sunroom's deep yellow chair on the phone with Kimberly, jolly Kimberly, the columnist. Mary Sue's phone had not answered.

"Did you have a pleasant trip to Indiana?"

"Faraway place it is. A little lonely. How was your vacation?"

"You don't want to know. I've been on the phone forever."

The sun was cutting into the sun room. His picked up the letter opener but did not drum with it. He could hear the parents unpacking suitcases in the far end of the house.

"Whom with?"

"Everybody. Mainly about nothing happening around here."

"Glad to hear it. And who would know but you?"

"Why me?"

"Columnist Kimberly. Knows all, hears all, tells all."

"Oh, the column, yes, but I don't tell all."

He tapped the letter opener once, then held it still.

"Any hints what you'll be telling next issue?"

"Oh no you don't. You'll just have to wait like everybody else."

"Jenny Crown and Jack both gave me hints already."

"They better not. I'll cancel their contracts."

He saw no way to read her thoughts. He wanted to trick her or force her to talk under threat of judicial mandate. He'd heard of truth serums, hypnotism. Beneath her rock of silence he sensed crawlers of immense horror.

He pleaded. "I just mean the tidbit column. Who went with whom, or something like that."

"Well, no hints from me." Then he thought he saw a hint of hesitation before she went on. "Actually, I don't think I'll be carrying any of that next time anyway."

"Oh."

"Miss Hazard wants us to try all different things."

Twenty Question's guest next night was playwright and producer Russell Crouse, who must have wondered what he had fallen into, since the panel correctly identified only two of the seven subjects, the worst record in the history of the show. Young Bobby had his mind elsewhere. He called Mary Sue at ten from WOR. Nobody answered.

Monday afternoon, he entered 206 briskly. She was opening books, eyes somewhat downcast, purple sweater, a smile managing to form.

He waved. "Hello."

While he was trying to remain calm even in the shadow of events now a week old, she did not appear to have those events in mind at all, as if every new day offered new directions.

She looked up. "Oh, hello." Then, after he was seated and his back was to her, she added, "How was Indiana?"

"Far, far away."

Mr. Chesterton began the class before any further words could bloom into anything. And, after class, Kimberly appeared and took over Mary Sue's attention. Then, oddly, Tuesday, Mary Sue was sitting two rows over when Bobby entered in deep conversation with Kimberly, as if their conversation Monday had continued for twenty-four hours. Bobby's brows were raised right into Wednesday when he joined Frank Cottman, Buzz, and Jack at lunch in the cafeteria.

Dark Frank, always probing the latest pieces of the larger scene, said, "You didn't fly?"

"Mother flies not. Her favorite phrase about it is, if you're on the train and you break down, there you are. If you're in a plane and you break down, where are you?"

Frank nodded in tolerance, "The plan is, you don't break down in the first place."

Bobby's own sandwich had come not from home but from the depths of the cafeteria's kitchen nearby. Although the pasty goo tasted the same each day, he was never quite sure what it was.

"I'll tell her. But the *Jeffersonian* wasn't bad."

Jack said, "Sleeper?"

"She won't go sleeper either. Coach all night. It wasn't bad. I carved my initials on a beech tree on my uncle's farm. My trip's highlight." He took a great bite from the sandwich and tongued it into ooze.

Buzz, looking into his soup bowl, said, "Bob leaves a mark wherever he goes."

"Sure." Bobby looked at him, not quite sure how read the compliment. Nothing seemed certain that day.

Buzz looked up. "It's hard to believe you came from a farm."

"Ah, those summers on the tractor." He finished the sandwich with a second bite, not quite more than he could chew. "What more occurred in this neck of the woods?"

Jack said, "Not a darn thing. The Junior Dance is next and that hasn't happened yet."

"I'm not sure I'm going," Bobby said, assuming that they would assure him that he should. Nobody said a word, so he continued, "I don't plan to attend every single dance."

Frank said with grinning assurance, "Who does? Other pastimes occur to me."

Bobby said to Jack, "Are you going to ask Jenny Crown?"

"Undecided."

Frank Cottman said to Buzz, "You going to the Junior Dance?"

Buzz nodded and looked down into his soup again. "Mary Sue Hurley."

Chapter 18

Canoe

Clobbered. Young Bobby had really never felt such a body shock before — the severe jolt first in the chest, centered just below his sternum in the solar plexus, and the wave of needles sweeping around his head to meet across his face in a shimmering climax. It reminded him of times he had touched a loose wire or a live light socket that had jolted its way up toward his shoulder. This time it shut down his thoughts and his speech for several seconds, long enough for Jack and Buzz to rise and depart for class. He did not hear Fred's comment very well, although he was sure it contained something with the word clobbered. He thought he responded with a little disclaimer to the effect that he had no valid claim anyway.

Kids that age face daily clobbering and the only difference between Young Bobby's distress and all the others was that it was his. Still. It was a hard rock in Young Bobby's path, away from light and toward deep cynicism, and it was never forgotten.

But the days kept dawning. During the two weeks before the Junior Prom itself, Bobby endured *Twenty Questions* broadcasts featuring guests Nat Holman and Billy Gilbert, played tennis, considered asking Jenny Crown to the Junior Dance, considered asking Honey Winderlick to the Junior Dance, went to the movies with Pete, *My Favorite Brunette*, and tried to discuss his distress with Kimberly, who assured him, "I don't know anything about it."

After school that Friday in April, the Junior Prom a few hours away, he played and won his first official tennis match, beating Swifty 6-0, 6-1, which wasn't saying much. Swifty had never played before. That evening at nine, he climbed on his bike and went for a ride to test his generator and headlight after dark, he said, and he found himself near the school, in the bushes near the gym, looking through the high, screen-covered windows at the dancers within. Peeper in the gym.

Okay, so much for women. It was back to Scouts, back to model airplanes, and next day back to *Twenty Questions*.

In fact, that next evening he was actually friendly with and listened to the left field lore of guest Charlie "King Kong" Keller. His mind even drifted to Angela, for an instant, got scared and drifted back.

Monday drifted by like a fog in the night. On Tuesday Mr. Chesterton's English class rode school buses to Trenton to see Olivier's *Henry V.* Bobby's former friend named Hurley sat in another part of the field, while another former friend named Honey happened to sit beside him elbow-to-elbow.

Honey: A developing friend named Honey sat beside him elbow-to-elbow.

There are those who might have called it a coincidence.

Honey: Those thinking coincidence don't know me very well.

She sat there because she wanted to be sure she understood all the words.

Honey: Who's forsooth?

Young Bobby hardly knew she was there. He wasn't even watching the arrows fly by, ignoring Agincourt because he was certain that Buzz and Mary Sue in their distant region were plotting.

Still, Honey's elbow wasn't to be taken lightly. You can't sit beside Miss Winderlick and dream dreams of the discarded lover, or any other dream for that matter, without her in them.

Saturday night he met guest Louis Calhern, meaning nothing. Then Monday in the cafeteria, at a different table, he was alone after Frank and Pete had departed toward class and was ready to leave himself, when Jack sat down across from him, saying, "Don't leave yet."

"Huh?"

"Listen, you want to go out on a blind date?"

A simple question, with pregnant overtones.

"A blind date would be new, novel, and exciting."

"Seriously. This Friday. Movies and then fool around. I'm taking Peggy Spivey. You're taking Honey Winderlich. She broke up with Duckworth. Or I guess he broke up with her and took out Marian Berk."

Bobby blinked. What goes on here? "Why me? Why not Lon or Buzz or somebody?"

"Don't ask. Come on. Yes or no. I'll have the car."

"The car. As in automobile?"

"Yes or no. I'm gonna be late."

Hot, hectic, bustling noon in the cafeteria, where all sort of debacles, explosions, liaisons, and alliances occurred, where trays clattered, noses twitched, and Venetian blinds cast cell-like shadows across the tables, Bobby suddenly felt like shouting out, "Yaa, Yaa, Yaa!"

"Okay, as in okay."

"Great. Details later."

When Jack parked near the Playhouse at six forty-five that Friday night in mid May and Bobby walked past the poster in the window that told passers by on Hulfish Street that the movie they would see, should they buy a ticket and enter, was *Saigon* with Alan Ladd and Veronica Lake, he looked beside him and saw somebody he was frightened to see. She even looked a little rougher than she had in school that day, too, maybe because she was wearing jeans and a man's white shirt and maybe because her smile was more laden with savvy. There had been calls from Jack that arranged the whole shebang, so he knew the schedule. Someone had suggested a moonlit canoe ride on Carnegie Lake, even though it was cloudy, humid, and breezy, and he had agreed, as if he had a choice, even though he had been in a canoe only twice before, one of them during Scout Camp in Brighton, Michigan, before the dawn of time.

Bobby also knew more about his date, from asking around. She was from a remote street called Western Way and her father was somewhere else. So much for research.

"Two in the loge, please."

"One sixty."

The arrangements had been simple enough, with Jack's car reserved, canoes planned, and paddles promised. That had all been accomplished before Tuesday. He didn't explain the state of blissful terror he was in all week and that he was saving all smiles for Friday night, one of which he carried all the way into the last row of the loge without any visible shaking from the fear inside him.

You have deduced, of course, the basic predicament Young Bobby faced. His name was Duckworth. Broke up or not, the possibilities were many and all dangerous — from a closeted encounter in the boy's room to a ringing match in the dust of the school yard, neither of which promised success.

He said, "Whom do we know?"

"More than we want."

The Playhouse seascape was drawn again. He murmured with near suaveness, "I see no Duckworth and Marian."

"Shut up."

The lights faded. The NO SMOKING sign appeared to appropriate applause. But Honey did not participate in such rituals. The darkness that followed hid her left hand, with its long tapered fingers, as they coiled around Young Bobby's modest right bicep and pulled it to her.

Bobby: I brought the usual flask containing upon this festive occasion a boodle of dry martinis.

Honey: Mine with a twist.

Bobby: (thinly) I usually start off at dawn with Scotch and soda just to cut the phlegm.

Honey: What's dawn? I don't get up till noon.

Bobby: Of course, I smoke like a chimney, mainly Luckies and Old Gold.

Honey: You can get me a couple of Ronsons in the bargain.

Bobby: I'll take you through the factory some day.

Honey: I'm not up days.

Bobby: I was arrested a little while ago for theft.

Honey: A year ago I was in reform school.

Somehow the Tom & Jerry felt merely humorous. Young Bobby did not fall on the floor or slump down to the horizontal. He couldn't have. His arm was anchored to tapered fingers of exquisite length and smoothness. The short subject was forgettable. The feature had something to do with former fighter pilots doing something or other in China or some place nearby where the supporting players looked Chinese.

In the car, headed down bumpy Murray Place, then Fitz-Randolph Road, then the curving gravel along the lake, Jack said, "You ever been in a canoe?"

"I think so," Bobby said. In the seconds of silence, Bobby's mind focused. "A canoe it resembled."

"How many times did you roll in?" Jack inquired.

You didn't have to be a champion of canoe maneuver to succeed here. But somehow he shied from carrying the image of an inexperienced kid, too.

"A Troop 43 outing in my previous incarnation, during which we spotted birds, explored the lake's shore line, and explored the birds that dwell along it."

Honey said, her hip to his in the back seat, "How deep is the lake?"

A world-weary woman of infinite experience? She was trim, tan, and pretty, but her whole package seemed coated with some secret lotion of maturity.

Jack answered, "Three feet at most. Ten feet at least."

Peggy Spivey, slumped alongside the driver, said, "I've never been swimming in it, you know."

Bobby said, "We'll change that."

The boathouse and dock were lighted by strings of bare bulbs, like a used car lot. The canoes, at sixteen feet, were old canvas types, internal ribs showing, with tiny caned seats on thwarts at each end, one of which supported a back rest, and a brace across the middle. Soft mats covered the keels. One red, one green, they drifted from the dock into the flat, black water. Agreed, back in one hour, when the rental ran out. Jack would head toward Harrison Street, Bobby toward Alexander. The young ladies were torn between positions as bow paddlers and reclining passengers. Both chose the latter configuration, lacking only a frilly parasol, and perhaps a frilly frock, to complete a languid summer scene.

The lake was more like a river, a quarter mile wide at most and three miles long. It was already black on the lake just yards from the dock. He could see little but the barest outline of the Washington Road bridge. The night sky was no help, with neither moon nor stars. The air was heavy and still. He took easy strokes, trying not to dribble on her as he crossed sides and not always succeeding.

He said, "If we get lost, you can start screaming."

The captain wanted very much to carry this off, both the girl and a little scene he was dreaming.

"I don't scream. Are you sure you've run a canoe before?"

She was thinking not only of the captain but of the dimensions of the lake itself.

"May heaven claim me, I surely have. You'll notice that my knees are properly on the canoe's keel. I feather the paddle with each stroke."

"Sing me a song."

He wasn't sure what that meant.

"Row, row, row your boat."

He did not have to put it to voice. They both assumed the melody.

She said uneasily, "Gently down the stream, I suppose. Shouldn't we be seeing the bridge?"

"We do. I see the bridge in all its stone finery."

It was a sleek, curved affair, made of the same Tennessee limestone by which much of the college was sheathed, with big half-round arches that you glided beneath, going, "Whoooeeeeeeee!"

"Oh, Bobby. Please."

"We passed the bridge in the proper manner, using the echo chamber to proper effect."

He felt himself drifting in a sea of happiness, not sure what other happy scenes lay ahead but confident all would be fine.

"Is that lightning?"

"I guess so." It was late now, warm and muggy. He knew that lightning on a lake could be fickle. He would be careful not to raise the paddle high. "My guess being that it's probably heat lightning."

They passed the University boathouse, drifted half a mile between two islands, and were circling beneath the Pennsylvania Railroad bridge, awaiting a Dinky to pass overhead, when the first drops came down.

They were big and gentle drops, slowed in their fall by the heavy air.

"Hey." That was Honey.

"We're in for it. The Washington Road bridge will require fifteen minutes of vigorous paddling."

"You'll think of something."

"I'll think of something of an emergency nature."

"It's raining harder."

She was calm but direct. This girl was used to men doing things for her without being asked, solving her problems and probably satisfying her needs if not drives.

"We face an emergency in the rain, to which I have a partial answer."

"Just paddle."

He was puffing as he paddled. "You request is being granted."

Between the bridges was a rivulet he recalled, perhaps four feet wide, that emptied into the lake near the university boathouse. During that Troop 43 outing, they had seen a Wilson snipe strutting there on the grassy bank. Young Bobby's nineteenth bird. If his figuring was correct, it was perhaps a hundred yards away. He pulled for the shore in long, dripping strokes, ruddering as he went.

"It's coming down, Bob."

"Our objective is nearby. In fact..."

He found the rivulet's opening, backed water, turned in, and pulled alongside close banks on both sides. The rain was gathering force. Bright lightning displayed bare grass. A tremendous clap of thunder followed.

Her voice was hard now. "So, we'll get soaked on land instead of in the canoe."

"We will not. We'll get beneath the canoe for maximum shelter."

A pause. A freeze. "I said you'd think of something, didn't I?"

He stepped ashore, a foot up, and pulled her after him. In seconds he had slid the canoe from the water, inverted it, raised one end to support it on the wooden back rest, and spread the rug-like keel pad on the grass beneath. It was beginning to come down hard when they slid into this long lean-to.

He whispered, "Irony. The keel is still in water."

"Never mind the water. Are you telling your mother about this?"

They lay on their sides end to end like the lovers he and Dick had come upon in the woods. That had occurred at life's dawn and it was now mid-morning. His ears were filled by the pellets of rain attacking the hull. His eyes were on the dark suggestion of her hair. He smelled its fragrance and allowed his eyes to close.

He heard her say, her lips an inch from his ear "This is pretty scary stuff. Even for me."

"Are you telling Duckworth?"

"Shut up." She gave him a quick squeeze, an event he had felt before somewhere. Then she sighed and admitted, "Ned would have paddled for the bridge."

An especially strong burst of rain wiped across the canoe, with a feeling of spray upon the back of his neck. He was afraid to press her against him.

Young Bobby was swimming in two fantasies at once and one was real. A sharp, hard crack of thunder came down. When it had rolled away, he heard her voice, a little calmer now, in his ear. "Let me get my other wrist loose." It slid somewhere and they were at ease in each others arms. "Now."

How he wanted to kiss her but he really was not quite sure how to go about it. He opened his eyes to see hers a few inches away clearly asking a question. So, he did. He kissed her, tentatively at first then surely. After a while he thought he heard a tone, a sigh, a moan.

She whispered. "Who kisses better? Me or Hurley?"

"That would be telling."

"You operator."

The rain settled into a strong steady sound. So did they. There was no time to it. Once she said, "The thing is, I know you didn't plan it."

He said, "It goes on my list of miracles."

It rained for half an hour and slackened about the time they were thinking of heading back, rain or no rain.

"We better keep still about this," Honey said. "Tell them we stayed under the railroad bridge or something."

"Stories of innocence."

"Nobody'll believe this happened. I'm not sure myself." She was standing, stretching.

They re-launched without a stumble. This time Honey became a paddler.

"Honey, I'm not sure whether this was a fiasco or something else from your point of view, but I'd like to ask you out again."

"Yeah. It'd be something if you ever topped this."

"I think you have a definite point."

He knew there must, somehow, some way, be a downside, some inevitable disaster to grow from this event. He looked all around the dark lake for it, ready to duck or paddle harder. Ned would await him on the quay.

Her paddle dripping, she looked behind her. "You'll think of something."

"Start with a movie? Next Friday?"

"Sure. That'll give you a week."

They returned to the boathouse without delay, paddling all the way. Peggy and Jack were waiting in the car. Bobby settled up, wiped his hair aside, and climbed into the back after Honey. "We got caught under the Washington Road bridge."

Honey said, "Yeah. What a drag."

Chapter 19

Haunt

"Don't tell me she's pregnant," Jack said indifferently.

Just chitchat, an obligato to Jack's removal of a ham sandwich from the brown paper bag. It was the following Wednesday. This was their summer luncheon venue, on the cement steps outdoors between the ag el and the side of the gym. Young Bobby was already on the steps when Jack arrived.

"Ho, there, Robert."

"Ho."

For various reasons of schedule and need, they hadn't seen each other to talk since riding home from canoes. So this sunny noon they finally had a chance to discuss Friday's strange exploits. Each felt a maturing confidence in his social stratum.

Jack spoke without ruffle. "Why the frown?" He had sat down a step above.

Both wore summer slacks above loafers with a short-sleeve shirt above that. Besides their lunch bags, each had a book in hand and a pencil in shirt pocket. Jack's right rear pocket also displayed half of a blue comb. In the near distance was laughter, shouts, doors, and the thonks of tennis to their left.

"So, where did you go, besides the railroad bridge?" Jack bit into the sandwich.

Bobby was shaking his head in resignation. "A place near heaven, or a facsimile thereof." He brandished half a mystery sandwich half gone.

"You didn't get very wet. I noticed that." He was now chewing, blunt and wide, a fire plug confidently on the corner.

Young Bobby's outdoor lunch consisted of two sandwiches and a daily dixie cup of ice cream, half chocolate, half vanilla. The cup's underlid always carried the photograph of a movie star. He read aloud the daily Caption. "Dana Andrews, starring in The Big Noof." He licked the frost from Mr. Andrews, pondering the elements of the world. "Being in heaven's vicinity next time is what she expects."

"This Friday?"

"Uhn."

" I think I can get the car again."

Bobby tore the wooden spoon from its wax paper covering. "But where will heaven's vicinity be?"

Jack still chewing, still indifferent, said, "That's your worry. I was thinking movie and DeLorenzo's."

"Movie and who?" The spoon always pierced the ice cream at the vanilla-chocolate demarcation line.

"Tomato pies in Trenton. Haven't you ever had tomato pies in Trenton?"

"No."

"She probably has, with Duckworth."

Young Bobby was not quite secure enough with Honey Winderlich to shed all worry over her former boy friend. With Honey alongside him, he still did not relish meeting Mr. Duckworth anywhere. "Would he be there with Marian?"

"How should I know? Fred is going, too. With Hurley."

"You're going with Spivey?"

"Jenny Crown."

Bobby smirked in wit. "Musical chairs. Musical dames."

"Yeah."

"I gotta say, Friday night was one of the most exciting things I ever went through. How am I going to top it?"

But Jack was hardly impressed. "Get two tomato pies instead of one."

Facing downward to the cement below, Young Bobby twisted his head, aiming his face upward at Jack with skepticism. Sure, tomato pies might be something new, but new did not guarantee Elysium.

Classes that week were mop-up sessions in anticipation of final exams the following week and commencement the week after that. Commencement, of course, would not concern Young Bobby until next year. Not directly at least. The teachers became more or less good guys, who often allowed change and fluid movement. Somehow, Young Bobby was allowed to move his room position in English to its original locale beside the windows.

Honey approved. Later that afternoon she turned around, not to borrow an eraser. "Will he ask us anything about Macbeth?"

They had spoken, of course, halls and class, with Honey repeating her tantalizing way of shaking her golden head at him in disbelief. But this was Bobby's first chance to offer her another night to remember and he didn't know exactly how confident to be.

He smiled. "The subject of long ago? I deem it doubtful. Probably figures nobody would get it right, which would lower the curve."

She pouted. "After I studied Macbeth for an hour."

He was not in exam mode and sought a segue from mundane school to the immediate problem. "The movie Friday is *The Iron Curtain*."

Honey was not ready for the immediate. "You can explain one thing. I know you can. How could those people in *Our Town* be talking when they were dead?"

She was the same girl in daylight, all right, but not the one he was imagining, a girl he had felt along most of her length. He liked the pencil eraser rolling along her lower lip, however.

"You speak of a heavenly experience, by goodly. What I have in mind for Friday evening will be designed for a heavenly experience as well."

"What?" She caught on, realized where they were. She tilted her head toward the memory and smiled. "We won't top last week, will we?" She folded her arms and hugged her elbows.

He covered his eyes with his hands, grinning without restraint. "Jack's driving again. We're going to Delorenzo's after the flick."

She tucked her chin in astonishment. "To Delorenzo's? Delorenzo's!" Her gentle forehead bore wrinkles. Then she shook her head slowly in awe. "You are amazing."

"I plan it to be something different and exciting."

"Oh, Bob. Not that. Don't you dig? That's where everybody in the place goes around kissing all the time." She thought everybody knew that.

He stared, saying while thinking of her lips, "Fred's going, too, with Mary Sue."

"Okay. You can neck with both of us."

Bobby was frowning at this throughout the remaining school day. It carried several images, depending on your lens. Was she suggesting an adolescent orgy with multiple neckers and neckees? More likely it was roguish sarcasm making light of her great rivalry with Mary Sue. Either possibility left him in some kind of school swim. Chest out, Young Bobby.

Friday morning Miss Eiseley announced during their final home room period that Mr. Woodrow was enlisting all members and former band members to volunteer for the coming commencement exercises a week from Wednesday at McCarter Theatre. He needed musicians for he commencement band. Mr. Woodrow was soliciting on behalf of such graduates-to-be as McFarland, Ham, Swifty, and even Duckworth. Later on, Mr. Woodrow even stopped him in the hall, near the auditorium, since Bobby had played trumpet in the band his first two years in school. But Bobby demurred. His schedule was just too tight.

That night in Trenton, with serious school behind everybody and exams' peril looming, Jenny Crown was saying, "Pepperoni gets stuck in my teeth."

"Mine, too," Fred Darkly added. One of his crooked fingers was digging into the yellowing ivory.

Delorenzo's was a dark dive on Broad Street near Centre. Although it was known as Trenton's Mecca for tomato pies, it was by no means the only tomato piery in the city. Whitey's on Olden, the Tik Tak out River Road, Tommie's in Lawrenceville also generated a following. But Delorenzo's was the darkest, the smokiest, and the most talked about in Mercer County. Those familiar with pizza might think that tomato pies were simply a variety. But they would receive from any maven of the things a chortle of beautiful condescension. A tomato pie was not a variety, or even a species, but a whole phylum unto itself, as different from pizzas as White Castles were from hamburgers.

Surrounded by minarets of orange soda, two pies lay on the booth's table like yellow-orange pools of molten goo. Sixteen inches. Hot! Bite a wedge and expect to stretch the mozzarella like a taffy pull. In various stages of such pulls were all six kids, girls on one side, dates across, each requiring arm-length space to complete an operation. Six never-parallel lines of force creating a euphoric mess.

After both pies were reduced to an arc or two and replacements were contemplated, Honey, on the outside, said to the young gentleman across from her, "So, this is supposed to be something heavenly?"

She was testing him and he was clearly failing. This night had to be a Topper but was, so far, merely an evening. Young Bobby was worried. He was anxious, as if he had two questions to identify the Eiffel Tower and knew only that the subject was a mass of steel in Europe.

Her image was closer in this pale light to his ideal. Her blue sweater, the matching ribbon in her hair, had magnetism for his eyes that kept them in place. They never swept aside toward the other sweaters across the table. Not even Mary Sue's. Honey finished a piece and, looking at his look, took a slug of orange soda right out of the bottle.

Jack, in the middle, beside Bobby, said to her, "Especially the second tomato pie with pepperoni."

She said, "Sure. Pepperoni. It spikes the whole evening with extra flavor." Her golden head tossed in confident irony.

Jack said, "I told Bob it would."

Which is when Jenny, beside her, across from Jack, said, "Pepperoni gets stuck in my teeth."

And Fred in the corner said, "Mine too."

The juke box was belting out "Four Leaf Clover" when the next pie arrived. Booth hoppers were beginning to move about the den. Bobby sensed depravity.

Mary Sue far inside said, seizing a piece of the new one, "I've never had tomato pies before."

Her attitude was definitely challenging, maybe ever aggressive. Beneath her sweetness, she might have a hidden streak of meanness, toward everybody, toward life, toward heaven and earth. But it never showed.

Honey said, "Bobby'll let us know when the experience comes off as heavenly."

But he never even thought of it. He had a hunch this evening was going to be bigger than the canoe and he began a secret antipathy toward his former love, Mary Sue. She was too nice to be real, too accommodating, and maybe felt herself above ordinaries.

Fred said, finishing a crust, "Comes off as heavenly?" He guffawed.

Bobby said, leaning outward from the booth and looking up and down the deep, dark room, "I don't see everybody going around kissing quite yet."

Honey said, "That comes later. When the Trenton Bennies get started."

Bobby nodded. "In the meantime, I guess we'll have to find heaven somewhere else if we're going to enjoy consecutive raptures."

While this banter went on as the slices disappeared, knowing eyes glanced. Coquettish heads tilted and dipped. Young Bobby was sensing nuances outside his range.

Fred was not only glum across from Mary Sue, Bobby's discard, he was taunting about it, as if they had never been an item anywhere. He hated the idea that his close friend had been with Mary Sue first and that he had to keep being friends anyway.

Fred said, taking a final slice, and still smirking, "You're going to enjoy consecutive raptures?" He was a little patronizing in this. Raptures were not exactly stuff of PHS.

Bobby nodded his way. "In heaven you don't get fun. Only raptures. And tomato pies..." He waved his arm to take in the lingering aura. "... is turning out to be merely fun."

"Merely?" Mary Sue said, finishing her wedge, tossing the residual crust to the pie platter's center.

Bobby turned his head to catch a sound. "I hear no claps of thunder, so it can't be rapture."

Jenny said, her eyes rising to somewhere secret, "I did hear about somebody getting caught out in a thunder storm."

One wondered why Jenny, who had a stunning figure and who was quite pretty, sometimes seemed to lack, and other times seemed to flourish, a coating of charm that tied the package together.

Mary Sue said, "I didn't."

Bobby said, eyeing his date, "Rumors. Right, Jack?"

Jack said bluntly, "I got soaked. You face less danger from pepperoni."

Well, this was merely true. But what did Jennie bring it up for? What did she have in mind?

Bobby sighed. "Danger, yes. But rapture? I'm not convinced."

Honey said, nodding with philosophical allure, "Yeah. You said you'd top everything and you've had a week."

Fred said, "Top everything?" He was stretching a wedge in his hand. "Are we getting personal?"

Mary Sue said, "Yes, Young Bobby. Tell us how you are going to top everything." This impartial vampire could still charm and needle at the same time. Her smile was so sweet, so daring and challenging, that Bobby was losing his place in the thought.

Honey said, "Including tomato pies."

Jack added, "With or without pepperoni."

Bobby sighed again. He looked from smeared face to smeared face. "Maybe." He took a very deep breath. "I've got a plan. Maybe."

Jack said, "Give."

Bobby looked across, taking in his date, Jenny, and the passionate, if duplicitous, Mary Sue. He nodded to himself. "I know where there's a haunted house."

Where else would a Topper be than in the shadows? And, beyond all that, those with any history in their lives at all will have examples of their own. Abandoned farm houses became tributes to the Depression. Deep in the woods lived witches seen only during the quarter moon. That old miners shack, the duck hunters cabin, the cracked pillars of the old plantation overgrown with vines and lore. But here, on the margins of ultra suburbia was an authentic mansion abandoned by time.

It was a half hour drive. Four piled in the back, Honey on Young Bobby's lap. From the depths of the back seat the night was very dark. The passing scene was obscured. He could hardly see that they were on State Road or even that they were passing his own house on the left, with the wooded hill of the frontier. He was deliciously surrounded by kids and a great deal of Honey.

He said, "Look for a lane into the woods. Through a red iron gate that's always open."

Jack slowed in the highway's darkness. In those days this state highway had little traffic near midnight on a Friday. The headlights swept left and found an iron gate painted red long ago. Jack turned onto the lane. He had to shift to low as they rolled up the steep hill. The headlights showed bushes at the sides. Trees made a canopy. Less than a quarter mile on, the lane petered out, as brambles closed in. Then it ended altogether, making Bobby wonder if this was the right lane. But Jack saw an opening in the brambles on the left and turned through it with a bounce. Beyond was a weed-covered parking area among huge trees that made wide shadows in the night. Jack seemed to hesitate. Then he stopped the car and turned off the headlights. When he cut the engine, silence enveloped them all. Outside, making an even wider shadow than the trees was the great bulk of the abandoned mansion about a hundred feet away.

The moon that night was high but thin. The light it offered seemed to accentuate the darkness by outlining tantalizing shapes without defining them.

"Well," said Jenny very quietly, "what do we do now?"

Her grey face at the front seat window was pale and wary. None of the four in back was moving or making a sound. Jack suggested in a whisper that it might be wise to turn the car around and point it toward the road.

But instead he leaned toward the windshield and scanned the dim view. "Is it supposed to be locked up?"

They were all whispering.

"I know how to get in." Bobby swallowed and couldn't quite move. The fear of Grimes was upon him.

There were small protests and questions. Were they supposed to enter? Were they even supposed to be there?

Fred said, "We didn't come just to stay in the car, did we?"

Mary Sue protested. How did they know somebody didn't actually live there? Honey allowed as how she would not want to encounter a cop then or anytime.

Jack broke the trance. "Who's chicken." A charge of chicken carried weight. They piled out.

But even then they merely stood their ground around the shadow of the car. They stared at the great black shape of the mansion but did not move toward it. Finally Young Bobby took the lead. He whispered, "Follow me. We can at least see if it's still open."

They eased — yes, eased — across the weedy gravel of the side yard. Ahead Bobby, orienting himself, discovered that the screened porch had not changed since that Saturday morning months ago, so far as he could see. But the same ripped screens that had appeared intriguing that cold spring morning appeared sinister this warm spring night. Every moon shadow became an ink blot. The potential of every void he saw was for danger. The others were close together, stepping with caution, legs bent, ready to flee.

Bobby's voice was low as he said, "See, the screen's gone. Come on." They moved into the deeper darkness of the porch. The kitchen door, as before, was pulled to but not latched. Six young bodies in a knot shuddered as he pushed it open with a tentative hand. It groaned as it swung, inviting them in.

Mary Sue whispered, "I'm staying here." Jenny agreed.

Bobby said, placing one foot over the door sill, "This is just the kitchen. Come on."

He crept in on his toes and paused just inside. The counters, the closet, the nooks were still there, barely visible in the thin light that spilled into the room. Then they were all inside, creeping forward by the inch.

Each short step they took became a major action, taken as if they were walking on a high plank, arms aside like a cat's whiskers. Bobby led. Jack and Fred were just behind an elbow away. The girls were just entering the kitchen door.

"I'm not going any father," Jenny said very softly as if she did not want anyone or anything to awake.

Everyone paused in a tableau for several seconds. Jack was beside Bobby now, the other four staring ahead over their shoulders. Silence. Another half step. The kitchen began to take shape from the gloom. And Jack said in an urgent whisper, "Look! Look there!" He pointed right ahead, possibly to the far end of the room, from which they all heard a sudden crash.

Three girls screamed. Three girls ran. Three boys followed.

Bobby asked as they crossed the screened porch, "What was it?"

Jack said, "I flipped a rock."

"Nice going," Fred murmured.

The girls were in the car and were not coming out. Protests, entreaties, threats. Forget it. They wanted to leave. They wanted their mommies. Jack had to explain his trick before they would consent to emerge.

As they piled again from the car, very slowly, with constant looks around, Bobby whispered to Fred, "Run ahead and hide in the closet." Fred expertly disappeared.

"I'll wait right here," Jenny was saying. She was closer to car than porch.

"I'm with Jenny," Mary Sue said.

Honey said nothing. She was O so nonchalant, one saddle shoe toeing the ground crossed beside the other.

Bobby led them, more briskly now, to the porch. They came, slowly to the door, and inside, still in a knot. "I saw this place in the day time and, believe me, it's nothing to worry about. Mostly just fallen plaster."

"Uh huh." That was Mary Sue, full of doubt.

"It's not that old," he went on, assuming the mantel of tour guide. "There's space for a dish washer. See, right there. You want to see the ball room?"

"No." That was all three girls together, even Honey.

"I do," Jack said.

Jenny said, "I'm going back to the car."

"While the going's good," added Mary Sue.

"Aw, come on," Bobby said more loudly. "You haven't even seen the ball room. And... hey, let's see what's in the closet." He pointed. "See that funny design on the door?"

To see it, they leaned forward with him as his hand grasped the knob. That was their position, straining forward, when the door opened and Fred, stiff and gruesome, fell outward, clutching and making a sound like an animal. "Uhhhhhh!"

Even Bobby recoiled. Jack jumped back into Honey, who was running wildly for the car, twenty feet behind Jenny and Mary Sue, whose banshee sounds were filling the county.

That was the end of it. They all assumed — almost hoped — that cops, if not the national guard, were on the way. They scrambled into the car, locked the doors. Jack hit all the controls at once and they careered through the brambles to the highway, willingly leaving behind flying dirt and burned rubber.

Word got around. Other groups in coming nights tested their mettle against gloom and haunt, on beyond the kitchen, eventually to alcoves and hidden closets on the third floor. But soon the groups seeking fright expanded to crowds seeking party, until collegians took over with beer and organization, so that the cops finally came and it was all over. But that one night, the consensus agreed, Young Bobby had come through. Another topper.

Chapter 20

Option

Saturday afternoon a neighborhood girl named Nicole Barbero came over to try to play *Twenty Questions*. This was an early move in Mr. Harris's game to find Bobby's successor. Nicole hoped to become a second Young Bobby, and she could play some. But her flair resembled a wet match. Mr. Harris's quest would continue.

The guest on the show that June 5 was the lovely Ann Blyth, who was nineteen, even older than Angela, on hand to push *Mr. Peabody and the Mermaid*. Mr. Harris had been expected at the show, hoping for a positive report on Miss Barbero but, since the report was negative, he didn't show.

For Bob, Sunday involved mowing the lawn. During each circuit, he analyzed and re-analyzed his current state of need. What about the coming summer? Of course, he imagined the shape and substance, mostly the shape, of Honey in every scene, with the summer's curtain at Labor Day, when he would return to PHS a senior and social king of the cafeteria.

After English exam the following Tuesday, which did little for Shakespeare, Wilder, or Bobby himself, he and Jack walked out past the flag pole circle of PHS to the waiting Plainsboro bus.

At the curb in front of the auditorium, Jack said, "What's next? The Fun House at Asbury Park?"

"To which I have never been and would wager that Honey has. I would wager she knows its every nook, from the topsy-turvy room to the rubber cell." He dodged some shoulders there in front of the auditorium as kids made way toward their busses. "I would wager that my demanding assignment now is to come up with a new capper of climax, to which I have been applying myself for half a week without result."

"I gotta hand it to you. The haunted house qualified."

Young Bobby nodded beneath his heavy responsibility. "But how to top that, a zenith in itself?"

Mary Sue, headed for the bus behind Jack's, walked up as Jack was saying, "Take her in to see *Twenty Questions.*"

Mary Sue, overhearing this, stopped and said, joining in a sunny presence, "Sure, Bob. Take her ice skating first."

Bobby held his ground and said straight ahead, "Suddenly I've forgot what we were talking about."

Mary Sue said, "I've forgotten I ever went to New York." She said it with little fingers of sarcasm thrusting forward, beyond savvy, approaching shrewd.

Jack said, "The trouble is, New York is for spending money. It's easier to spend fifty bucks in New York that five bucks in Trenton."

Bobby said, "The trouble is, she wants to go, Honey does, letting that eager fact be known some time ago."

What the devil was this Mary Sue hanging around for anyhow. One explanation was obvious, but maybe too obvious. Bobby liked explanations that were simple, or, better yet, elegant.

"That's what you're known for," Mary Sue said. "Eager facts."

"She wants to go to New York like your sister did."

Mary Sue said, "She's forgotten it, too." She flopped her light jacket over her shoulder like a cape.

Bobby, crossed a toe to the ground, taking showy ease.

Jack said, "Ice skating's over, McGuire. You've got to come up with something else."

"How about the Gilbert Hall of Science? We could learn about the origin of chemistry sets. And we'll get there early in order to enjoy the historical attitudes of Grants Tomb, the Statue of Liberty, and Coney Island."

"Coney Island's an idea," Jack said. "I didn't know that's right there in New York."

Bobby nodded. "Requires a subway ride."

"I think you've hit it," Jack said. His hands went to hips to survey the possibilities. "Coney Island. Nathan's Famous. The Parachute Jump. Wouldn't mind going myself."

"Welcome you'd be."

Abruptly Jack turned to Mary Sue. "Wanna go to Coney Island Saturday, Mary Sue? How about it?" Jack was so maddeningly bullet proof, so insouciant. If she said no, he wouldn't care at all.

The whole scene was just too hectic to believe. Too busy to feel confident. Voices echoed all over the drive and the flag circle and among the sides of the yellow buses.

Bobby warned, "She'd have to bring her sister along."

"Not anymore. I'd love to."

Jack nodded. "Good. We'll make arrangement."

Bobby said, "Okay." He thought over the possibilities as one hand was massaging his mouth. "I'll ask Honey tonight. We can all go to the show afterward and home together on the train."

"Sure." Mary Sue said with a grin. "On the diner."

Bobby was not sure how to accept that lick of sarcasm. Maybe as a healthy rib dug between old friends.

Saturday, June 12. No diner. Instead, they rode in before lunch, which they took in a Times Square Automat. By noon they had fed nickels to slots for a tableful of Gotham delights. Jack delighted with nouveau relish on some strange sandwich. Young Bobby, although he had been in an Automat just once before, assumed the old timer's role by his flawless slide of quarters into the changer's marble trough.

Mary Sue was probing a club sandwich as she said, "A funny place to spend the end of school."

That sounded slightly out of whack to Bobby. For one thing, it wasn't quite the end. Three half-days remained, as well as the coming year. Second, it implied there might be a better place to spend the end of school and that maybe she knew what it was.

The Automat room reminded him of the gym with its high windows, high lighting, and high decibel level. He had a glass sugar cylinder in one hand and was sliding it every which way. He found himself looking at it. Somehow, for some reason, he knew he didn't want to look right at Mary Sue.

Jack said, "What happens if you don't go back next week? Do they flunk you?"

"Actually, I can let you know," Honey said. "Because I ... got a job. You know. Atlantic City. Waiting table at Hogates. At the shore for the summer, and it has to start Monday. Mr O'Dell gave me permission."

Bobby inwardly recoiled almost as violently as he had that watershed day long ago in the cafeteria, that noon when the planet changed orbit. Waitress at the shore! Yes, she would fit there, waiting tables at Hogates, cadging drinks after hours at Boardwalk bars. He may have sighed. The summer had suddenly vanished just as spring had so long ago.

There was a difference, of course, the kind of difference your hand feels when it touches the hot stove the second time. That hand has grown a callous. But it still hurts.

Mary Sue said, "I might as well go back next week, since … I mean, I'm an usherette for commencement Wednesday night anyway."

Young Bobby stared.

He wished that he could claim that he got an idea right then. But he didn't. It took most of the day. It took much of the ride on the Brighton Beach Local. He simply envisioned her striding up and down the aisles of McCarter Theatre. She had mentioned it for one reason, he thought amid the sways and bumps, but, when that deduction focused itself, the portion of his mind dealing with alliances suddenly got jammed into confusion.

By the time they had swung the reverse turnstiles and had crossed Brightwater Avenue to the Boardwalk and down to the right to Steeplechase Park and were riding the horses on their roller coaster rails, he had decided that she had mentioned it when she had because she wanted him to think it over, not talk it over. Only those with the code would understand the full import of her announcement.

The idea bloomed sometime during the stupendous fright of the Cyclone. They nosed over the top into the first fall only to see that it was so steep that the rails ahead were tucked under them out of sight. Well, there's your metaphor, Charlie. Never ride a roller coaster when you can't even seen the tracks ahead of you. Never mind. Sometime during that four seconds of terror he decided that she was trying to tell hm that, despite the duplicity, the strict rationing of herself that she had practiced, she wanted him to know that he was still in her autograph book.

By the advent of the Wonderwheel, while they held on inside one of the inner cars as it started one of its terrifying outward swings into space, he had decided what the point of it was. She was telling him how he stood, without admitting it. At that time, kids admitted nothing. It was all reserve. You had to assume things and could get clobbered on account of assuming anything. The Parachute Jump drop with Honey beside him was an eternity not a flash.

By seven o'clock, after four plates of spaghetti at Toffinetti's, they had walked up Times Square to 52nd Street, turned left to the Mutual Guild Theatre, and had mounted the stage steps. Young Bobby, again missing the dramatic seating in the front row of his love, whoever she might be, stashed his three guests there before the audience was allowed to enter.

Backstage, he said hellos to Herb Polesie and Bill Slater and then encountered the circle of training. The trainee that evening was Basil Rathbone, on hand not so much to plug a movie as to plug his own radio Holmes on Mutual. Bobby stepped forward and took a seat at the far arc of the circle. His hand was trying to be nonchalant by fondling change in his trousers pocket, which brought a frown from Mother and from Dad at the same time.

Dad said, "Bobby, have you met Basil Rathbone?"

He grinned and said in a loud voice, "Hi. Where's Doctor Watson?"

The actor did not flinch. He nodded. "Believe it or not, that is the most asked question I've encountered for the past eight years." That was Holmes. Oh, yes, that was Holmes talking, my dear Bobby.

When the training broke up a few moments later, Dad and Mother separated themselves from the group and gathered Young Bobby into a secluded corner near a harp case.

Dad said, "Mr. Harris is due any minute with some announcement, according to George." In the theatre Dad often affected that forgotten accent actors used in early talkies, part English, part social register, almost mincing.

Mother said, "The western tour in August."

Bobby had heard little more discussion of the great 1948 publicity tour than he had of anything else regarding the show. If it really happened, well, he would go, especially since his summer had gone off to a restaurant at the shore. Standing there in the gloomy theatre, he thought he could afford to adopt a very casual attitude toward the whole scene, including Mr. Harris.

Dad said, "Chicago and Denver at least." He looked over Bobby's shoulder. "Here he is."

George Adler was with him. They made a five-part circle by the harp case. George said with pride, "It's on. Ronson is going for the tour."

Dad said to Mr. Harris, "I think it will be a success."

Mr. Harris had lit a cigarette in a holder with a Ronson Adonis. He was shaking hands all around as he held the smoking thing aside. Bobby had to wrinkle his nose as he took his turn.

Mr. Harris was gracious. "I'm sure it will be."

Mother was smiling. "We'll make sure. Won't we, Bobby?" Her breathy, lower-lip-under smile.

"I guess so."

Mr. Harris said, "I thought you'd be as thrilled as I am." Here in public, outside his bed, bedroom, and apartment, the gentleman appeared more in tone with the portrait of the Jewish businessman, with an obviously artificial tan, white hair, and expensive clothes that somehow sagged about him.

Bobby said, "I've already been out west."

Dad said to the gentleman, "We've already spoken about it. He'll be happy to take part."

George said, "And we're kicking it off next week. Before we go west, we go east. Flo is expecting full coverage for the event."

Mother said, "Tell us about the event."

"A yacht party out of the north shore of Long Island on Mr. Aronson's yacht," George said.

"Full coverage is right." Mr. Harris nodded. "Several photo sessions. Deep sea fishing in the sound. Overnight Wednesday after your news and back by Thursday afternoon."

Dad said, "Sounds interesting."

Bobby said sharply, "This coming Wednesday?"

Mr. Harris looked at Bobby. "Angela Rhome is booked, if that may be of interest."

"It certainly is. But not to me, since I won't be there."

Every eye was a slit. Mr. Harris said, "But this is part of the tour."

George said, "We can't build it on a piecemeal basis, Bobby."

Mother said, "I don't see how you'd want to stay home by yourself for two weeks, Bob. Do you?"

"Depends."

"It could come to this," Mr. Harris said. "And I hate to say it. In now or out for the rest."

Dad said, "Don't you want to go out west again?"

"Look. I guess so. But I'm committed for next Wednesday. I promised Mr. Woodrow I'd help out with the music at commencement."

They goggled.

Chapter 21

Stare You Down

Princeton University's McCarter Theatre has had several reputations. Acoustically, two old grads held lifetime tickets for the only seats from which one could hear anything said on the stage. Artistically, big Broadway shows opened there out of town, bringing the big time to the small time. Historically, Tallulah Bankhead had thrown either a fit or a bottle or both into the pit. None of those events was on Bobby's mind that Wednesday evening. Neither was "This Is My Country" or "Land of Hope and Glory," even though he had stayed after school the first two days of the week to rehearse them with the Senior Band. Instead, his thoughts focused on the aisles and the usherettes upon them.

Bobby: My thoughts focused on one usherette and the formal gown she was wearing.

The trouble was, he had no idea what to do about it.

Bobby: I had no idea what to do about it.

Strangely, his idea was aimed at the future rather than the usual present.

Bobby: Maybe we could salvage something for the summer.

After B. Woodhill Davies had presented several dozen diplomas, after the alma mater, one of many written by Mr. Woodrow over the years, had been sung, and, after deft aisle search, Bobby had found Mary Sue back stage, wearing a skirt and sweater, packing her formal into a small suitcase. He had recognized the formal in pain, the same formal he had seen through the windows of the gym in another age.

Looking up, she waved and smiled. Hope sprung. "In the Elgar I thought I heard your trumpet above the rest," she said. "Want to walk me uptown?"

"Sure. Meet you in the lobby."

So, he stashed his horn with the school's other instruments, and got the former aisle person and through-the-gym-window person at his side. They entered College Road. Ahead it entered the university, now largely abandoned, and would pass the pool and Brokaw Field. But they turned left onto University Place, up which a haunting march had been held some thirty years before, this side of paradise. Most of the commencement traffic had long departed for parties, but a few cars cruised the street, their lights washing over the strolling boy carrying a suitcase and the plump girl alongside him, who was saying, "Where shall we go?"

She was hinting at some great, adventurous, maybe even sinful, choice. Bobby was sure of it, or hopeful of it. But he had no idea what to say to respond to her spunky, breathy exuberance.

"Peacock Inn for a drink."

"Impossible."

"One dry martini."

"Why not two or three?" Not sarcasm. Just her note of melancholy.

"Only on Saturday."

Several silent steps followed that claim. Then, "I had a drink once."

"Where at?"

"Oh, I don't remember."

"How can you not remember?"

"My father told me about it one night among several of his. I must have been pretty young." How much younger than seventeen could she have ever been?

"A funny thing for a father to do."

He wasn't sure what he might be treading on here. There might be some hidden bit of truth ahead on this road. She still seemed spunky but with an added note now of resignation, a little weary, and somewhat remote from where they were.

She looked sideways at him. "In your opinion?"

"A funny thing for a father to do, noting that my father would about as soon give me a drink as he'd give me a convertible."

"Your Midwest upbringing. With my father, drinking whiskey is routine."

"My father drinks Old Forester."

Bobby was sensing something antagonistic here. He was sparring against his will. He also felt her pace accelerating, as if that were a contest, too.

The street lights, often hidden by leaves, offered sparse light at best. Passing on their right were limestone and brick, university buildings in various shadowy facades. On their left, they were passing Dickinson Street and then a line of old three-story houses the Princeton Theological Seminary used to house missionaries on leave.

She finally said, "Where shall we be?"

He felt he ought to offer something special this night, something with rapture built in. But past raptures, the kind Honey had either inspired or fallen into, seemed remote now. His mind flitted up and down the places of Nassau Street he knew without finding anything that suggested rapture. "We might as well hit Renwicks's."

"Okay. But Dutch."

"Sure." He understood. She was making no deals. "Hey, detour," he whispered urgently, stepping sideways into the dark. They stood on a flagstone walk that led at right angles toward Blair Arch.

"What's this, a short cut to the skating rink?"

"Didn't you see him?"

He had seen ahead of them the wide, short silhouette of Jack Harnesall rounding the corner from Nassau Street onto University Place. Even if Jack's date with Mary Sue in New York had been a transient alliance, he did not want to see Jack now. Bobby held his breath in the shadows and saw that the silhouette walking by was even wider than Jack's with a short mustache.

He whispered. "False alarm."

"Was that your father out looking for you?"

So, she could be a bit sarcastic, which meant he must revise all his approaches and lines. He did not want them heading into different understandings. He was having trouble penetrating her little world as it was.

"No. Sorry. Phantoms all over."

"Point one out."

"Phantoms all over since I was spooked by the Grimes place."

A police car with its red lights flashing glided up the street past them, hesitated at the corner, and turned right onto Nassau Street. He saw her face in its red bolts as he tried not to flub this liaison, to find something she might want to hear.

"How was it living in Knoxville? High school in the deep south?"

"It wasn't deep. Most of the people we knew were from California or Chicago."

It seemed unreal, this response. He was beginning to feel helpless, worried that whatever he might ask would bring them no closer. He was beginning to believe that this girl was not who he had thought she was. And maybe never had been.

In a moment they turned onto Nassau Street around the great gothic building on the corner known as Commons, where most students ate.

"Were you super glad to get back to Princeton, New Jersey?"

"Not super."

When she was younger, she must have lacked this little hint of sadness that mixed in with her jaunty smile. He wondered what sort of life her parents had provided and that had led to the sadness.

She said, "Improvements always seem to have some drawbacks with them."

"What kind of draw backs. When we moved here from Detroit, I thought I'd hit paradise."

"During the war. Right?"

"I thought I'd hit paradise during the war. Three years and seven months ago. Dad rose in the ranks of newscasters because of the war, I guess. So, I thought the war was the greatest thing that happened."

"The war didn't do good things for everybody." She paused. Was she recalling a gold star in her window, cheating on rationing, lack of chewing gum? "But Princeton is nice, I have to admit. It's old but made of old things made to last. Look at that lovely row of buildings and stores over there. I love that block. Even Public Service has brick and white wood. And so does Renwick's, the little candy shoppe, and even Skirms."

"Renwick's food is fair at best, but it feels comfortable. I always get good service because Harry Renwick is a friend of the family."

"You're used to that, aren't you?" That sidewise smile of hers. Was it disguising contempt? Ridicule?

"*Twenty Questions* makes some thing different although it really doesn't amount to that much in itself."

Without knowing why, he suddenly thought of Ruby turning down the cards, as if the secret of the cosmos would turn up somewhere in the stack.

"But you're still on the radio." The charge. Your honor, we rest our case.

"I'm still on the radio, for another year. I try not to make it a big gun."

"How could you make it a big gun?"

"Oh, go to their parties. Like tonight. There's a party on a yacht with models and photographers and big guns from Ronson."

"Why didn't you go?"

"I'll tell you some time."

They jaywalked across Nassau Street.

She splurged with a grilled cheese and Coke. He had his usual. She smiled at him across the table in a winning way and later smiled in a different way to the waitress when she ordered separate checks. "I meant it about Dutch."

He was beginning to glow in her company. She seemed more substantial than the last time they had boothed at Renwick's. Her narrow smile was whiter now, less of a kiddie blur. Her even teeth smaller, closer to perfect. "Now you can walk me home."

"My pleasure."

He was thinking about where to neck. How to steer them that way, toward some comfortable venue. He would show her he was still a force in her life. But she was so fluid. Hard to grab. Like a ghost.

They rambled down Nassau beneath the great trees alongside Mrs. Palmer's wall. Traffic was light except for the tall, tan Trenton Transit bus that chugged by on its way out Stockton. The wall curved around the corner onto Bayard Lane and on down past the Greenholm enclave where Ross Markham used to live, past Avalon Place, and the big Libby House. She lived down Bayard Lane in a garden apartment complex the university had developed called Stanworth, which began where the street started down a long steep hill. He was figuring his coming walk home. About a mile and a half. No sweat.

They turned right into the area of brick walls, passed two dim buildings, and turned left toward a corner doorway. He said, "It's dark as a pocket here."

"We're supposed to leave porch lights on, but people forget."

They approached a small porch. Above it was a dull orange light.

She said, "Wait here a minute. I've got to take Christie for a walk." He handed her the suitcase. She went in and came out quickly with a small dark dog on a leash. "There's a little park in the back." In the dark they were whispering, walking across the courtyard, around the opposite apartment building, and into a narrow alley.

He looked about. Little was visible. He felt a nudge of sweat. Panic.

Highwaymen. Juvenile delinquents on the prowl. She was setting him up for rumble. "It's even darker than a pocket back here."

Mary Sue started humming. Abruptly she turned through a gate Bobby could not even see and, once through it, bent down and released Christie from the leash. She leaned back up and on back. "But look at the stars."

He did. They were spectacular. His night atop Kittatinny Ridge for astronomy merit badge came back. The proscenium here was narrower but the density and intensity equaled what he had seen from Skyline two summers before. Both their faces up, they drifted together. "I see Vega, Capella, Aldebaran. There's Cygnus."

She said, "Where's the Big Dipper?"

"Behind all those trees."

She turned, face still up dim as a ghost, only now he was looking down into it. Her eye caught his. She said, "I bet I can stare you down."

Sure. He kissed her. After three months. Calm, cool lips, not as thin as long ago. Drawing back, he did not know what to expect. She had not moved, or changed. Their lips went together again. His hands took her arms now in gentle grips. Of security? Confirmation? When he drew back, she turned away abruptly. "Oh, Christie!" The dog was prancing beside her like a phantom of the jungle. She snapped on the leash.

They turned back to the gate. He said, "Sorry. My fault." They went through the gate. "Wasn't it?"

"That's the sixty-four dollar question."

"I mean Jack's my good friend and all."

"Jack's not..." They rounded the building toward the courtyard. "It was nice of him to take me to New York. He's ... a friend."

They started across the courtyard diagonally. "Let me say something I hope isn't too forward."

She stopped and turned. "What? Bob McGuire being forward?"

"Seriously. I mean, up to five minutes ago I was looking forward to a bleak summer."

"I know. Honey gone to the shore."

"Besides that. I means she's ... a friend. But now..."

"Summers can be very bleak."

"So, well, now..." He felt himself stumbling into another chance to be rejected.

But she interrupted. "And so am I." She laughed. "Not that. I mean I'm going away, too. For the summer."

"What?" His valve sprung open. Air rushed away.

"I am. I'm spending the summer with my aunt in Denver."

"In ... Denver?" He goggled.

Chapter 22

Red Rocks

Three weeks and more later, looking out the roomette window at two in the morning, according to his Lusserna, he relaxed into the berth's tight sheets with a new fact of life. Young Bobby was always on trains. To New York on the 4:17 Saturday, July 10, to Chicago on the *Pennsylvanian* after Dad's Eleven O'clock News Saturday night, and now the *Denver Zephyr* in the wee hours of July 12. He was too thrilled to sleep. He wondered where Mary Sue was at the moment, and, of course, he knew. She was sound asleep in a house on South Marion Street in Denver, about five hundred miles away. And he was on the way to her.

It sounded corny thinking it. Or romantic. He was going to have a date with his girl friend out west. Really out west. In those days Denver was not just another stop on the jet. It was truly Out West, west of Dodge, where the West began. Men wore boots to work. You could have your picture taken in the saddle of a bucking bronco right out the end of Colfax Avenue. It was one of those faraway places. Trysting there with a girl was a rough equivalent of meeting her today in Paris. Majorca. Bali. And they were going to do it. Nothing could stop them. He had leaped the hurdles. He smiled through the train window across the dark plains as he relived that first exchange after she told him her summer plans.

"You're what? You're *what*?" He had stared at her in the darkness. She was a lunatic. She was kidding. Taunting.

"Right after the Fourth."

"In Denver? Denver, Colorado?"

"I'm flying out from Newark. DC-6, United."

"And you'll be there the whole summer? Is that what you said. You'll be there the whole summer?"

"Into mid-August. What's all this about?"

"Well, Mary Sue, believe it or, I'll be in Denver, too. At the same time! I'll be in Denver the same time as you are. We have a publicity tour coming up."

She stared. Why was she silent? Thinking of Jack. Buzz. Still, he had to blurt. "Can we go out? I mean, would you go out with me in Denver?"

"Hey. Wouldn't that be fun? And so romantic."

"I just can't believe it. The coincidence. We'll be in Denver, Colorado, at the same time."

"Rapture, maybe?" So she would be amusing. Gently sarcastic.

Their tryst would come Tuesday night, August 10, later phone calls arranged. Call to confirm.

He had skipped home down Bayard Lane, a mile and a half of giddy, giggly dance. He flew into the kitchen, grabbed the telephone, and put it down. It was midnight. Too late to call the yacht? He supposed so, but wasn't sure. Hello, Mr. Harris, please. Bobby McGuire calling. Please tell him that I will be taking the publicity tour after all. What yacht? What port? He cursed himself. He had Angela's number but she would be aboard, pining her little calculating heart out. But he couldn't wait for a night and a day, tossing and fretting, and pining himself.

But, of course, he did. He waited a day in turmoil. It was all night and all Thursday morning before he called Dad at WOR and said, "Guess what. I'm going."

"Oh?" The pondering Oh. "Aren't you a little late?"

"I truly hope not. Maybe I should call Mr. Harris."

"No. Don't do that. He was miffed yesterday that you didn't show up."

Ah, these wayward adults. "I told him last Saturday night I wouldn't be there."

"I know, but he was miffed anyway."

He pleaded his case. "I told him I wouldn't be there because I'd already confirmed I'd be playing." Not saying when. "I couldn't go back on my word."

"Let's have George handle it." George Adler, dumping ground. "This is for sure now. We have train tickets and other arrangements to make."

"Sure it's for sure. Do we go to California first or Colorado?"

"California. We're not firm as yet on Colorado."

"What?" Air hissed from his valve again. "I thought mother wanted to go there more than anything."

"It's a toss up though. KFEL was interested but the audience there isn't as large."

"It's practically on the way."

"You sound more interested in Denver than you do in Hollywood."

"Who wouldn't be? Denver's out west, and I've wanted to go out west ever since Tom Mix. The other's just Hollywood."

"We'll work on it. I'll call George right now."

"Is mother coming home early?"

"No. We're having dinner at the Artists and Writers and she's coming home with me."

"I'll leave a light in the window."

Young Bobby, helpless, paced the house, the yard, the woods at the frontier. Supper was soup and a sandwich he didn't want to eat. He would kill an hour on the phone with Mary Sue but she had gone somewhere. He called Jack but he wasn't home. He even called Fred Darkly just to mention casually that he might be having a date with Mary Sue Hurley. Where? Why, in Denver. You know. Out in Colorado. Nobody home. He sat slumped in the yellow chair like a bomb.

The phone rang.

"Hello, is that Bobby McGuire?" An older voice, the timbre of adults calling his Parents, but this one had asked for him.

"Speaking."

"This is Sam Harris."

"Who? Oh! Mr. Harris. Hello."

"I was so pleased to hear from George Adler that you will join the tour, after all." That corporate oil. They all sounded so calm and controlled. But what always followed calm? Cut that kid down. Axe him. Release, he's out.

"Yes. And I'm really sorry I couldn't make the yacht trip. I just couldn't shake that conflict."

"Well, that's over now." Gears shifted, Hydra-matic. Dynaflow. That second coupling. "I've already alerted our people and those at Mutual of the coming tour. And there's another item in connection with the tour I'd like to address, which is why I'm calling."

"Such as what?"

"College."

"College being a year off and more."

"I think college selection is merely months away. And I want you to make me a promise."

"In connection with the publicity tour, you mean?"

"Well, it's all in one great Ronson lump."

Okay, let's get this straight. "I still don't want to go to Princeton. I don't know why, but that I don't want to go to Princeton is decided."

"I understand. Your life is your business. Ronson is my business. And in that connection I want you to promise me this: should you maintain your opposition to a college within shouting distance of New York, that you'll find us a new teenager before you leave the show. Will you do that?"

"I will do that eagerly, but what can I do?"

"Which is an attitude I like to hear. We've been auditioning possibles here and there, as you know, and we'll be holding more formal auditions during the warm-up before each show beginning in September. But I have a feeling they aren't going to produce another Bobby McGuire."

Find one in the circus. Call Dr. Frankenstein. "So, what can I do?"

"Your friends. Your friends at your school. Surely you know of one among them who can play the game."

"That's right. Maybe one. I'll work on it."

"Good. Work on it and keep me informed. Will you do that?"

It was an anti-climax. He'd been ready to fight for Denver. "Sure I will, Mr. Harris. I'll start working on it right away."

Then three weeks passed, void, edgy, vapid. Mary Sue had to visit somebody in Cape Cod. June 19 the guest was Faye Emerson. The week after that it was Ilka Chase. Thursday, July 1, Mr. Lennox of The Music Shoppe climbed onto the roof and installed their first television set, a ten-inch RCA for $350. Saturday, July 3, came James Dunn pushing a picture called *Texas, Brooklyn and Heaven*. The Fourth of July held nothing explosive. The Fifth he went to Aqueduct and won five dollars on Better Self to show, wondering as his horse finished third, if Mary Sue was heading west. July 10, Dale Carnegie. Very influential.

And so it came to pass that this kid arrived in the western outpost of Denver, capital of Colorado, the city on Cherry Creek, the place of Molly Brown and the Brown Palace, long before Rockies, Broncos, and smog transformed it into just another mall. He and his parents were graciously met upon de-training by special representatives of the Burlington, KFEL, and the Albany Hotel.

The man from the Burlington hoped the *Denver Zephyr* was everything they had hoped it would be.

Burlington Man: I hoped the train was everything they hoped.
Frank Bishop of KFEL hoped they would drop by for a little interview.
Frank: I hoped they would stop by for an interview.
And the man from the Albany hoped their stay there would be most comfortable.
Albany man: Not staying at the Brown Palace? These people must be real penny pinchers.
All the while young Bobby, hardly awake that morning, smiled away the sand in his eyes, felt comfortable with the Zephyr's diner's lavish French toast in his craw, and was ready to ask piercing questions.
Bobby: Anybody know where South Marion may be?
He found it a day later. First he saw sights. That same day they toured Buffalo Bill's grave and curio shop, Echo Lake Lodge and curio shop, and Mount Evans, highest road in the country, and curio shop. Dinner that night at something called Joe's Awful Coffee. Tuesday, north to Boulder, Estes Park, and Trail Ridge, after which Tuesday evening floated into view.

He waited for her in the lobby in his newest Palm Beach, sprawled on one of the modern couches they had there in their art deco motif. He didn't wait long. When he first saw her, she was moving through the brass revolving doors and striding with athletic confidence across the lobby. She looked absolutely stunning. Her white dress was dazzling but it was her movement, her bearing, that was so striking. Behind her was this older woman, her aunt obviously, who Bobby could hardly notice, since Mary Sue came right up to him, a foot away, before she stopped. He'd always reveled in that little trait. He would almost flinch in case she didn't hit her brakes in time.

Her smile was dazzling, too. Dark lipstick, onyx ear rings, eyes almost black. "Fancy meeting you here." The surface of her was freshly happy.

"Fancy meeting you here half way across the continent." Grab now? Shake hands? Smooch? His arms were flailing, trying to find some way to show how euphoric he felt without actually grabbing her.

"Bob, this is my aunt."

He bowed and she smiled. She had to be off since she was double parked and off she went.

Mary Sue cocked her head at him, like an archer with a cross bow taking aim. "So, what raptures have you planned?" Facing him, almost facing him down. Challenge. Show me.

"I got tickets for Red Rocks."
"How can we get there?"
"Cab."
"I'm impressed."
He would have been hard pressed to identify this girl as the one he had first seen in Miss Hazzard's room. Even in this modern public place he noticed something elusive, almost contrived about her, as if she were in her own groove, or at least seeking one in which to spin.

Turning toward the revolving door on her own as if she knew the way, she seemed far ahead, him behind. Hey. Was it her at all? The one who had penciled in and erased his name from her autograph book, probably in that purse she was gripping. What else was in it? Comb? Passport? Compartment for the microfilm? Bobby was one mile high.

A cab was at the curb. He opened its door for her, thinking of how soon inside he should encircle her and crush her in some solid necking. Jack and Fred would get a full report, exotic love west of the Mississippi. Have to show the gang this late comer to the game had a full stack in front of him. But in the cab they talked of her flight and his train, leaving him somewhat behind with his old fashioned mode, making excuses. "Mother always wants to go on the train."

"So how do you like Denver?"
"The city itself? Pretty plain. How come it's so flat? I thought Denver was in the Rocky Mountains."
"I was surprised, too. Red Rocks is. Red Rocks is in the mountains."
Something disturbing faintly stirred. Was she claiming turf?
"You go there a lot I guess?"
"Once so far. This will make twice."
"How far is it?"
"Just beyond the western edge. Twenty miles."

She knew so much. At least, the cab was finding its way without her directions. The talk's edge dulled some as they moved. He was nervous about something.

He said, "I mean, Red Rocks was just an idea. We don't have to go there."
"But you got the tickets, and that was nice."
"But maybe not quite rapture?"
"Don't you want to hear the symphony. I thought you liked classical."
She turned to him and took one of his hands in both of hers. Was this Angela? Girls have a network. Unfair.

She said, "Your trouble is, you've always have this crazy desire to please."

"Probably without knowing about it. I might take a poll and find out how some people seem to doubt it. So, I would like to go, if you won't be bored stiff. I mean, there's only so many thing we could do, you know, with my parents and your aunt around and all."

"You're always so worried about control."

"Just trying to avoid disaster."

"Well, I love Red Rocks. I looked up the program in the paper and I can hum you the opening bars of every piece they're playing."

"Now I hope it's a good orchestra."

The amphitheater revealed itself in changing tableau as they approached, first the steep turns and ascents as they left Colfax Avenue, then all the mountain rock itself in smooth finish, near and distant, then the forged place it had become, with its subtle lighting, the quiet traffic careful not to disturb the scene, and finally the vast, curved rows of benches and their aisles like the ribs of a fan focusing on the stage far below, with the enormous rock cliff backing the stage and the lights of Denver below, beyond, and around it. He was over a mile high.

During some soaring passage of the strings, *Valse Triste* perhaps, he looked aside. She was there. She was with him in this place. Chin in hand, elbow on knee, she was smiling at the music. He eased his arm behind her like a slanted cross member for her back and she leaned toward him, fitting into his arm and shoulder as if they had been ordered to fit.

After applause died and intermission began, she murmured, swaying slightly toward him, "Is this the life?" She shrugged her near shoulder, a touch, a nuzzle. This small animal was burrowing, feeling out its territory.

He said, "Another entry on my list of miracles."

She pressed in against him. "I'd like to see the list."

"My list of miracles is very short. I haven't really done as much as some people seem to think."

"Yes, you have."

"Maybe in New York. Some. But not much at PHS. I've really hardly ever even gone out."

"Are you going to be going out this coming year? This fall?"

"I'd like to. This coming fall I'd like to take you out every night in the week." Betsy Baldwin's plea to the student council jolted into his head. Date every night? Young Bobby? Gee, Ma.

She laughed. "Now that is flattering."

Bobby almost felt himself relaxed now. His small, wiry arm muscles loosened their hold on themselves. "But every night in the week I'd guess you'd be going out with guys who know the score better than me. Big athletes. Lon or Jack. Or Buzz."

She asked softly, "Why are you so defensive about who you are?"

"Heck. I'm just a country boy come to the city."

"The word is that anybody gets a date with Bob McGuire is doing pretty good."

He snorted. "Well, if that's right, it's just because I don't go out much. What I mean is, a place like this, a night like this, I just feel I'd like to be a bigger gun being here with somebody like you."

"That's pretty silly. You should have heard yourself described last fall, when I was new. This boy was that way. That boy was this way. Then your name would come up."

"And Bob was every which way."

"No. Your name would come up and they would all agree. Well, Bob is, uh, different."

He snorted. "Uh huh. So was Tiny Tim."

"And, in case you didn't know it, *Twenty Questions* would never even come up."

He was startled. "It didn't?"

"Just sort of an asset you came with, like having a rich family, or being fast on your feet, or maybe you can draw."

"Surprise if true. I always give off the impression I think I'm better than anybody else, for some reason. I blame it on the show. Maybe just an excuse."

"You're not that way after five minutes."

"Thanks. It's sort of frustrating I admit."

She let her arm slip around him, took his shoulder in hand, and pulled herself up and kissed him tenderly right on the ear.

The conductor entered, bowed, turned.

At the end, as the orchestra rose and mingled, Young Bobby and this girl, this Mary Sue, stood and just looked. His arm was around her waist, hers around his. He said after while, "I suppose we'll have to go."

Afterward, it was all little signs on the way down the mountain. In the cab, bumping along Alameda Boulevard, they held hands. He walked her to the door of the bungalow. As they kissed goodnight very carefully — no fumbling at the church — one of her hands curled around the back of his head.

She said, "When we get back, call me."

Young Bobby was two miles high.

Chapter 23

Senior

Wednesday, September 8, Young Bobby, dumb, struggling, and shy in corduroys, red sweater, and loafers, entered this cathedral of learning like a mid-century statue of Romeo not quite set in stone. He entered the Tower door, permitted seniors, turned right into the main hall, and felt almost exhilarated by the bustle and the sense that he belonged here.

Halfway down he ran into Fred Darkly. Fred wore a tan buttoned shirt, pants like Bobby's, and oxfords. Fred was everybody's idea of a model high school student.

Fred: I was still everybody's model of an ideal high school student.

Fred was as active in the school as Bobby and just as smart.

Fred: I was more active than McGuire, just as smart, but not as lucky.

In fact, there was some evidence he resented him.

Fred: I hated his guts.

They were going opposite ways down the crowded main hall. On Bobby's right, lead casement windows still looked out upon the flag pole in the circle, one year older now. Although the halls had not been used since June, an aroma of red cleaning granules pervaded the air.

Bobby swung back and shouted, "Hey, Fred. We've managed to run into each other on the first day of school."

Fred said, "Seen the new girl?"

"What new girl?" He swayed with the current. "I don't need a new girl."

Fred's eyes rolled upward. "That means you haven't seen her." He swung back and was gone. Bobby wondered why his cronies' eyes were always rolling.

As a senior, Young Bobby's favorite ride was this Hudson convertible, here in front of the PHS auditorium.

He had called her when he got back. But getting back had been delayed by a week with a second family trip. They went to Lake Placid, a charming village at the time, especially at the Mirror Lake Inn. They fished, swam, rode up a ski lift, met Kate Smith, and ate a lot of food. But even when they returned a week later, Mary Sue was still in Denver. It was late August before they could talk again. While he waited, Ralph Kiner, Jack Pearl, Frank Buck, and Joe E. Brown came to the Mutual Guild Theatre to distinguish themselves as no better at playing animal, vegetable, mineral than any other guests. And no worse. These also came: a dozen bright kids from New York, all dressed up in kid suits, pushed by mothers, and all trying too hard to be new Bobbys. Bill Fineshriber frowned. Maybe *Twenty Questions* didn't need a juvenile. "If we're going to change the panel, let's do it now before Bobby is no longer young."

Dad said one night backstage, "Isn't there anybody you know can play this game?"

"There is. One. You know him. And he'll be going to Princeton."

Now seventeen, Young Bobby during this period also passed the world's most major adolescent milestone. On Lamberton Street in Trenton, he operated the family's new 1949 Ford, the first one in town, in the proper manner. He answered the written queries correctly. He read E, OFLCTC, with reasonable accuracy. For his trouble the State of New Jersey issued him a piece of paper in a cellophane case. He considered it a proclamation as big as Lincoln's.

That Wednesday in September, Bobby swept into 219 as if he were mounting a stage. It was a Miss Gilman's classroom, a bank of windows on one wall opposite a black board on the other. Chair/desks were in ambiguous rows. The teacher's desk was up front. Flag in one corner. Bible on a lectern. The previous year Bobby had fostered Dick Mickleson's election. Bobby described Dick as "too nice a guy from Stoutsburg." After waves and hellos to the kids and finding a seat in the middle, Bobby drew Dick aside.

Behind his hand he whispered, "Kimberly."

"I figured as much."

Mort Manion, leaning in, said, "Seen the new girl?"

"Girl? Not interested." New girl. What was happening to everyone's priorities? Didn't the school, the world, know he was spoken for? But still.

The bell soon rang and they jammed out to class.

Fourth period, back in 219 Miss Gilman said, "Bob, will you please handle the election."

Bobby rose. "I am proud to nominate Kimberly Manners."

Dick rose. "I'm proud to second."

Then dead silence, as Bobby expected. "Any more nominations?" asked Miss Gilman. "Nobody else?" She looked about, slightly surprised, gently waving her board pointer all the way around to the blackboard, its white chalk still whole and unbroken.

Bobby said, "Hearing none, Kimberly Manners is elected by acclamation."

Sixth period, after lunch, Bobby saw a new face. A pretty face, dark brown hair, and a silhouette called "a lot of woman." He would admit that he blinked.

After class, in the hall, Bobby asked Fred, "Is that who you meant? That big girl?"

"Yeah." They walked along, lockers at their elbows. Fred continued, "Something new for PHS, isn't she?"

Bobby said, "New for PHS I'm sure she is. Reminds me of a young lady named Angela, only more of her."

They swung around a traffic patrol member. Between classes the student patrol anchored the hall intersections like pylons.

Bobby added, "Looks very, uh, mature."

"Which is more than I can say for you."

Finally, just before school was over for the first day of his final year, this senior student finally found that other new senior, Mary Sue Hurley. She was coming out of the front office with a sheaf of papers in her hand.

She stopped still. "At last. There you are." She seemed frantic, but not about him.

"Mary Sue. You've been hiding. I've been roaming the halls looking."

She took a breath. Looked down. Looked up. Raised the sheaf of papers. She frowned and said as she was shaking her head, "It's my transfer papers. It's a mess and there's nothing I can do about it."

"What? Transfer?" The valve was on the edge of releasing all his air.

"I'm being sent away to private school. Starting Monday. Near Philadelphia." She nodded grimly.

"You … what? You…" He took a breath, planted his feet on the hall's terrazzo. "Reminds me of…" He stared down the hall and saw nothing in it. So, he closed his eyes. "Never mind."

Crushed, deflated, ruined, he thought, new girl. Ah, new girl. New girl.

Afterword

Mary Sue asked Young Bobby to the Halloween dance at the Baldwin School, Bryn Mawr, Pennsylvania, and found a blind date for Lon, who went along. Most of the evening he and Lon were known as "The Two." They were the only males there from a public high school. Altogether it was a close-in, uncomfortable adventure. He never saw Mary Sue again. Then, a year almost to the day after Mary Sue told him she was going away — the first Saturday Bobby was away at college — Johnny McFarland, using the name Johnny McPhee, replaced Young Bobby as the juvenile panel member on *Twenty Questions*.

THE END

BearManorMedia
PO BOX 71426 · ALBANY, GEORGIA 31708

ARCHIVES OF THE AIRWAVES
Roger C. Paulson's epic encyclopedia of Old Time Radio
This seven-volume set from historian Roger C. Paulson, twenty years in the making, promises to be the most complete OTR encyclopedia ever written, featuring biographies of even the most obscure series and stars. A must for any fan of radio!
$21.95 EACH. SEVEN VOLUMES

THERE'S NO BUSINESS LIKE SHOW BUSINESS...WAS
by Alan Young
You've heard Wilbur speak about *Mr. Ed* — Now read what Alan Young has to say!
$14.95 ISBN 1-59393-053-4

CORDIALLY YOURS, ANN SOTHERN
by Colin Briggs
Written by a regular contributor to *Classic Images*, this first book on Ann Sothern contains many rare pictures from the author's personal collection.
$24.95 ISBN 1-59393-060-7

FIBBER McGEE'S SCRAPBOOK
If you want to know more about Fibber McGee & Molly...
From Fibber McGee's (Jim Jordan) early years, to his final days. Includes a seven page biography of Fibber McGee and Molly and Jim Jordan, plus over 100 reproductions of original newspaper and magazine clippings and photos. Not sold in stores!
$15.00

THE RONALD REAGAN MURDER CASE
by The Firesign Theatre's David Ossman
A comedy mystery novel. Radio star George Tirebiter discovers that the apparent murder of Ronald Reagan's movie double could have been an early CIA double-cross, fabricated by Bill "Wild Bull" Casey! Could our beloved ex-President actually be his own stand-in?
$19.95 ISBN: 1-59393-071-2

HOLD THAT JOAN
THE LIFE, LAUGHS AND FILMS OF JOAN DAVIS
by Ben Ohmart
One of the funniest, most overlooked comediennes of the 20th Century. The star of television's *I Married Joan* and film classics *Hold That Ghost*, *Show Business*, *Thin Ice* and many more, very little has been documented about Joan's comical career — until now.
$24.95 ISBN 1-59393-046-1

SON OF HARPO SPEAKS
by Bill Marx
Not merely a Marx Brothers book, but an intriguing journey down an amazing highway of discovery, and love. This is Bill Marx's story.
$24.95 ISBN 1-59393-062-3

RUSS COLUMBO
THE DEFINITIVE BIOGRAPHY
by Tony Toran
The only detailed biography of Russ Columbo the man, the singer, and the enigma.
$29.95 ISBN 1-59393-055-0

ADD $2.50 POSTAGE FOR EACH BOOK

ORDER THESE BOOKS AND MORE! VISIT WWW.BEARMANORMEDIA.COM

www.ingramcontent.com/pod-product-compliance
Ingram Content Group UK Ltd.
Pitfield, Milton Keynes, MK11 3LW, UK
UKHW021313180426
11947UKWH00015B/1196